# Playing with the Book

## Victorian Movable Picture Books and the Child Reader

— Hannah Field —

MINNESOTA

UNIVERSITY OF MINNESOTA PRESS

MINNEAPOLIS

LONDON

*Playing with the Book* is supported by a Publications Grant from the Paul Mellon Centre for Studies in British Art.

The University of Minnesota Press gratefully acknowledges the generous assistance provided for the publication of this book by the University of Sussex.

A different version of chapter 2 was published as "The Story Unfolds: Intertwined Space and Time in the Victorian Children's Panorama," in *Space and Place in Children's Literature, 1789 to the Present,* ed. Maria Sachiko Cecire, Hannah Field, Kavita Mudan Finn, and Malini Roy (Farnham: Ashgate, 2015), 165–92; copyright 2015.



Published by the University of Minnesota Press
111 Third Avenue South, Suite 290
Minneapolis, MN 55401-2520
http://www.upress.umn.edu

Printed in the United States of America on acid-free paper

The University of Minnesota is an equal-opportunity educator and employer.

25 24 23 22 21 20 19 10 9 8 7 6 5 4 3 2 1

---

LIBRARY OF CONGRESS CATALOGING-IN-PUBLICATION DATA

Names: Field, Hannah, author.
Title: Playing with the book : Victorian movable picture books and the child reader / Hannah Field.
Description: Minneapolis : University of Minnesota Press, 2019. | Includes bibliographical references and index. |
Identifiers: LCCN 2018026873 (print) | ISBN 978-1-5179-0176-9 (hc) | ISBN 978-1-5179-0177-6 (pb)
Subjects: LCSH: Toy and movable books—Great Britain—History—19th century.| Toy and movable books—Great Britain—History—20th century. | Children's literature, English—History and criticism. | Children—Books and reading—Great Britain—History.
Classification: LCC Z1033.T68 F54 2019 (print) | DDC 096.0941—dc23
LC record available at https://lccn.loc.gov/2018026873

And in children's books, even children's hands were catered to just as much as their minds or their imaginations.

—*Walter Benjamin, "A Glimpse into the World of Children's Books"*

# — Contents —

— Introduction —

# Novelty Value

Famously, the Victorian era was a boom time for children's books. Indeed, the changes the period wrought are important enough to require their own epochal terminology, as the flourishing of juvenile publishing between 1865 and World War I is often called *the golden age of children's literature.* The phrase has a variety of connotations. Particular treasured texts, such as the Alice books, might spring to mind, or particular book formats—gilt embellishments on richly embossed covers. Particular models of childhood might also seem important, especially those that glow with pleasurable nostalgia, as in Kenneth Grahame's memoir of his early life, published at the end of the nineteenth century and titled *The Golden Age.*

But around the same time, a second, less familiar set of books was also materializing. Take, for instance, a slim volume made around 1895. The cover illustration shows a ruby-nosed clown unfurling a banner on which a title appears in multiple languages: *Novelty! Metamorphoses Picture-Book/Neuestes Verwandlungs-Bilder-Buch/ Nouveauté! Livre de metamorphoses* (Figure I.1).[1] Between its covers, the book contains an array of odd figures—a long-faced woman with a bird's torso; a bear smoking in evening dress, chicken feet peeping out below its skirts; a pudding-faced boy in emerald-green stockings and high-heeled shoes (Figure I.2). More notable even than the appearance of these strange characters is the *manner* in which they appear. As the English subtitle states, this is a metamorphoses book, or, in common parlance, a lift-the-flap book. The pages of *Novelty!* are divided vertically into three, each section representing one part of a body, and the child reader lifts the flaps to create the diverting transformations—all of them made possible by the configuration of the book's leaves. What were the appeals of such an object to its child owners and readers? How did children use it? How does the fact that *Novelty!* does not conceive of itself as instructing its child readers—as bestowing an important lesson—affect the answers to these questions? And what can this obscure item—powerfully summoning as it does the word *novelty* in its subsidiary sense, which became current at the time Queen Victoria came to the throne, that is, "an often useless or trivial but decorative or amusing object, *esp.* one relying for its appeal on the newness of its design" *(Oxford English Dictionary)*—tell us about children's literature and childhood in the nineteenth century?

*Novelty!* is just one example of a large and understudied subgenre of Victorian children's literature: novelty and movable picture books that dramatically alter the form of the bound book. The production of these items began in the eighteenth century, when publishing firms including Robert Sayer released harlequinades (another type of lift-the-flap book). But thanks to an expanding market for children's books and new technological developments in papermaking and printing, the nineteenth century saw a huge increase in both the number of novelty books published and the variety of their formats. Children's panorama foldouts unraveled often continuous scenes across a number of panels (Plate 1). Pop-ups incorporated three-dimensional paper tableaux, with particularly sumptuous examples mounted from midcentury onward, each one like a miniature theater (Plate 2). Dissolving-view books transformed one image into another using a system of interlocking slats, which were activated by a tab at the bottom of each page (Plate 3). Mechanical books embedded movable figures in the pages, part of the long tradition of blurred boundaries between objects in a child's world—including, most obviously, the boundary between books and toys (Plate 4). Indeed, the scope and variety of the achievements of movable book artists, otherwise known as paper engineers, at the fin de siècle mean that collectors and scholars may now refer to that period as the golden age of *movable* books for children.[2]

Novelty picture books show that attempts to write about and for children differently in the nineteenth century comprise material experiments with format and publishing models as well as experiments in genre and style—the publication of

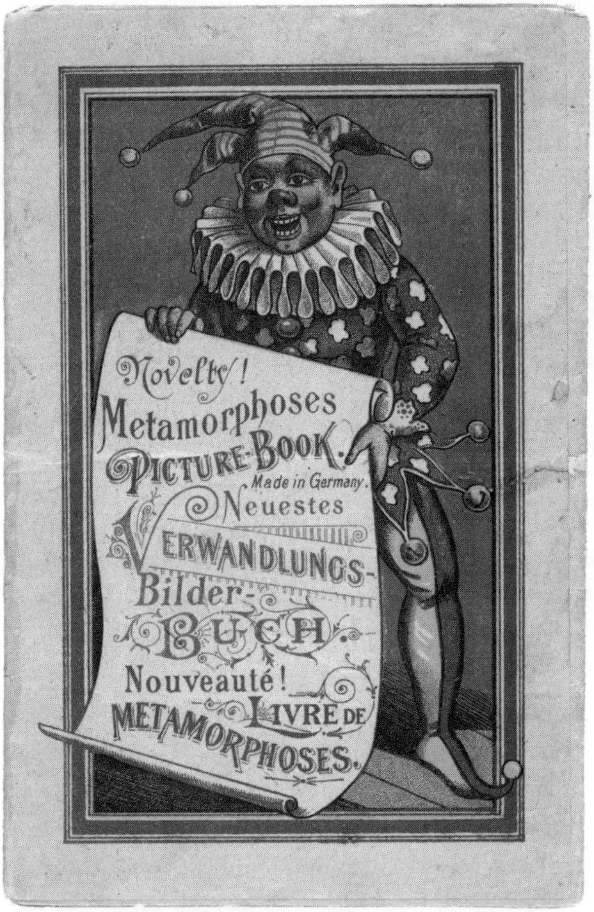


FIGURE I.1. This rare lift-the-flap picture book conjures a model of Victorian children's literature as silly, formally playful, and above all else novel. *Novelty! Metamorphoses Picture-Book/Neuestes Verwandlungs-Bilder-Buch/Nouveauté! Livre de metamorphoses,* circa 1895. Rare Book and Manuscript Library, Columbia University in the City of New York.

the first mechanical book with movable figures for children as well as present classics.[3] Compared with their more famous contemporaries, novelty books provoke a different set of associations: ephemerality over durability, experimental and playful formats over established ones, and silliness over seriousness (sometimes), but most of all the attractions of a book's material form over the merits of its content. Children's literature often invites children to consume books with unique attention to their material properties, with the picture book in particular trading on sensuous features including colorful illustrations, luxurious papers, and unusual formats. Novelty books amplify this tendency. They make the child reader aware that their

FIGURE I.2. When the child reader opens *Novelty!*, she can fold flaps up and down to create a host of different, mismatched bodies. *Novelty! Metamorphoses Picture-Book/Neuestes Verwandlungs-Bilder-Buch/Nouveauté! Livre de metamorphoses,* circa 1895. Rare Book and Manuscript Library, Columbia University in the City of New York.

meaning is inextricable from the book's physical format as well as the interaction of its words and pictures. They render impossible any commonplace model of idealized, abstracted communication associated with the book. In short, they foster an inescapable sense of the book as a material object—one that has troubled as well as pleased commentators.

At the same time, picture books are distinctive material objects because they are treated as such by their young readers, who are as likely to gnaw on pages as they are to pore disinterestedly over them. Novelty picture books court such propensities in the child reader, constructing a process of reading that is dependent on both physical action (pulling a tab, lifting a flap) and intellectual activity—they *embody* reading, so often thought of as a dematerialized and disembodied experience. They supply a means of refining and adjusting many of the assumptions commonly made about the manner and motives of reading: the conception of reading as absorbing, for example. Marks of the ways children did *not* read novelty picture books—ripping, tearing, coloring-in, and more—are ubiquitous in surviving copies. This archive of damaged novelty picture books undermines the reasoning that has (historically and in our contemporary moment) justified support for children's reading and intervenes in the power structures that concern much contemporary scholarship on children's literature. This is because Victorian novelty books for children provoked a physical reader whose actions on or with the book dispelled or even destroyed the messages given by word and picture.

Novelty picture books are a subject germane to the growing concern with material form in the study of children's literature, especially the picture book. The recently published *Routledge Companion to Picturebooks* devotes an entire chapter to materiality.[4] Within the study of early children's literature specifically, a strong commitment to tracing the physical makeup of children's books and its role in the development of juvenile publishing (as well as its impact on the child reader) is visible in the work of Brian Alderson, Andrea Immel, and Katie Trumpener.[5] Some impressive investigations of eighteenth- and nineteenth-century novelty picture books have been undertaken. Jacqueline Reid-Walsh's online archive "Learning as Play" provides interactive digital versions of many historical movables, as well as an explanatory apparatus drawn from Reid-Walsh's own research.[6] Stand-alone articles and essays on movable books, some focusing on individual paper engineers, have been published by leading children's literature critics, including Michelle Ann Abate and Margaret Higonnet.[7] This new work on novelties builds on the scholarship of Ann Montanaro, the Rutgers University librarian and expert on movables whose bibliographies of pop-up and movable books are indispensable, as well as on Peter Haining's *Movable Books: An Illustrated History* (1979).[8] Because novelty books resemble toys, fresh perspectives on the material culture of childhood also provide angles for investigation, in particular, Robin Bernstein's concept of the scriptive thing in *Racial Innocence* (2011).[9] Moreover, damaged copies of novelty books provide distinctive source material for the current flourishing of work using archival evidence to tease out how actual children read in the past, exemplified by M. O. Grenby's *The Child Reader* (2011), Courtney Weikle-Mills's *Imaginary Citizens* (2012), and Patricia Crain's *Reading Children* (2016), as well as Karen Sánchez-Eppler's provocative short meditation on the childhood book destruction that took place at the Evergreens (the Amherst home of Emily Dickinson's brother and his family).[10]

Nonetheless, novelty picture books remain outliers to literary criticism (even children's literature criticism). They are typically dealt with in discrete articles, or in collectors' guides and bibliographies, rather than in full-length critical studies such as this one. More pressingly, they are outliers to definitions of the book itself, a signal example of what Walter Benjamin called "booklike creations from fringe areas." (Benjamin, an avid collector and scholar of children's books, took a special interest in novelties, documenting "books in which doors and curtains in the pictures can be opened to reveal pictures behind them," paper doll books, flip books, and the "well-known pull-out books"—probably panorama foldouts—in careful detail in one early essay. His sensitivity to childhood objects and the way these are handled make his writings important to my discussion throughout this book.)[11] But it is novelties' very unusualness as books and as objects of study that allows them to offer fresh insights into both children's literature and the broader history of books and reading in the nineteenth century.

*Playing with the Book,* then, is about three things: the book as a material object; reading as a physical, embodied practice; and the child in the nineteenth century. In the remainder of this Introduction, I focus on the first—the material book. I begin by tracing the ways the novelty picture book has been defined in terms of either its specific formal innovations or its general difference from other books and by outlining the historical developments in nineteenth-century print culture that allowed different novelty books to be produced. I then turn to a series of critiques of novelty picture books—as nonbooks for nonreaders, as gimmicky, as failed aesthetic wholes, as exploitative in their appeals to child consumers. Such objections prove not so much the value of the novelty book as the norming of children's literature itself around particular ideals: the disavowal, despite the aforementioned fact that children's literature has always been packaged with careful attention to its material qualities, of books for children that become *too* materialized. This in turn lays the groundwork for chapter 1's investigation of the child readers of novelty books and their physicalized reading practices. The anxieties surrounding novelty picture books as overly materialized shade into anxieties surrounding child readers as overly embodied.

## Novelties, Movables, and "Nick Nacks": Definitions and Histories

Right from the outset of children's literature criticism, defining the novelty book proved vexatious. The first edition of one now-standard history, F. J. Harvey Darton's *Children's Books in England* (1932), makes glancing mention of some formats of movable picture book—expressly, the paper doll books produced early in the nineteenth century by Samuel and Joseph Fuller—after noting the development from 1780 onward of pedagogical games that were sometimes bound as books by the Abbé Gaultier, the French priest and education reformer.[12] When Darton's history was updated in 1982 by Alderson, the eminent bibliographer and historian of children's literature, an appendix was added containing details of the "amazing range of gimmickry" released by the London firm of Dean and Son—self-proclaimed originator of the movable book (and certainly its most prolific producer at midcentury)—and the later publications of Ernest Nister, an Anglo-German chromolithography and publishing firm that made many children's novelties.[13] (Both of these publishers appear repeatedly throughout *Playing with the Book,* with chapter 4 devoting particular attention to Nister.)

While Darton focuses on historical shifts and developments, most other definitions of novelty books are formal. Elsewhere, Alderson describes *movable book* as "a generic term which encompasses the intrusion of modelling processes upon the conventional book-block," having earlier noted that such a "general rubric" in itself may comprehend considerable variety.[14] In her contribution to *The Oxford Encyclopedia of Children's Literature,* Montanaro classifies movable books as those "supplemented with innovative movable paper mechanisms."[15] The Children's Books History Society adds nuance to the category by distinguishing between novelty and movable books: novelty books are those with "distinctive treatments of the book's leaves," while movable books are volumes with an "additional mechanism."[16] Here, I use *movable book* mostly in this sense (although the phrase *movable picture books* in my subtitle includes novelties in its ambit), but I employ the term *novelty book* to cover both movable books and books with unusual formats that do not have moving parts, such as the panoramas discussed in chapter 2.

These definitions share a traditional bibliographic flavor, enumerating a few or many formal permutations of the category *movable book* or *novelty book,* perhaps naming some publishers associated with each one. And yet they expose a problem of definition that is also visible in general statements such as this one made by Montanaro: "For over 700 years, artists, philosophers, scientists, and book designers have tried to challenge the book's bibliographic boundaries. They have added flaps, revolving parts, and other movable pieces to enhance the text."[17] Montanaro's account, initially specific ("flaps, revolving parts"), descends into "other movable pieces" as a response in kind to proliferating innovations and adjustments of format. The designation *novelty and movable books* spans a huge range of printed objects. Indeed, to adapt David Hall's critique of the phrase *history of the book,* perhaps the sheer variety of items under the heading seems "too nebulous and sweeping to exert interpretive power."[18] But as critics, collectors, and historians note this material diversity, the nonspecific nature of the catchall word *novelty* proves valuable. Importantly, novelty and movable books are defined in the negative—not by what the formats grouped within the category share with one another but by what they do not share with other sorts of book. Another definition is a case in point: in his *English Children's Books* (1954), Percy Muir includes novelty and movable books under the chapter title "Nick Nacks."[19] Its beguiling quiddity aside, Muir's term suggests an important characteristic: the novelty book's allegiance to items other than books.

Despite their distinctiveness, novelty books may not have thrived as they did in the nineteenth century if it were not for a number of wider historical developments. Most obviously, novelty picture books form part of the familiar story of what Seth Lerer calls the *docere et delectare* of children's literature—the sense that children's books should delight as well as instruct their readers.[20] (The latter element is rather more incidental where the nineteenth-century novelty book is concerned.) This move toward the delightful was in turn intertwined with the children's picture book, of which the novelty book is a subtype. Picture books became prominent in the nineteenth century thanks to celebrated illustrators, such as Randolph Caldecott; prolific publishers, such as Routledge; and new technologies, such as chromolithography.[21] They also reflected new understandings of childhood: the possibility of a consumerist, consumerized, leisure-filled middle-class childhood, confirmed in part by the existence of luxury items such as picture books.

Novelty books represent the close quarters shared by children's books and toys; in the words of Beverly Lyon Clark, "From the start, children's literature was imbricated with material culture."[22] This spans both the tie-in toy—from the pincushion and ball offered with John Newbery's *A Little Pretty Pocket-Book* (1744) to the packaging of children's books with toys representing their characters in the twenty-first century—and adjustments to book format that make the children's book itself a sort of plaything, as is the case with the novelty book. The links between children's books and toys affect not just the representations that children's books contain but also the uses to which the books are put in relation to other objects, as Bernstein recognizes when she calls for scholars to embrace the synergy between books and toys in order to generate new understandings of children's literature and culture. Bernstein observes, "Books and toys jumble together in children's rooms, in their beds, and in their play."[23] In the case of the novelty book, the two are not so much jumbled together after the fact as they are made hybrid at the production stage, so that the question "Books or toys?" poses difficulty (as Reid-Walsh has pointed out).[24] In turn, this leads to patterns of usage that are different from those seen with other kinds of books—notably, patterns that indicate an adjustment of the very idea of what reading is.

Not every factor in the nineteenth-century rise of the novelty book relates to the juvenile market, though; the novelty book was also involved with general trends across publishing and printing in Victorian Britain, such as the extraordinary popularity of illustrated books and the achievements of their creators. As Gordon Ray notes in jingoistic fashion, "England held its own in book illustration with any country in the world" during the period.[25] The pervasiveness of illustrated print was matched by the public appetite for printed pictures—an appetite that also takes its meaning from Victorian visual culture more broadly. Richard Maxwell writes that a "hunger for visual stimulation" shifted from such locations as the street corner and the pageant to the book itself: "a subjective but also a socially determined space; an idea but also an object that could be touched, opened, explored, and owned (portable property *par excellence*)."[26] Illustrated books reflect not just a particular nineteenth-century publishing market but also a distinctive approach to visuality, spectacle, and the material object, all of which unite in the private and mobile space of the book.

The interface between visual culture outside the book and the visual culture of the book can be approached from the other direction, too, as illustrated books might represent or engage with popular entertainments. These intersections constitute instances of what Michael Booth has termed the Victorian "miniaturising of spectacle." (Booth's concept also pleasingly conjures the prevalence of changes in size within Victorian writing for children.) This shift, Booth argues, stemmed from the fact that viewers were "accustomed to see the wonders of the world unfold before them as they turned the pages of a book or magazine."[27] Such intersections of the book with the visual arts and popular entertainments require the simultaneous tracing of what Martin Meisel calls, in his landmark study *Realizations* (1983), "formal similarities" and "expressive and narrative conventions."[28] Meisel's multifaceted approach—he is as interested in structural echoes as in outright references, and he gives space to speculative examination of the ways in which certain visual modes shape narrative patterns—influences a number of the readings of novelty picture books that I offer here.

Children's novelty books are exemplary both as instances of miniaturized spectacle and as ready testaments to the flexible approach needed in any consideration of the full range of intersections between nineteenth-century print and other arts and entertainments. Novelty books often positioned themselves as direct competitors with, or formal re-creations of, visual spectacles such as the magic-lantern show and the moving panorama. The midcentury volume *Dean's New Book of Dissolving Views,* for instance, equated itself to a magic-lantern effect in its title, but also in the specific changes made by the pictures, which included summer to winter and day to night, both signature transformations of the inventor of the dissolving view, Henry Langdon Childe (see Plate 13).[29] In contrast to these explicit and direct parallels, children's panorama picture books relied on multiple and diffuse echoes between their own contours and a variety of different panoramic entertainments.

The novelty book's explicit and implicit links with entertainments such as the dissolving-view projection and the panorama have led media historians and theorists to explore the relationship between novelties and Victorian visual culture, including the evolution of photography and cinema. For instance, Eric Faden calls children's pop-ups the first "moving pictures," noting numerous connections between early cinema and movable books, such as their attempts at "negotiating a balance between linear storytelling and visual display."[30] John Plunkett has charted the attempts of novelty publications "to replicate—or structure themselves on—the viewing experience of peepshows, panoramas and the magic lantern" in order to make a larger argument about the pervasiveness of optical recreations: "Magic lanterns, peepshows, and dioramas did not just stand as figures for the working of the imagination; they offered a visual format that could be imaginatively translated into other media, from children's books and toys to satirical prints."[31] Helen Groth discusses movable books as "explicitly inter-medial forms" that "encouraged reading as a form of interactive episodic play, transforming the codex into an instructive miscellaneous entertainment where extracts and abridgements of familiar tales, legends and myths could be endlessly recycled."[32] This rich vein of scholarship underpins *Playing with the Book,* particularly chapter 3, which concludes with a comparison between fantasies of three-dimensionality in the stereoscope and the pop-up book, and chapter 4, which uses theoretical accounts of the cinematic dissolve to unpick the relationships between the paired pictures in Nister's dissolving-view books for children.

I avoid, however, discussing novelty picture books here solely as they pertain to nonbook visual technologies and entertainments, or as most notable as part of the prehistory of cinema. Conflating the history of cinema and the history of publishing threatens an error of the sort Markman Ellis critiques with reference to the eighteenth-century panorama: the substitution of a teleology for the "recalcitrant historical complexity" that attended the emergence of entertainments such as the panorama and the dissolving view.[33] Novelty books are particularly vulnerable to such (technicist) positioning of visual entertainments. Hence in this volume I give them space and time on their own account, recognizing the distinctive sorts of perception and playfulness they demand of their child readers, instead of locating them in a genealogy of visual culture that might imply, for instance, that the dissolving-view book is a failed intermediary or evolutionary dead end between dissolving-view lantern effects and the cinema. This is important, too, because the embodied, physicalized reading demanded by novelty picture books takes its significance from its relation to specific factors in the history of children as readers and to specific sensory factors in reading—particularly touch—that may be marginalized by an interest in optics alone.

All books are, of course, material objects, but not all books are "materialized"—that is, not all of them show off and highlight and trade on their material form. By behaving in this way, novelty picture books take part in the wider nineteenth-century publishing trend of using material ingenuity to ward off textual ephemerality. "Victorian 'text,'" writes Gerard Curtis, "was constantly being refigured to avoid its symbolic and ephemeral disposition in order to promote a more tangible, and everlasting, reality/materiality—exploiting, wherever possible, text's constituency with the visual, tactile and visceral. This was achieved through such devices as paintings from the novel, ornate bookbindings, initial letters, advertising graphics, bookplates, graphic illustration and frontispiece portraits—even perfumed books."[34] Movable parts and unusual formats further exemplify Victorian "visual, tactile and visceral" strategies for refiguring the book. These strategies were responses to the feeling of overabundance in publishing—a proverbial complaint that increased over the century as mechanized printing became the norm—and the associated disposability of printed matter. Augmenting or showcasing their own materiality allowed books to make a special claim in an overcrowded market, and the links between children's books and toys made the juvenile market a natural home for these practices.

Novelty books intersected with other types of "materialized" Victorian books, too, as was the case with the gift book, typically an anthology of short texts packaged with illustrations in a decorative binding for the Christmas market. Gift books and novelty books for children shared publishers: in Michael Twyman's history of the fin de siècle chromolithographed gift book, three publishers of movables are mentioned by name.[35] Both types of books sought to control the way they were bought and used (that is, as gifts). Scholarly readings of the gift book also illuminate the novelty picture book, such as Lorraine Janzen Kooistra's idea that gift books yoked together the "scopic regimes of spectacle, visual art, material culture, and social status," and Kathryn Ledbetter's point that gift books constituted "ornamental drawing-room attractions."[36]

Technological developments enabled the production of the nineteenth-century novelty picture book. This is true of later picture books as well, as Nathalie op de Beeck has shown in her study of modern American picture books, but it takes on special relevance in the case of children's printed novelties.[37] Key shifts included the move from handmade to machine-made paper enabled by the invention of the Fourdrinier machine in the early years of the nineteenth century. (The machine was in "almost universal application" by 1837.)[38] Paper and card are especially important to the movable book: it is strong card that enables the production of works such as the intricate, multimedia mechanical books made by renowned German paper engineer Lothar Meggendorfer, which utilize card, paper, and metal screws. (Papermakers, writes Alderson, are the true "founders of 'the movable book.'")[39] These technical developments have aesthetic implications, too. Meggendorfer's books are famous for their naturalistic movement, which is largely unparalleled in other movable books. In *Always Jolly!*, the motion of an angler drawing a fish up from the water conveys strain as much as do visual cues such as the man's determined stance—legs apart, head thrown back—and is entirely dependent on the flexible yet strong card that realizes the effect (see Plate 4).[40] Indeed, it is not just that rudimentary motions were standard in movable books before the production of certain papers and cards; the effects produced were even less likely to last than those in later examples, as attested by the condition of extant Victorian books with moving parts made from paper.

Changing methods for printing books, and in particular for coloring images, also enabled or stymied the novelty book's reach. Although the first steam-driven printing press was invented in 1812, at midcentury a firm specializing in novelties might still be, in the words of Iona and Peter Opie, "the scene of almost frenzied activity, of picture-colouring, paper-sticking, of card-cutting, and of head-scratching, as [the publisher] sought to keep ahead of their rivals in the field."[41] The Opies' account focuses on Dean and Son, imagining in particular Dean's premises at 65 Ludgate Hill, which the firm occupied from 1856 to 1871.[42] The Opies expose the hand-coloring that dictated the production of the mid-Victorian movable book—a method of production that affected both the quantity of books produced and the quality of the finished product. For example, a thousand copies of one of the first mechanical books, *Dean's Moveable Mother Hubbard,* were printed in February 1857; the color was sometimes haphazardly applied.[43] Later, Dean and Son became able to produce more sophisticated effects. A book in the company's 1890s Surprise Model series, with its rounded, convex pop-up forms, was noted at the time of publication as "an extraordinary bit of mechanism, working automatically and producing quite startling effects" (see Figure 1.6).[44] The volumes in this series stood into the twentieth century as the "most ambitious and fragile of nineteenth-century pop-up books," in the Opies' opinion.[45] Across the century, the firm's movable books were supported by an extensive marketing apparatus, both internal to individual titles, as in advertisements on endpapers and back covers, and external to them, as in newspaper notices.

Nister, a printer-publisher, and Meggendorfer, an illustrator and paper engineer, are the producers most associated with the golden age of movable books at the end of the nineteenth century, and their respective productions represent an increasingly sophisticated technical system for producing movables. As Nister collectors and scholars Julia and Frederick Hunt have documented, delegates of the British Department of Science and Art of the Committee of Council on Education visited Nister's chromolithographic print works in Nuremberg in 1896.[46] There they observed steam-driven presses large enough to be manned by two workers.[47] Parallel technical innovations in printing methods allowed one million Meggendorfer movable books to be produced by 1902.[48] The scale of the various printing operations producing movable books for children—like the scale of printing operations producing other sorts of juvenile publications—altered drastically over the course of the nineteenth century. Nonetheless, as Michael Dawson and Geoff Fox have demonstrated, even today movables continue to require what Dawson calls "a high degree of hand assembly."[49] Moreover, while my focus in this volume is on Victorian children's literature, the books discussed were often made in Germany, thanks to the dominance of German firms in chromolithography for the juvenile market—fin de siècle movables represent an international children's publishing industry, as I explore in chapter 5. The flourishing of novelty books in Britain ended when World War I cut German printers off from overseas audiences.

The technological shifts that affected the production of novelty books were multifaceted. For instance, in an 1897 article in a technical publication, Ernest Nister proposed applying the newly popular three-color principle to chromolithography, thus reducing "the large number of printing plates hitherto required in producing a good chromograph."[50] While the invention seems to have been little taken up—Geoffrey Wakeman and Gavin Bridson, for instance, have to provide an explanation of it in their historical guide to nineteenth-century color printing—Nister's hybridized patent process suggests once more the need for complex understandings of technological change.[51] This holds true not just for the technologies used to produce novelty and movable books but also for the book *as a* technology developing via the trajectories of individual novelty formats.

Aesthetics and technology intertwined as Victorian artists anatomized the effects that different modes of producing color illustrations might have on the child reader. Take hand-colored children's books. At the end of the century, renowned illustrator Walter Crane bemoaned such productions, available when he began working as an illustrator thirty years earlier, as "not very inspiring," characterized by "careless and unimaginative wood-cuts, very casually coloured by hand, dabs of pink and emerald green being laid on across faces and frocks with a somewhat reckless aim." Such slapdash efforts are undesirable for children, according to Crane, because of the "ineffaceable quality of . . . early pictorial and literary impressions."[52] Crane incorporated technical details within pedagogical concerns, but altered techniques for the production of color illustrations affected children as workers as well as children as consumers in the nineteenth century. The fact that children worked as colorers is visible in the driest of documents (evidence given to the 1818 Select Committee on the Copyright Acts reveals a "young lad" coloring works for the artist and printer Thomas Fisher), as well as in children's literature itself, as when a young girl finds a job as a colorer at Benjamin Tabart's publishing emporium in Eliza Fenwick's *Visits to the Juvenile Library* (1805).[53]

Later writers tended to romanticize the connection between the publishing practice of hand-coloring and child labor. Darton states of hand-colored children's books, "The colour was put on by droves of children working together; so many put on the red patch, so many the blue, and the prints were passed on thus till the final gay thing was completed," an assessment he seems to borrow from Andrew Tuer, a fin de siècle antiquarian and children's book aficionado: "The colouring was done by children in their teens, who worked with astonishing celerity and more precision than could be expected. They sat round a table, each with a little pan of water-colour, a brush, a partly coloured copy as a guide, and a pile of printed sheets. One child would paint on the red, wherever it appeared in the copy; another followed, say with the yellow, and so on until the colouring was finished."[54] The association between the child and colored pictures is so pervasive as to make even a story of child labor delightful or, to use Tuer's preferred word, "quaint."[55] Comparable fantasies of book production underscore the novelty book's vexed relationship, triumphal yet escapist, to the industry and technology that enabled its existence—particularly as the sometime focus on workers is concerned. Moreover, the "quaint" child colorers hint at the division between children who work (sometimes making novelty picture books) and children who consider representations of workers in novelty picture books, which were often expensive.

The vogue for illustrated books, the intimate relationship between print and other popular entertainments, and new technologies that affected the appeal or success of printed materials place novelty books within a specifically nineteenth-century history of the book. But the children's novelty book must also be located within factors that are fairly specific to it. One of these is the invention and patenting of new mechanisms to enable movement on the page. The cover of the Nister dissolving-view book *Playtime Surprises* bears a note reading "ENTERED AT STATIONERS' HALL, PATENT APPLICATION NO 10870," also listing "D. R. G. M. No 11486" for the imprimatur *Deutsches Reichsgebrauchsmuster* (German-registered design).[56] The patent, recorded in 1899 under the title "Improvements in So-Called Revolving Changing Pictures," was classified as a pictorial toy invention related "to changing pictures consisting of two superimposed pieces of cardboard &c. cut into sectors so that a partial rotation draws one set from under the other."[57] One of the figures accompanying the technical description of the improvements showed both the signature starburst effect of the changing pictures and the sort of subject that it might be used to depict: children playing.

Clare Pettitt has drawn attention to the distinction in nineteenth-century legal definitions of originality between "the mode in which an artwork was executed" and "the raw ideas contained therein," with their attendant cultural assumptions; as Mark Rose has shown, for some time these debates had ranged over form and content, "style and sentiment," in attempting to anatomize just where intellectual property resided.[58] The illustration included in Nister's patent collapsed the distinction between the revolving pictures (a "mode" of the picture book) and the depiction of children and childhood (the "raw ideas" the picture book comprises). The final statement in the patent, however, was, "The pictures may be used singly or bound into a book." Hence this question of "mode" of execution becomes a wider formal one, raising the issue of the interface between ephemera and bound books—particularly as the inclusion of such pictures within books, and as accompaniments to stories, changes their formal implications as well as the ways they are used. How did novelty books, with their marked resemblance to other objects, challenge the book's very definition?

## Picture-Book Theory and the Trouble with the Material Book

When the book historian Simon Eliot asks of nineteenth-century print culture, "What do we mean by a 'book'? Anything above a certain length? What then about part-works and pamphlets? What about broadsides? Should we include maps? Where do newspapers fit in? What about music and prints? What about ephemera?," he seeks to prompt bibliographical debate—to encourage scholars to realize the diversity of the period's printed matter.[59] Such a debate, however, becomes tinged with urgency in the case of children's novelty picture books, which, as Kathy Piehl has observed, are dogged by the question of whether they are "worthy to be called books at all."[60] The formal variety of novelty books has sometimes spurred a cultural deliberation over the category *book* itself, how far its boundaries can be pushed before it loses its meaning. Moreover, the question of how the physical entity of the book should be defined can also constitute a question of what we want a book to be, and of how certain books might pose a threat to these wishes—as Piehl's choice of the word "worthy" recognizes.

I conducted much of the research for *Playing with the Book* at the Bodleian Library, University of Oxford, using the Opie Collection of Children's Literature. The Opie Collection is one of the most significant children's book resources in the world. As is true of many children's literature archives, the holdings come from a substantial private collection: that of the scholars mentioned above, Iona Opie (1923–2017) and Peter Opie (1918–1982).[61] The collection comprises some twenty thousand items collected by the Opies over decades of scholarship, as well as acquisition records and bibliographic notes kept by Peter Opie. After Peter Opie's death, Iona Opie agreed to sell the Bodleian the collection for half of its valuation of one million pounds, and the library acquired it in the late 1980s following a huge public appeal led by Prince Charles.[62]

The history of the Opie Collection reveals the difficulties in preserving novelty picture books, of which the Opies collected a significant number. First of all, the move from the Opies' home to the Bodleian created a division between books and toys that was not present in the Opies' original collection. As renowned scholars not just of children's literature but also of children's culture, the Opies had many toys and games as well as books; these did not migrate.[63] Their absence makes novelty books—which had their own special wing in the Opies' home, called "the Temple of Fancy" after the early nineteenth-century London emporium belonging to the creators of the first paper doll books—seem aberrant rather than part of the continuum between book and toy that is constitutive of children's literature.[64]

But the Opie Collection's novelties occasioned more specific unease as well. When the Bodleian acquired the collection, Alderson (who had provided the valuation of the books) presented the library's acquisition as a legitimation of children's literature criticism: "If children's books are to be treated as objects worthy of study . . . there can be nothing but satisfaction that a great private self-indulgence is to be institutionalized in the Bodleian Library."[65] But Alderson's encomium to the collection's movement from "private self-indulgence" to national treasure evokes the novelty only to dispel its charms. While "a hundred . . . will nod and find justification for the whole enterprise in Meggendorfer's cunningly engineered *Lebende Tierbilder,* with articulated movement of the pictures as you pull the tabs," Alderson is dismissive of this logic. The Opie Collection is instead valuable for the following effect: "We are given an insight into the making of . . . readers."[66] Alderson displaces material understandings of children's books—those that naturally stem from the novelty book—with the internal shaping of the reader and the culture.

His ideas mirror those of the Opies themselves, who wrote an essay about novelty and movable books titled "Books That Come to Life" in the mid-1970s. Novelty books' popularity with collectors had, the Opies wrote, deleterious effects: "Before we know where we are, the non-readers amongst us, who seemingly include the majority of visitors to antique supermarkets and buyers at Sotheby's children's-book sales, are valuing these non-books above real books, and paying for them as if they contained the gems of our literary heritage."[67] The buyers of novelty books, the Opies implied, had been captured by a gimmick—something appealing at first sight, but ultimately valueless. (This bait and switch is vital to the gimmick, of which Sianne Ngai has recently written: "We describe it as cheap or aesthetically impoverished only because something about it seemed so truly shiny with value.")[68] In fact, the term *gimmick* haunts novelty books and underpins the mistrust with which they are sometimes met.[69] The book artist Martha Carothers, for instance, warns: "The risk of novelty devices is that a book may become just a collection of gimmicks. When properly used, a novelty should explain, describe, or entertain, at the same time piquing the viewer to action, both physical and mental. Otherwise, it becomes a trick feature without significant meaning."[70] For Carothers as for the Opies, gimmickry comes back to a sense of overmaterialization. The material properties of novelty devices are not always harnessed in line with, or subservient to, traditional notions of value, which inhere to a book's capacity "to explain, describe, or entertain," rather than its material forms.

This sort of charge of gimmickry carries more weight when leveled at nineteenth-century novelty books than when aimed at contemporary ones. (Meggendorfer is an important exception to this rule, as chapter 5 explores.) Twentieth- and twenty-first-century paper engineers such as Jan Pieńkowski and Robert Sabuda have created exceptional movable picture books that fit within established models of value in children's literature. Pieńkowski's pop-up book *Haunted House* won the Kate Greenaway Medal for the most distinguished picture book of 1979, for instance, while Sabuda has reflected on his practice as a paper engineer in *The Lion and the Unicorn,* one of the leading scholarly journals devoted to children's literature.[71] By contrast, the verbal and visual texts of Victorian novelty books often parallel the books' unmanageable physical contours: they trouble tenets of textual value by being poorly executed, haphazard, composed in line with their formal gimmicks, crudely humorous, or sentimental (sometimes all at once). They are examples of the special categories of nineteenth-century book identified by Leah Price: categories in which "a book's textual content is judged particularly worthless *and* its material properties are judged especially valuable."[72] Novelty books *overmaterialize,* which is to say, the appeal of their gimmicky formats often exceeds the merit of their content.

Central concepts in children's literature criticism show that even when scholars consider overtly "materialized" forms, such as the colored picture book (referred to as a *toy book* in the nineteenth century as a matter of course), certain principles of selection tend to marginalize those books in which, for example, form overwhelms content. Hence Perry Nodelman begins his landmark monograph on picture books: "The first noteworthy children's storybooks that have a similar balance between words and pictures as do contemporary picture books were books illustrated by Walter Crane, Kate Greenaway, and above all Randolph Caldecott in the last third of the nineteenth century."[73] The idea of balance recurs in more recent scholarship on contemporary picture books, as, for example, when Lawrence Sipe and Caroline McGuire state that "picturebooks are aesthetic wholes, so carefully designed that everything in the book is the result of someone's choice," or when Barbara Kiefer devises the formula "the integrated nature of the design of the total book."[74] An interest in balance or complement between picture and word—in picture books as carefully curated and holistically designed—suggests that picture books are serious. It revalues the picture book as an art form: a valuable endeavor.

But this interest also excludes many picture books from consideration. Ideals of balance and integration disavow other models for putting visual and verbal texts together; as W. J. T. Mitchell has observed of word–image relationships more generally, "Difference is just as important as similarity, antagonism as crucial as collaboration, dissonance and division of labor as interesting as harmony and blending of function."[75] In the nineteenth century, such differences and antagonisms were a generic feature, rather than an exception to the rule: Julia Thomas calls the Victorian illustrated text "a divided genre, in which image and word fail to coincide."[76] Forms of dis-integration—of perhaps contradictory messages from picture, word, and format; of picture overwhelming word, or of format overwhelming both pictures and words—characterize Victorian novelty books, meaning that some existing frameworks for studying the picture book fall short when brought to bear on this unusual subtype.

The relationship between markets and novelty books is also significant. With their material innovations and interactive modes of cocreation, Maria Nikolajeva observes, twentieth- and twenty-first-century movables blur "the boundary between art and artifact." Nonetheless, only a few represent "examples of the highest artistic quality"—the rest are "mass-market goods."[77] Like the ideal of balance, Nikolajeva's distinction in part reflects the long and definitional struggle in children's literature criticism to cement the place of children's books as a worthwhile subject for scholarship and object of aesthetic consideration. Any divide between "artistic" and "mass-market" books reproduces, however, a tendency noted by the book historians John Jordan and Robert Patten: the literary critical principle that "to consider publishing as a culture industry, with all that such a perspective implies about its commercial motives, would depreciate the publishers' products into mere commodities."[78] This is a particularly tricky assumption when dealing with children's literature, which, as Alderson remarks, "has been governed by publishers to a much greater degree than in other fields of literary endeavour."[79]

What if the history of the children's picture book were rewritten, and, instead of balanced examples of word–picture interaction and illustrious practitioners of picture-book art, novelty books were placed front and center? A short test case for this question, which I explore at length throughout this book, can be provided by the earliest printed novelties for children: eighteenth-century harlequinades.[80] Harlequinades are made from two printed sheets, with the top sheet segmented into flaps; any individual panel of the harlequinade contains three different images, depending on whether none, one, or both of its flaps are lifted (Figure I.3).[81] The reader turns a flap up or down at the salient moment in the story to reveal a new image and block of text. The relative obscurity of the format makes it seem—as novelty books always seem—a subcategory of the picture book. In fact, the relationship (temporally at least) goes the other way: harlequinades appeared *before* the picture book *tout court* as it developed in the nineteenth century; they are the picture book's precursor.[82]

Harlequinades reshape picture-book history in a number of ways. First, they unbind the picture book, showing the inseparability of children's literature from what Cathy Lynn and Michael Preston call "the other print tradition": ephemera.[83] The relationship is multidirectional where nineteenth-century print is concerned, as novelty items may subsequently be classified as ephemera—for example, Maurice Rickards and Michael Twyman include the Fuller paper doll books and children's paper panoramas in their *Encyclopedia of Ephemera* (2001)—while at the time of their production, movable books shared techniques and publishers with ephemera such as pop-up Christmas cards.[84] Like children's novelties, ephemera are classified not by shared features but rather by a sort of unmanageable diversity, "as various as the insects with which they share their name," to quote Timothy Young. (Young also notes, as I have done where novelty books are concerned, the negative weight of definitions of ephemera as "non-book material.")[85] If the history of the picture book begins with the harlequinade (a

FIGURE I.3. Eighteenth-century harlequinade books, such as *Queen Mab; or, The Tricks of Harlequin* (1771), require the child reader to lift the flap in order to continue the story. Beinecke Rare Book and Manuscript Library, Yale University.

movable made up of flat sheets of paper), ephemera take on new significance. Rather than occupying their traditional place, "mapped by hegemonic print culture as its low 'other,' disparaged, and marginalized accordingly," ephemera become central to one of the most iconic and beloved print traditions in children's literature.[86]

Second, harlequinades elucidate the cross-pollination between children's books and nineteenth-century visual culture at large. The harlequinade is named after the popular theatrical interlude in the pantomime and often mentions particular productions in its colophon; indeed, harlequinades are a valuable source of information about historical staging.[87] Such publications, along with later theatrical movables—for instance, mechanical books such as Nelson Lee's *Royal Acting Punch and Judy*—may represent the dynamic of the souvenir, by which "the public, the monumental, and the three-dimensional" are converted "into the miniature, that which can be enveloped by the body, or into the two-dimensional representation, that which can be appropriated within the privatized view of the individual subject."[88] Novelty books might, then, memorialize children's attendance at particular theater productions, or perhaps *parents'* attendance.[89] As such, they show children's literature as part of a network of entertainments, all of which generated material objects and all of which (to recall Bernstein) script particular interactions with the book.

Finally, harlequinades can demonstrate the importance of format, in addition to words and images, to the study of the children's picture book. While declarations about complementary pictures and words in the picture book are commonplace, discussion of morphology—the shape, size, *form* of the book—has until recently been more marginal.[90] By contrast, the harlequinade's alternative name, *turn-up,* shifts emphasis from a central character (Harlequin) and his connection to eighteenth-century theater to the book's material constitution: "Turn up, to find how from this scrape, / Our Comic Genius can escape," "Turn it down and you'll see further," and so forth.[91] This device—resembling what Nikolajeva and Carole Scott describe as a "primitive" page-turner—instructs the reader to manipulate the book and hence carry the story forward.[92] Whether primitive or not, the harlequinade's page-turner instruction demonstrates the vital importance of the movable book's material form. Child readers can understand the story, as told in words and pictures, only once they have mastered the novel material parameters of the book.

Harlequinades show the adjustment of knowledges that can happen when novelty picture books shift from their peripheral place in the history of children's literature to take on a starring role. They break down the boundaries between children's literature and ephemera, and between children's books and the wider cultures of entertainment in which they appear. Most crucially, they insist that material form need not (should not) be a second-order consideration in discussions of the picture book. Book format and its varying impacts on the child reader are, then, the key concerns of *Playing with the Book.* Chapter 1 presents an introduction to the distinctive embodied reading experience offered by novelty picture books, linking this to the history of children as readers in the nineteenth century. In this chapter I provide detailed evidence, drawn largely from the Opie Collection, of how children read novelty books and the challenges their reading practices pose to some common assumptions about the power dynamics of children's literature. The movable's fragility demands explicit instructions: injunctions as to how, physically, to read, and guidance about correct and incorrect use. I counterpoint these instructions with sustained examination of new and unconventional archival evidence of children's reading—ripping and tearing, coloring-in, dirt, and reconstruction. Such evidence, regularly displaced by marginalia in scholarly considerations of reader usage, should be given greater import in the study of children's reading practices, illuminating as it does children's nontextual understandings of their books.

While chapter 1 ranges across different types of novelty books, each of the remaining four chapters treats an individual format, addressing its unique reshaping of picture-book form and its demands on (and offers to) the child reader. The chapters broadly follow a progression both chronological, circa 1835 to 1914, and formal, moving from simple to complex innovations in shape, size, or page. Chapter 2 centers on the panorama. The children's panorama is a long foldout that, once extended, resembles a scroll, each part of the image or text block proximate in physical space. The resulting simultaneity has structural implications for both visual and verbal narrative. This chapter uses theories of narrative and space to explore how various configurations of the panorama book for children shape, or refuse, visual narratives, considering panoramic alphabet books, histories of royal succession, and fictional tales both original and preexisting. The chapter's final section raises the point that children may not have read some Victorian panoramas at all, but instead pasted them up on walls—an alternative model of spatializing stories.

Chapter 3 treats the most familiar of novelty formats: the pop-up book, in which three-dimensional scenes spring up from the page. Taking as its foundation Walter Benjamin's synesthetic statement that children's "eyes are not concerned with three-dimensionality; this they perceive through their sense of touch," the chapter brings the pop-up book into dialogue with models of surface, depth, and the illusion of three dimensions drawn from three nineteenth-century visual modes—landscape painting, the theater, and the stereoscope.[93] The pop-up book makes tactile what is achieved purely by visual means in other arts. The child reader physically enacts the three-dimensionality of the scene, which is a layered product of techniques of perspective and actual manipulation of the picture plane within the book. Ultimately, the reader's production of the pop-up's three-dimensionality is vital to the sensorium of childhood created by this kind of novelty book.

Chapter 4 is at once an investigation of a particular format and a case study of an influential producer of children's novelty picture books. The dissolving-view book interlays two pictures by way of a system of interlocking slats; the mechanism means that one picture changes or dissolves into another when a tab is pulled. At the end of the century, the publisher Ernest Nister was particularly famous for producing dissolving views. Nister is a frequent character in his own publications, and this chapter uses these appearances to reveal embedded ideas of what a children's book should be and where it should come from—a version of Leah Price's history of *a* book, in which "accounts of print culture" might be "narrated from the point of view not of human readers and users, but of the book."[94] Part of the story a Nister dissolve tells about itself involves connecting the two parts of the dissolve, hence the chapter traces the relationship between the dissolve pictures in a series of close readings of movable images that considers not just their local content but also the publication process of reusing and remixing images that led to their production.

Finally, the mechanical books discussed in chapter 5 blend the book and the toy: paper figures, mounted on the page, move at the pull of a tab. This chapter examines the ways in which the famous mechanical books by Lothar Meggendorfer (a celebrated caricaturist) present dehumanized characters equated not with individuals but with professional, subcultural, and racial types. This typifying tendency is read in light of the works' formal resemblance to the mechanical toy, the automaton, and the puppet. The (white) child reader's power over the mechanical figures in each book signals the child's mastery of certain adult character types, most pressingly, racial stereotypes, as a sustained examination of two Meggendorfer illustrations of black figures demonstrates.

Building on existing work across a number of fields—children's literature, the history of the book, Victorian visual art and material culture—*Playing with the Book* uses novelty and movable picture books for children to intervene in such areas of study as the book as a material object; the relationships between word, image, and format in illustrated books; the phenomenology of reading; and the child as reader. Nineteenth-century novelty books exemplify the alternative materialist and materialized ways of creating books that define juvenile publishing. They also, as we shall see in chapter 1, illuminate the alternative modes of reading sometimes granted to or fantasized for the child in Victorian Britain.

—Chapter One—

# The Three Rs

## Reading, Ripping, Reconstructing

One of the earliest and strictest lessons to the children of the house being how to turn the pages of their own literary possessions lightly and deliberately, with no chance of tearing or dog's ears.
—*John Ruskin, preface to* Sesame and Lilies

And my ambition *now* is (is it a vain one?) to be read by Children aged from Nought to Five. To be read? Nay, not so! Say rather to be thumbed, to be cooed over, to be dogs'-eared, to be rumpled, to be kissed, by the illiterate, ungrammatical, dimpled Darlings, that fill your Nursery with merry uproar, and your inmost heart of hearts with a restful gladness!
—*Lewis Carroll, preface to* The Nursery "Alice"

Two prefaces to Victorian texts by canonical authors, both addressed to parents, and both laying out particular visions of the young reader—but they could not be more different. For Ruskin in 1871, learning to read means learning not to dog-ear pages as part of a fastidious socialization process that involves subtle modulations of children's behavior and movement as they come to handle books "lightly and deliberately." By contrast, in 1890 Carroll envisages a whole host of unconventional usages—thumbing, cooing, dog-earing, rumpling, and kissing—that an audience too young to read will find for the last installment in his Alice series.[1] Despite their varying viewpoints, though, both quotations offer moments of instruction in reading that are also instruction in *not* reading, if reading is conceived of as a purely mental activity: each writer imagines a child's ideal *physical,* rather than intellectual, engagement with a book.

Ruskin and Carroll represent two poles in the cultural attitudes toward children as readers in the Victorian period, extremes that can be traced to the end of an earlier age. In his comprehensive history of child readers at the birth of children's literature—between 1700 and 1840—M. O. Grenby concludes that, just as the attraction of children's books "was frequently based less on text than physical appearance—pretty binding, miniature size, moving parts," so "their owners often understood them as material rather than textual entities." Material understandings of books were entrenched in young readers, and this very issue of materiality resulted in what Grenby describes as an "ongoing, attritional war" between children and the adults who governed their reading. By the Victorian period, however, the consensus around child readers had changed somewhat, as "Romantic revaluations of childhood as a phase to be cherished, rather than hastened and overcome, led at least in some quarters to a relaxation of the injunctions against children's physical relationship with books." (To this end, Grenby cites the rumpled and disordered books of Carroll's preface to *The Nursery "Alice."*)[2]

Because of their linked attributes of interactivity and fragility, novelty and movable picture books hold a special place in this history of children's reading. True movables, in particular, place specific bodily movements at the heart of the reading experience while also demanding careful handling from their child readers. Moreover, there is rich archival evidence in particular copies of how child readers disobeyed these dictates—either deliberately or inadvertently. The material traces of children's often destructive reading practices have the potential, as Karen Sánchez-Eppler has noted, to intervene in the debates over agency that structure much children's literature criticism.[3] With this proposition in mind, in this chapter I range across formats in order to explore how novelty books foreground, imagine, or display the child as reader. In the process, I consider theoretical models of embodied reading and their relationship to the child; depictions of reading in novelty books' words and pictures, including the instructional poems that are a generic feature of nineteenth-century movables; and unconventional archival traces of children's reading—coloring-in, rips, tears, and other marks of damage. Such evidence shows the distinctive ways that children read (and did not read) the novelty book in the nineteenth century, while also suggesting what such specific practices might have to do with children's reading more broadly.

## "The Smallest Thumb and Finger": Children, Novelties, and Embodied Reading

The novelty's nonbookness—its troubling of the usual contours for the book, surveyed in the Introduction—links persistently to a parallel sense of its nonreadness. As David Lewis has noted in a contemporary context, "Pop-ups and movables tend to produce a degree of unease amongst children's book critics and scholars for they often do not seem to offer much in the way of a reading experience."[4] In fact, the Victorian novelty picture book diversifies the reading experience by recognizing reading as comprising physical acts as well as intellectual ones, or even refusing the opposition of the two. Take, for instance, a movable book titled *The Children's Wonderland,* produced around 1900 by Ernest Nister.[5] The volume contains multiple components: a series of short, unrelated poems composed by the prolific Nister author Helen Marion Burnside; line illustrations by Florence Hardy; and full-color dissolving-view movable pieces—segmented-disc dissolves, where the slats that interlock the two pictures form a circle or wheel. (The colored pictures that make up the dissolves, which are frequently repurposed across Nister volumes, are usually unattributed.)[6] While in 1896 the word *wonderland* inevitably recalled the otherworld fantasy story for children, the book focuses on more naturalistic subjects, including learning to read and playing with animals, all of them mediated through the movable mechanisms. Hence, in the opening poem, it is the narrator's "delightful task" to transport the reader into the children's wonderland, where the dissolving-view mechanism allows one picture to change into another. The end of the poem underlines the physical procedure of moving through the book, rather than imaginative travel into the world of the story powered by the (adult) narrator of the poem: "The smallest thumb and finger here / Can always let you through!" This section explores the thumb-and-finger reading demanded by the novelty picture book: how it relates to specific conceptions of Victorian readers and children as readers, and how embodied reading shapes the power dynamic among child, adult, and book.

A number of historians and theorists of reading have sought to embody the reader as a way of correcting models of reading as exclusively intellectual or abstract. Georges Perec once issued a directive "to bring reading back to what it primarily is," reimagining reading not as dematerialized but instead as "a precise activity of the body, the bringing into play of certain muscles, different organizations of our posture, sequential decisions, temporal choices, a whole set of strategies inserted into the continuum of social life which mean that we don't read simply anyhow, any when and anywhere, even if we may read anything."[7] (Michel de Certeau later deployed Perec's idea in his account of reading as "a wild orchestration of the body.")[8] More recently, in his work on pictures of reading, Garrett Stewart has affirmed that "however much the subjective horizon may be expanded by it, reading is always a putting in of body time as well, including the prolonged, fluctuating engagement of the nervous system and its multiple affective and physiological registers."[9] Perec's "precise activity of the body," de Certeau's "wild orchestration of the body," Stewart's "body time": these writers seek to embody what seems disembodied, externalize what seems internal, about reading. This is a mirror image of the action performed by book historians concerned with the material book, as the regained body of the reader corresponds with the regained presence of the book as an object.

Leah Price structures her examination of Victorian reading around the question "What meanings do books make even, or especially, when they go unread?"; she argues that reading was embodied and physicalized as often as it was intellectual in the period. Unread books are a peculiarly common fixture, as Price notes, in nineteenth-century texts, even at a linguistic level. Victorian novels compulsively prefer "manual phrases like 'turned the page' or spatial phrases like 'sat with a book before him'" to "the mental verb 'read.'"[10] Price proposes three "operations" that books undergo in Victorian literature: "Reading (doing something with the words), handling (doing something with the object), and circulating (doing something to, or with, other persons by means of the book—whether cementing or severing relationships, whether by giving and receiving books or by withholding and rejecting them)." In the case of the novelty book, handling—the physicalization of reading—goes beyond turning the page or hiding behind a newspaper to constitute the text on every level. Moreover, as Price notes, Victorian children's literature is "materialist" whereas fiction *about* children is "idealist," using the child to epitomize "the good reader's out-of-body experience" rather than physical pleasure in books.[11] In other words, books for children and books about children for adults imagine the child reader in different ways. The former make space for reading as a physical process and (an associated point) book production as a commercial enterprise. The reading habits of actual children also lead to a sense of this distinctiveness of the child as reader: echoing Price's handler of books, Grenby chooses the term *user* over *reader* in *The Child Reader.*

A number of factors in children's interactions with books—particularly the interactions of very young children, such as the implied audience for novelty books—further speak to questions of embodiment and physicality. The young reader is in the process of coming to terms with reading as a special activity and the book as a special entity. The book is an object unlike others that young children encounter, as Perry Nodelman remarks:

> An infant's first task on handling a book for the first time is to figure out its unique function. This particular object, unlike all the others that adults willingly place in babies' hands, is not a toy and not food. Its significance is not its shape or its taste or its texture but, rather, the variations in tone and color on its surfaces. It is not to be chewed or ripped apart; it is meant to be looked at. Most books for babies are printed on cloth or on thick cardboard in the understanding that their intended audience has not yet learned this basic skill.[12]

Nodelman's summary of the first encounter with the book is evocative, but it also hints that a materialized understanding of books is incorrect, a stage to be transcended. And yet the persistent material parallels between picture books—especially novelty books—and other objects make the book's "unique function" seem less certain than might be supposed. Moving this model away from a telic progression toward reading as intellectual activity, we might think (after Lewis) about what Catherine Snow and Anat Ninio call "contracts of literacy." These comprise regulations concerning the book itself ("Books are different from other objects") and regulations concerning reading ("Books are for reading, not for eating, throwing, chewing, or for building towers").[13] The contracts of literacy, always conveyed to the child by the adult, typically replace physicalized usages, such as action and manipulation, with intellectual ones, such as contemplation of the ideas a book contains. But as Lian Beveridge has inventively documented, babies' physical uses for books—such as, in Beveridge's example, biting—may in themselves be "a form of reading and even a form of literary appreciation," one that is simultaneously acknowledged by the sturdy laminate of the modern-day board book and discouraged by adults who believe that "books are not for eating."[14]

The philologist Armando Petrucci has posited that the characteristic ways in which children read (and do not read) demand a new iteration of what he calls the *modus legendi,* or reading mode. In a theoretical assessment that echoes Grenby's carefully historicized account of children's reading, Petrucci characterizes the practices of young readers in terms of "a physical relationship with the book that is much more intense and direct than in traditional modes of reading. The book is constantly manipulated, crumpled, bent, forced in various directions and carried on the body." This manipulation results in an altered subject–object relationship between book and reader: "One might say that readers make [the book] their own by an intensive, prolonged and violent use more typical of a relationship of consumption than of reading and learning."[15] Petrucci's sense that childhood book use is not best thought of in terms of learning is particularly provocative considering the fact that, as Patricia Crain argues, children's reading has been conceived of as so involved with the classroom that historians of reading have seldom considered how children read outside an educational context.[16]

The child's *modus legendi* is different once again when it comes to novelty books. (This is apparent in the further nuancing of terms for the child reader of novelty books beyond *handler* or *user*—Jacqueline Reid-Walsh has proposed *interactor,* taken from Janet Murray's accounts of digital narrative.)[17] In the case of conventional books, the habits Petrucci describes are outright transgressive, but the novelty book serves as a heightening apparatus for the child's physical understanding of books and reading—it constantly engenders such behaviors. The book is manipulated, as when the reader pulls a tab to animate a page. The book is bent (and potentially crumpled and forced) when the reader folds back a flap to reveal the continuation of the story. The book may be carried on the body—it may even be designed in this way, as when Samuel and Joseph Fuller attached wrist ribbons to the protective sheaths of their paper doll books.

Engendering this physicalized, embodied reader constitutes the novelty's greatest intervention in the questions of agency, audience, and authority—encapsulated by Marah Gubar in the question "Given their status as dependent, acculturated beings, how much power and autonomy can young people actually have?"—that famously structure the study of children's literature.[18] Commentators have located movable books within these debates before. Margaret Higonnet has examined the relationship between narrative structure and reader agency in unusual book formats for children, while Reid-Walsh has written about agency versus activity in different novelty formats, arguing that simpler book-objects, such as the harlequinade, offer greater opportunities for agency than those in which complex mechanisms are concealed from the child reader.[19] But the *modus legendi* for novelty books—in which the child understands books materially, is a physicalized and embodied reader, and so forth—has implications that go beyond the specifics of format (important as those may be) or the contents of individual titles. Across formats and across titles, the physical reading demanded by the novelty book has the potential to lead to the book's disintegration, and to the attendant disintegration of whatever it is that the book teaches to or expects of its child readers.

To expand: Victorian novelties present their unique versions of the prohibitions that typically govern children's reading. They often give explicit instructions as to the handling of the book (gently, without tearing, and so on) rather than the lessons to be gleaned from its contents. Such injunctions, which are particularly common in the complex movables made by Lothar Meggendorfer at the end of the century, construct the reader physically. A further central dimension to this involves a material paradox, however: no matter how careful the reader is, the movable book is always liable to be torn, ripped, or destroyed. The nineteenth-century movable book forbids its destruction while its material properties make that destruction almost inevitable. The fragility of these books combines with their textual guidelines for usage to produce a reader in excess of the book, just as the novelty book presents a physical book-object in excess of its content.

The best model for making sense of these properties of the novelty book comes from Robin Bernstein's recent remapping of the material culture of childhood. Bernstein orients her discussion around the concept of the *scriptive thing*: "an item of material culture that prompts meaningful bodily behaviors." Books are always scriptive things: "To use an English-language, printed book as a book, one must open the covers and read words from left to right."[20] The book-as-object, in other words, requires its reader to follow—or perform—particular orders so that it works. In turn, "literary-visual content combines crucially with the book's physical properties and the sequential actions that those properties script for the reader," as Bernstein brilliantly shows using E. W. Kemble's *A Coon Alphabet* (1898), which relies on the script of page turning to intensify the violence against black subjects depicted in its pictures and words. The point, though, about any of the scripts that things issue is that "individuals commonly resist, revise, or ignore instructions," as the "resistant performer understands and exerts agency against the script."[21] In the case of the novelty picture book for children, the questions of scripts, resistance, and revision that Bernstein outlines are relevant and pressing.

The child's physical interactions with the novelty book, both scripted and unscripted, are a potential site of resistance, a way of eluding or reshaping common demands on or expectations of children's reading. In Walter Benjamin's words, the child's material engagement with her books makes the "true meaning" of children's books "very different . . . from the tedious and absurd reasons that induced rationalist pedagogues to recommend them in the first place."[22] Material acts on or with the book—Benjamin discusses scribbling and coloring-in—undermine the didactic reasoning that has often underpinned children's literature and justified support for children's reading. They provide concrete, evocative evidence of the complicated question of agency in children's reading; they testify to a physicalized *modus legendi* that is both distinctive to the novelty book and indicative of how critics might challenge canards in the larger history of children's reading.

We can explore this state of affairs by returning once more to *The Children's Wonderland.* Nister's illustrators adopted a particular house style, characterized by what Joyce Irene Whalley and Tessa Chester dismiss, in their history of illustrated books for children, as "generally insipid pink-and-blue prettiness."[23] (The picturesqueness of Nister's plump, middle-class children is of just the sort that Benjamin himself disparages when he rails against "the depressingly distorted jolliness of rhyming stories and the pictures of grinning babies' faces supplied by God-forsaken, child-loving illustrators.")[24] *The Children's Wonderland* is indeed full of illustrations of pretty, rosy-cheeked children asleep, embracing one another beneath a tree, or dressed up in furs for a visit to a snow palace, and because the working practice at

Nister was typically to commission writers to compose in line with illustrations, the tone of the text follows suit:

> The moment rather strange is
> When the scene so quickly changes
> Into Christmas-time, and here, dears,
> Are the children who were *there,* dears!

We might assume that the children reading *The Children's Wonderland* will resemble those depicted within its pages—powerless in the face of the sentimentalizing voice of the poem, with its identical rhyming *dears.* But the foregrounding of the child's physical operation of the paper mechanism elsewhere complicates this picture, as the pleasures of "thumb and finger" reinstate the body of the child to the book. This does not occur in relation to outright depictions of the child's body, which, as Anne Higonnet notes, has often been coded as the fantasized nexus of childhood innocence.[25] Instead, the child's body materializes *outside the book* as the conduit for reading as a physical practice that leaves material traces. These traces in turn allow us to see children as unpredictable agents who do not just read the words and look at the pictures in novelty books but also paw the books, throw them, scribble on them, and perhaps ultimately destroy them.

## The Scenes of Novelty Reading

As I have said, though, nineteenth-century novelty picture books exercised various techniques to delineate the sort of embodied reading that was acceptable. One of these techniques—common in many branches of children's literature—was to model reading directly, in pictures or in words. As Crain has shown in her account of visual tropes of children's reading, including the "child-in-a-window-seat-with-books" and the "standing-book-in-hand child," such depictions provide implicit guidance as to what, how, why, when, and where children should read.[26] For example, to return to *The Nursery "Alice"*: if Carroll's preface to mothers clearly frames the book's entire contents, E. Gertrude Thomson's cover illustration of Alice asleep beneath a tree does similar work (Figure 1.1). In the image, an open book, colored illustrations just visible on its pages, lies at Alice's side. Floating on a cloud in the background are characters from the story: the Mock Turtle, the Gryphon, the pig baby, the White Rabbit, and the Dormouse. With its discarded book, Thomson's illustration promotes a lax use of *The Nursery "Alice,"* perhaps echoing the play of Carroll's "dimpled darlings" in their nursery. Thomson shows Alice accompanied by a book with pictures, invoking one of the most celebrated of the heroine's pert opinions: "'And what is the use of a book,' thought Alice, 'without pictures or conversation?'"[27] No such statement exists, however, in *The Nursery "Alice"*; by 1890, illustrated books are simply the correct reading material, the default answer to the question of what a child should read. Location is important, too: Alice reads outside, like various eighteenth- and nineteenth-century child readers real and imagined who are documented by Grenby and Crain.[28] There is no adult present.

The fact that Alice is asleep, dreaming instead of reading, gives a further tacit instruction because dreaming and reading, as Garrett Stewart has provocatively remarked, "are each other's doubles."[29] (This is especially true of childhood cultures at the end of the nineteenth century, as bedtime stories link books with dreams.)[30] Thomson's illustration at once recalls and dispels the ending to the earlier *Alice,* which centers on Alice's dream. Here, Alice's dream is private, the result of her own silent reading, whereas in *Alice's Adventures in Wonderland* the dream occurs as Alice sits beside a reader, her sister. Indeed, Alice's sister possesses her dream at the end of the novel through a switch in perspective whereby the narrative suddenly inhabits the sister's thoughts: "Her sister sat still . . . thinking of little Alice and all her wonderful Adventures, till she too began dreaming after a fashion, and this was her dream:—."[31] This frame is absent from *The Nursery "Alice,"* which simply begins, "Once upon a time, there was a girl called Alice: and she had a very curious dream." The book ends without the sister, with advice to the child reader as to how she can have a dream like Alice's. "The best plan is this," the text counsels. "First lie down under a tree, and wait till a White Rabbit runs by with a watch in his hand: then shut your eyes, and pretend to be dear little Alice."[32] Rather than displacing reading onto an adolescent or adult figure, *The Nursery "Alice"* safeguards acts of reading and not reading for the very young audience Carroll imagines in his preface.

Victorian novelty picture books, especially movables, have special recourse to the scene of reading. In part, this is because, as Seth Lerer has observed, movables "never let the child forget that they are books": their self-conscious materiality becomes a springboard for self-conscious representations in word and picture, such

FIGURE 1.1. E. Gertrude Thomson's cover artwork to Lewis Carroll's *The Nursery "Alice"* (1890) uses Alice to hint to small children at how they might read. Copyright the British Library Board, General Reference Collection Cup.410.g.74.

as metafictional depictions of reading or readers.[33] The scene of reading may also be necessitated by unusual formats and requirements: How should the reader operate the novelty book? Finally, though, early novelty books dramatized scenes of reading in order to publicize their own merits. Stewart has suggested that depictions of novels within nineteenth-century novels are a form of "self-advertised privilege," and Grenby observes an analogous, if more explicitly commercial, trend in the ways that eighteenth-century juvenile publishing touts the benefits of reading the new literature specifically *for* children in order to carve out a market share: "The promises of the transfiguring effects of reading were designed to work as an advertisement for the whole new genre of children's literature, convincing adult consumers of its utility, cost-effectiveness and indispensability."[34] Novelty books might (perhaps jokingly) proffer depictions of reading that bear little resemblance to their likely employment

FIGURE 1.2. The pop-up book *Comical Kittens and Their Frolics* (circa 1896), despite being an entertaining novelty, shows a scene of instruction on its cover. Phyllis Hirsch Boyson Collection of Children's Literature, Archives and Special Collections, University of Connecticut Library.

as pleasurable, luxury objects. For example, the cover of the pop-up book *Comical Kittens and Their Frolics* (circa 1896) uses a schoolroom conceit: a schoolteacher cat picks out letters, which spell *Comical Kittens,* for three kittens (Figure 1.2).[35] While two visibly inattentive kitten pupils counter any optimistic assessment of how effective the instruction provided by the book will be, *Comical Kittens* jokingly elides the fact that novelty books do not pledge pedagogic value and would not typically have been taken to school, let alone read there. (Although Grenby gives one example of an early nineteenth-century harlequinade with an ownership inscription indicating educational use, novelty books were and are leisure items.)[36] The scene of reading the novelty book may imply educational and other usages as a form of tongue-in-cheek self-promotion, more in line with wishful thinking than a consumer guarantee.

At other points, novelty books dramatized scenes of reading in order to bring their texts in line with alluring popular visual entertainments, rather than children's literature per se. Thus Nister's *Magic Toy Book,* an unusual title with spectral images visible—like watermarks—when the pages are held to a light, begins with a "magic-lantern party" where an aunt gathers children around her for stories illustrated by magic-lantern projections. (This was Nister's first novelty, sold for one shilling and sixpence at Christmas 1890, according to Julia and Frederick Hunt.)[37] The dust jacket to another book, the pop-up titled *Our Peepshow,* shows a man carrying a peepshow box on his back and three children following in his wake, suggesting that the book is not a text to be read but a technology for viewing images.[38] The first page opening, or double-page spread, in the book gives two different contexts: that of a staged performance, with the separate voices of "The Children" and "The Peepshow-man" laid out like a play in the text, and that of a traditional book, in an image at the bottom right-hand corner of the recto, with the Peepshow-man pointing at a closed codex lying flat.

*Our Peepshow,* however, does not settle on one mode for the book. Each component of the volume provides a divergent answer to the question of what the book is or what it can do, and by consequence of how it can or should be read. The text refuses to give any definitive cues. When the Children ask the Peepshow-man whether the rhymes "will . . . tell us without a doubt / What the pictures are all about?" he replies:

> If they neither fit nor scan,
> You must not blame your old Peepshow-man,
>
> But take some paper and ink from your shelves,
> And write the rhymes for your dear little selves.

As Verity Hunt says, this poem dismisses the labor of Nister's writers by "suggest[ing] the existing rhymes are not only dispensable, but positively unimportant."[39] But these lines also lay out a flexible ideal for children's reading, as *Our Peepshow*'s status—split among peepshow, book, and home theatrical—becomes less a problem to be solved than an enjoyable lack of fixity to be appreciated by children who can decide for themselves what words and pictures mean.

Details of the poses and locations for children reading in novelty books—what Kate Flint calls the "phenomenology of reading: the spatial positioning of the reading body"—can yield considerable information, too.[40] Consider a static black-and-white illustration of one girl reading to another in the pop-up *The Robins at Home* (Figure 1.3).[41] This version of reading aloud is horizontal in its emotional ties: two children reading together, rather than being read to by a parent or other authority figure.[42] The two girls read outside, sitting on a garden bench; the reading girl has her lips slightly parted and holds the book carefully without cracking the spine; the other little girl bends her neck to look at the book, the angle suggesting her attention, and has crossed her legs at the ankle. Both girls rest one foot on a bar at the base of the bench. These are leisured yet engrossed young readers, fit representatives of what Stewart dubs "the foundational balance of the reading body—at attention and rest at once."[43] Their attentive reading, conveyed through their pose, suggests that *The Robins at Home* will provide a traditional childhood reading experience—losing oneself in a text, while at the same time sharing that absorption with another reader—and the illustration gives no visual hint that the book being read is unusual, although the accompanying poem implies that the girls (like the child readers outside the book) peruse *The Robins at Home.*

The emotional connections between adults and children that (movable) books can foster might be explicitly moralized within a text. The title story in *Peeps into Fairyland,* a particularly sumptuous 1890s pop-up, concerns parents who are too busy or too tired to tell their children stories but find an alternative storyteller in the form of a local eccentric called Old King Cole. This frame story for the collection presents the tales in *Peeps into Fairyland* as "the stories that King Cole used to tell." Aside from the fairy-tale-like insistence on a prior degree of authenticity, the story displaces a scene of reading to a scene of listening: "And then the old man begins, and, closing his eyes, tells them one by one the tales they love, while the afternoon darkens, and the firelight flickers on their listening eyes as they cluster round the old man's knees."[44] Roger Chartier draws attention to "formulas of oral culture" that are "inscribed in texts destined for a large public," problematizing a division between oral and written language; however, he notes that such devices "[assure] the return of multiple texts in oral forms, where they are destined to be read aloud," too.[45] *Peeps into Fairyland* operates within such a loop, the proposed oral origin and the gemütlich

THEY were happy little children,
And they had a pretty book,
And they dearly loved to read it,
And at every picture look;
They began at the beginning,
And they quickly looked it through,
Then they cried, "Oh! it is finished;
Now whatever shall we do?"

"If 'twere mine," then said the Robin,
"And I'd looked at it myself,
I should shut it up and put it
Safe away upon
the shelf!
Then when I got
up next morning,
It would seem almost
like new!"
"Oh, dear Robin,"
cried the children,
"That's the very thing
we'll do!"
*Clifton Bingham.*

FIGURE 1.3. This generic depiction of two girls, from the 1890s pop-up book *The Robins at Home*, represents reading as an affectionate, bonding practice. *The Robins at Home* [189-?]. HISTCHIL Unclassified, Rare Book and Manuscript Library, Columbia University in the City of New York.

particulars of firelight and the children's "listening eyes" at once mitigating the book's unusual material presentation and demanding its reconversion into the oral through reading aloud.

The Victorian novelty book returns again and again to reading aloud—a mode that associates reading with emotional connection. In part, this association relates to what Chartier identifies as the "sociability" of such a scenario: reading aloud acts as "a fundamental counterpoint to the privatization of the act of reading, to its retreat into the intimacy of solitude."[46] Reading aloud is so mythic as to seduce even critics and scholars, who, as Price explains, search for moments of reading aloud because they "[restore] a social dimension to an activity now more often parsed as individual or even individualistic. . . . In reconstructing sociable forms of reading, book historians make one reader knowable to another."[47] The scene of reading aloud rehabilitates not just the activity of reading but also the study of reading, which so often seems a battle to capture the irrecoverable. Each of these discussions bears special relation to adults reading aloud to children—what Flint calls that archetypal "comforting, bonding practice"—if only because children remain one of the privileged categories of reader who is read *to,* both in the nineteenth century and today.[48]

The depiction of reading aloud in the novelty book has a crucial added significance as the single most sentimental version of the scene of reading available. The scene of reading aloud is a nostalgic trope, one that gains new purchase once this mode of reading is at risk of being lost. Imagined touchstones of traditional reading experience are all the more important in those types of children's books, such as novelties and movables, that unsettle or trouble standard practices of reading. For example, on the cover of *Fireside Pictures,* a mechanical book produced by Raphael Tuck, a small, golden-haired girl sits on a man's knee (Figure 1.4).[49] There is no information in the text as to the identity of either figure, and this image, like many others that depict reading, lacks a mise-en-scène, instead spotlighting the reading pair by means of a hazy backdrop.[50] The readers are both seated on an oversize, wood-framed leather chair, the girl's left hand held in the man's left hand. The reassuring solidity of the chair complements the sturdy patriarch in a tailcoat who sits on it. As our eyes are drawn to the cover of the book held in the man's right hand, we discover a recession of the reading scene: the image on the cover of the pictured book also shows a blond head and a gray head side by side.[51]

The cover of *Fireside Pictures* legitimates an unusual technology of the book and an unusual mode of reading in two ways. First, it suggests that the book can be shared between generations despite its unconventional form. Second, it locates the mechanical or tab-pull book within a traditional scene of reading. The title *Fireside Pictures* provides an even more specific (and nostalgic) location of reading, one that is echoed in the book's incipit. This is not just reading aloud, but firelit reading as, in Maria Tatar's words, the "luminous space" of the *veillée,* or evening gathering.[52] This scenario is often repeated, as in the Nister dissolving-view book *The Fairies' Playtime,* which ends in an "old easy-chair" by the fire: "Here, while the fire dances and shines on the wall, / We'll meet with those old friends we love one and all."[53] The accompanying line illustration depicts a child sitting on her mother's lap, their archaic

FIGURE 1.4. *Fireside Pictures,* a Raphael Tuck title from around 1900, allies the mechanical book with a traditional scene of reading aloud by the fire. The Bodleian Libraries, the University of Oxford (2015), Opie EE 81.

medievalized costumes suggesting that the scene of reading *The Fairies' Playtime* might have occurred hundreds of years before the book was published.

While *Fireside Pictures*'s cover image justifies the movable book by way of the affective connections it can foster between adult and child, it also presents a scene of reading by way of a scene of action: the girl's right hand gently grasps a tab that protrudes from a page of the book in front of her, about to pull it and manipulate the picture. The reader poised in this way belies the clear discrepancy between the intimate *veillée* over a movable book on the cover and the actual contents of *Fireside Pictures,* which, instead of offering a text composed with the same delicate charms, contains the slapstick mayhem typical of mechanical books. A naughty boy who becomes ill after eating too much Christmas pudding, for instance, is examined by a

FIGURE 1.5. The charms of *Fireside Pictures* are much less genteel than the cover implies, as the movable illustrations make visual jokes about naughty boys and their bodies. (Note also the doctor's detached hand in this particular copy.) The Bodleian Libraries, the University of Oxford (2015), Opie EE 81.

doctor, and the mechanical movement reveals a comically oversized movable tongue (Figure 1.5). This spirit of discord and misrule hints at quite a different set of appeals, and quite a different set of uses, for *Fireside Pictures* than the cover implies.

## Indestructible, Destructible, and Destroyed

In the nineteenth century as today, children's embodied reading summons the worry that children will rip or tear their books. This is why adult supervision governed children's physical usage of books as well as which books children read or how they understood them, as is confirmed not just in adults' instructions about children's reading (Ruskin's horror of dog-ears in *Sesame and Lilies*) but also in memories of what it was like to read as a Victorian child: one of Flint's cohort of Victorian women readers, Mary Carbery, recollects such instruction in action as "her father taught her to handle a book—how to take it down from a shelf, how to replace it without squeezing it, how to turn the pages slowly and with respect."[54] Despite the special physicalized reading acts demanded by the novelty picture book, parallel passages of general instructions for book handling are found there, too, as when the last verse in *Comical Kittens* tells its readers to "shut [the book] up carefully, and put it away, / To look at again, on the next rainy day." Such instructions for reading, while reminding us that the book is a material object and that reading is a physical practice, could apply to conventional book formats as well. Other novelty books, however, contain very specific exposition and hints on physical positioning—explicit instructions that can be counterpointed with the implicit guidance provided by depictions of reading.

For instance, a bright-red instruction is printed at the top of every page in the four titles in Dean's noteworthy Surprise Model series of pop-up books: "BEFORE OPENING EACH PAGE PLACE THUMBS WHERE MARKED, HOLD FIRMLY AND OPEN WIDE."[55] Color illustrations of thumbs appear on the outside edges of the page opening, inscribing the reading body on the book itself (Figure 1.6). But Dean's instruction is striking for its concision when compared to the directions given in a range of other novelty books from across formats and across the century. For instance, *The Paignion,* a rare, complex set of Regency paper dolls with accompanying scenic pages into which cutout figures could be slotted, explains, "As the figures are moveable, the children may arrange them in a variety of situations, to personate and illustrate any scene in domestic life that is familiar to them."[56] An early twentieth-century series of panorama fairy tales released by the publisher Raphael Tuck instructs the user: "To make the Panoramic Pictures, insert the figures, which will be found in the pocket attached to this book, into the spaces which are marked with numbers corresponding to those upon the figures. A variety of scenes, however, can be formed, and unending pleasure provided, by placing the figures in innumerable positions, and sometimes in one picture background sometimes in another, so that constant change and interest is obtained."[57] The exhaustiveness of the instructions themselves represents a way of laying claim to innumerability, variety, and enduring "change and interest" in these panoramic pictures—the novelty book's assertion of its renewability as well as its up-to-dateness. *The Motograph Moving Picture Book*

(1898), an unusual movable that shows the occasional link between novelty formats and avant-garde art movements in the nineteenth century (its cover image is designed by Henri de Toulouse-Lautrec), also gives an instruction on each page: "Place the star on the Transparency exactly over the star above the picture, and see that the Transparency comes directly in contact with the paper; then move the Transparency slowly up and down over the picture."[58] R. March's penny silhouette play *Cinderella and the Glass Slipper and the Pantomime,* produced in the early 1900s, is yet more prescriptive. "Paste the sheet of black figures on a piece of card (not too thick) then cut out neatly each figure," the reader is counseled, and "now procure a piece of very thin paper (which should be coated with paraffin to make it transparent)."[59] Across examples, novelty book instructions imagine children's reading in terms of movement, assembly, recipe, or spell, depending on the format.

The "true" movable book (that is, the book with added mechanisms) in particular requires both a set of unfamiliar movements for reading and an increased level of care in executing these movements, as these instructions reflect. For example, *Living Nursery Rhymes,* a midcentury mechanical book produced by Dean and Son, begins with "LIVING NURSERY PICTURE NOTES" that lay out the book thus: "Hold down the picture flat in the book (not loose) before pulling the shafts down or pushing them up, and the movement will work well and last long, and give four times the delight of an ordinary toy book. Also, if in reading the rhymes to very young children the action be imparted to the picture when at the proper place in the verse, the interest of the child is intensified, as author and artist have found by experience."[60] The word "Also" signals a change from instructions to the child to instructions to the adult, placing the book in the context of familial usage. In line with its format and audience, *Living Nursery Rhymes* asks to be approached with substantial adult supervision. The title takes little about the physical practice of reading for granted either, providing very technical details expounding fine points of movement and positioning: page flat not loose, pulling and pushing at the same time, and so on.

All of these instructions prohibit ripping and tearing, and they constitute a generic feature of the period's novelty books. In fact, these instructional poems are a version of Bernstein's scripts or "set of prompts that the plaything issued"—one directly told to the child reader, rather than implied.[61] As Dean's *Living Nursery Rhymes* reminds the reader with a motto that evokes the book's own fragility (an ironic inversion of Edward Bulwer Lytton's "The pen is mightier than the sword"), "PAPER IS

FIGURE 1.6. Dean and Son's unusual fin de siècle rounded pop-ups, the Surprise Model series, had printed thumbs at the outside edges of each movable illustration to guide the child's hand. Copyright the British Library Board, General Reference Collection 12806.l.74.

NOT IRON."[62] Nonetheless, the historical paradigm of children's reading proposed by Grenby—the "relaxation" of rules regarding children's book use—actually allows a certain joy in such destructive acts in the nineteenth century when they are undertaken by children, as opposed to the well-regulated horror that Grenby and other critics, including Andrea Immel, detect in the eighteenth.[63] The transgressive pleasure associated with children's more vigorous styles of reading gives us both Carroll's dog-eared *Nursery "Alice"* and Becky Sharp's rapid defenestration of her presentation copy of Johnson's dictionary from Miss Pinkerton's Academy.[64] In a less well-known example, even a seemingly conservative writer such as Charlotte Mary Yonge might gleefully imagine a scene of book destruction:

"There, it is not indestructible!"

"What mischief have you been about?" The question was needless, for the table was strewn with snips of calico.

"This nasty spelling-book! Lucy said it was called indestructible, because nobody could destroy it, but I've taken my new knife to it. And see there!"[65]

A review in *The Athenæum* upon release singled out the novel in which this scene appears, *The Young Step-mother; or, A Chronicle of Mistakes* (1861), for its depiction of "three of the most odious children it has ever been our fate to meet with, either in a book or in real life."[66] Yonge's narrator, however, does not necessarily share this opinion. While the eponymous young stepmother Albinia worries about the boy Maurice's naughtiness, the narrative tone is droll: "Maurice did not appear on the way to penitence." A little later, Maurice's father restores the boy's knife ("If mamma wished the penance to have been longer, she neither looked it nor said it"), and the adults jokingly threaten one another, "Take care I don't come on you with the indestructible—," the terminal dash typographically mimicking a cut or tear.[67]

The scene, with Maurice's dubious repentance and abortive punishment, and the indestructible book a source of fun, allows the adults a degree of pleasure in the resistant child reader. But it also imagines that the child reader may respond to such a book as a challenge, as the phrase *indestructible book* presents not so much a promise as a stern imperative (You will not destroy this book) and a hopeful entreaty (Please, please, do not destroy this book). Yonge herself later writes about something similar in *What Books to Lend and What to Give* (1887), when she notes of young readers in real life, "Some are much more willing to listen to, or read, what is not too obviously written for them. A book labelled 'A tale for—' is apt to carry a note of warning to the perverse spirits of those to whom it is addressed."[68] The same might be said of the more formal descriptions or instructions for use issued with the movable: the specificity of the injunctions makes them more likely to be ignored.

Yonge's destroyed "indestructible" book is a dig at a particular Victorian publishing trend. Darton's Indestructible Elementary Children's Books were advertised around the time *The Young Step-mother* was published.[69] Ward and Lock had the New Indestructible Picture Library, "profusely illustrated by Eminent Artists," while Dean and Son released a raft of such imprints, including the Sunshine Series (sometimes "'Shunshine' Series"), "nondestructibly mounted" for a shilling—sixpence for the destructible version—which were billed as the "cheapest and best books in the world" despite the spelling mistake in the advertisement.[70] F. J. Harvey Darton suggests that Dean invented "printing on untearable holland," and the firm made such printing a feature of its marketing: a later incarnation of the Dean firm trademarked an image of two dogs fighting over a rag book as one of its logos.[71] *Indestructible book* was at once a factual term for a book made using a new technique of production—with pages typically cloth-mounted, as Maurice's "snips of calico" testify—and a broader claim for the longevity that such a book might have within a child's affections.

Indestructible books provide evidence of persisting anxieties around children's material understandings of their books in the nineteenth century—anxieties that the specific properties of the novelty book heightened. Even when attempting to advertise movable books as, if not indestructible, at least sturdy, publishers made concessions to the fundamentally fragile material dimensions of the book and the likelihood of its destruction or malfunction. For instance, in the 1860s, Dean denounced its competitors by claiming that the movements in its mechanical books "*are, by an improved plan, worked upon thin Copper Wire, and, therefore, are not liable to get out of order. As, however, other publishers have attempted Imitations of similar Moveable Books,* BE SURE YOU HAVE DEAN and SON'S MOVEABLE BOOKS."[72] Another example adjusted the claim slightly: "The changes are strongly secured, and not liable to get out of order."[73] Again, the advertisements might have had the opposite effect to the desired one, as they introduced by antithesis the idea of a movable book "liable to get out of order," or a movable book with parts that are not "strongly secured." The movable book comes to seem a work in progress. On the same sheet as the first advertisement, simpler claims for the utility of other children's books—the Reverend John Cumming's *Ministering Women, Their Lives, Perils, and Devotion* is described as "a strong, serviceable, and lasting present"—diminished Dean's puffs for its Improved Moveable Books yet further.

When the publisher failed to make an indestructible movable book, prefatory material exhorting the child reader to cautious handling was the next line of defense. The promissory tone of the set of notes in *Living Nursery Rhymes* makes kind treatment of the book into an exchange: in return for her care and correct manipulation, the child is assured of the continuation of the peculiarly specific amount of delight (or Lockean *delectare*) to be derived from the book—that is, four times as much as from other children's books. Other examples approach the same subject with more charm than wheedling. There are countless versions of such demands in Meggendorfer's publications, chiefly because as the ingeniousness of movable books increases, so too does their fragility. Meggendorfer's *Comic Actors* has a prefatory poem that anticipates movable figures so captivating that the child will cry, "'Tis really hard . . . / To think them only paper."[74] The figures nevertheless *are* paper, and paper needs certain treatment: "Your fingers must be slow and kind / And treat them well while using," "Turn the leaves and use them well / And don't be over zealous." *Always Jolly!* is even blunter, its opening verse worth giving in full:

> Within this book, my own dear child,
> Are various pictures gay.
> Their limbs move with gestures wild,
> As with them you do play.
> But still they are of paper made,
> And therefore, I advise,
> That care and caution should be paid,
> Lest woe and grief arise;
> Both you and pictures then would cry
> To see what harm is done,
> And sigh would follow after sigh
> Because you've spoilt your fun.

Meggendorfer's "Introduction" provides very specific information about the physical book, the content of its words and pictures, and the usage to be made of it. This has the corollary effect of encouraging a reflexive awareness of the fictiveness of the representations the book contains: the figures "move with gestures wild" (the rhyme pairing "wild" with "child"), lifelike enough that the reminder "But still they are of paper made" is required. Self-consciousness about the book as a material object, and of reading as a physical act, seems the necessary offshoot of the book's format.

Meggendorfer is notable for releasing his movables in different languages, often with considerably different content, but instructional verses appear across editions, making them—and the destructive energies they foretell in the child reader—something of a stable generic property. For instance, Meggendorfer's mechanical book *Aus dem Leben* (From life) uses the word *zerreißen* (to tear) to characterize undesirable usage but also makes a more general point about ownership: children should respect books but also their other possessions in order to be happy in the future.[75] These guidelines embed a lesson in book usage within a broader instruction in good conduct—carefulness, caution, conservation—recalling what Courtney Weikle-Mills has identified as a Lockean pedagogical emphasis on affection (here, care) in children's relationships to their books.[76] The potential for a book to be ripped or destroyed was, however, especially relevant to the movable book because of its fragility, meaning that care was enjoined with special fervency.

### Thumbing through the Novelty

The joke a hundred years later is that novelty picture books bear witness to treatment quite different from what the books themselves exhort. This section examines such material evidence found in individual novelty books contained in the Opie Collection. Ripping and tearing, coloring-in, dirt, and reconstruction—the material traces of how children read novelty books—are not the types of evidence commonly invoked by historians of reading. Many of the fine studies of book usage, including children's book usage, that might be expected to reflect on these matters often ignore, displace, or simply remain silent on such evidence. In part, this is because, as Sánchez-Eppler has pointed out, finding and documenting children's book destruction is an impossible task; Sánchez-Eppler wryly sums up the challenges thus: "So here is a method—search book dealers for children's literature in poor condition."[77] Nonetheless, in neglecting evidence of destruction, book historians enforce a hierarchy: writing is always a better response to printed text than nontextual responses. Nineteenth-century novelty books, because of the rich material practices they demanded, can challenge this hierarchy. They also, on a practical level, provide an archive of books just destroyed enough to still be readable.

H. J. Jackson's two foundational books on nineteenth-century marginalia both omit nontextual evidence of reading. In *Marginalia* (2001), Jackson writes that "'notes' are to be distinguished from asterisks, fists ☞, exclamation marks, word by word translation, and similar signs of readers' attentions." Indeed, Jackson chooses "to concentrate on original discursive notes that express a reaction to the text or an opinion about it." "On the whole," she goes on to remark some pages later in a specific discussion of the child reader, "preschool children are not real annotators.

Coloring black-and-white illustrations does not count."[78] Nontextual responses to a book instead form a preliminary stage in a move toward writing: "Before they can read, children may scribble—pretending to write—or draw pictures in books that come their way, but as soon as they can read and write, they write their names, often over and over again in the one book."[79] Jackson sets up a timeline in which the young child's earliest engagements with books are false steps because they are nontextual.

Even as scholars critique Jackson's methodology where children are concerned, they may display a bias toward textual marks. Lerer calls the children's annotations he explores "barely legible, tantalizingly irrelevant to the texts before them, evasive, duplicitous, or just plain weird," in direct opposition to Jackson's criteria, which he distills as "intelligibility, relevance to the text, and honesty." His argument, however, that "children's writing has its meaning in relationship to adult writing" and to writing as a taught subject leads to a scriptural bias: writing receives much more attention in Lerer's article than drawings, for example, which he also examines.[80] The same is true of Gillian Adams's work, which in its focus on "children and the development of writing" via an examination of marginalia in the medieval and early modern periods mirrors Lerer in purpose if not in period.[81] Scholars acknowledge the distinguishing properties of children's marginalia. "Might the copiousness of children's marginalia," asks Grenby, "be due to children not yet having learned to treat their books with the reverence that adults generally developed?" and Crain observes that "many child book taggers go in for excess and superfluity, as they exploit and appropriate the physical form of the book—that it opens onto blank pages and white spaces, and that it closes up again, concealing whatever is inside it."[82] Like Cathy's voluminous notes in the margins in *Wuthering Heights* (1847)—a favored example for the historian of reading—children's marks in their books sometimes threaten to overwhelm the text they purportedly annotate, as opposed to the more decorous markings of adult annotators.[83]

For this reason, children's marginal annotation is frequently read as a subversive act. Lerer sees children's marginalia as "charting relationships of authority between child and book: between the institutions of control and their playful subversion, between the authority of the canon and the autonomy of the reader."[84] According to Crain, "In laying claim to their books as personal property, child scribes (and sometimes adult inscribers) creatively engage and profoundly transform the expressive form of the book."[85] Within these dynamics, it is significant that—to quote Jackson in *Romantic Readers* (2005), the second of her books on marginalia—"certain forms of writing in books had been immemorially approved as study methods."[86] Grenby's list of "reading strategies designed to facilitate and consolidate the instruction children could receive from books" includes a number of writing strategies, such as the creation of an index, the inscription of "Hints in the Margin," and the copying out of extracts.[87] The child readers of novelty books did respond to them with more writing, as Reid-Walsh has shown in an essay examining "a flap book that has been inscribed with several girls' names, a paper doll book that has an extra episode inserted into the narrative, and a toy theater play script (and set) that has been completely reworked."[88] But if more writing was the prescribed response to certain types of texts, might other sorts of responses—the sorts generally elicited by movable books—be yet more subversive? While the annotator responds to the book in kind, the reader who rips or tears or colors or dirties a book engages with it in a different register entirely.

After all, writing is only one mode of damaging a book. "For every pencil mark in the margin," remarks Price, "ten traces of wax or smoke; for every ink stain, ten drink spills."[89] (Billy Collins traverses similar territory at the end of his poem "Marginalia," when annotations made by a teen reader give way to enigmatic "greasy looking smears.")[90] Such marks, as Price suggests, point to "the wide range of nontextual and sometimes even noninterpretive (which doesn't mean noninterpretable) uses to which the book is put."[91] Her statements are especially evocative in the case of children, as annotating may not be germane to the materialized and materialist practice of their reading. Paying attention to nontextual marks in novelty books challenges such privileging of the written over the drawn, the ripped, or simply the "thumbed," recognizing in the process that children's material and physical engagements with their books reconstitute the meaning of children's literature.

To begin with ripping and tearing in the Opie Collection's novelty book holdings: Dean's mechanical book *This Is the House That Jack Built* is full of dismembered mechanical figures.[92] Legs with no torso disappear into the blackness of a doorway. Jack pats a headless and tailless cat—the same one praised in the rhyme for killing the rat that ate the malt, a feat it is patently unable to do in its present condition (Plate 5). As I discuss in my Conclusion, a copy of the Meggendorfer mechanical book *Curious Creatures* has been so decimated that the instructions to the original factory assembler, which should be concealed beneath movable parts, are clearly visible.[93] Such instructions for assembly are likewise visible thanks to damage in a copy of Dean's

Surprise Model pop-up book *A Visit to the Country*.[94] In Meggendorfer's *Tiny Tim, Prince of Liliput,* a rivet is missing from a double-page spread showing Tiny Tim with a frog; only a little pinprick on the page remains to suggest the loss.[95] Whole transformations in Nister dissolving views are broken—in *Playtime Surprises, Pleasant Surprises,* and *Something New for Little Folk,* to name three examples.[96] (In each case, the revelations promised in the title may not be quite what the reader expects.) The Tuck panorama fairy-tale book that promised "constant change and interest" is in such bad condition that a cataloger of the collection (perhaps Alderson) appended an apologetic note to the book: "This copy is in very very poor condition and has eleven of the figures missing! I am, however, keeping it as it is the only copy of a figure-panorama which I have seen."[97] The movable book is a site of destruction and malfunction; its familiar spirits are ripping and tearing. This state of affairs is paradoxical, as ripping and tearing are in some cases unavoidable offshoots of handling the book, however carefully one does it—symptoms of the book's material configuration.

The title page of the ripped and torn copy of *A Visit to the Country* reproduces the gloriously chromolithographed cover image in black-and-white line, much of which has been colored in with pencil (Plate 6). The very presence of coloring-in tells us that the book was used "in fairly informal settings where there was ready access to writing materials—most likely in nurseries and schoolrooms."[98] Presuming the child who colored *A Visit* had access to more than orange, red, blue, and brown pencils, the choice of colors could be suggestive: the colorer has not followed the cover template, making, for example, the sky in the image blue, not orange (the cover shows a sunset scene), and leaving the little girl at the center of the image uncolored. The contrast between this picture and the rest of those in the book suggests that coloring-in could be a usage approved by the publisher: as Benjamin says, the black-and-white line illustration "seems incomplete and so can readily be filled out."[99] Considering the damage to the book elsewhere, what is the relationship between sanctioned and disallowed treatment of the book here, between children's constructive and destructive book use (what Lerer call devotion and defacement)? Does coloring-in span the two?[100]

The many dirty marks on movable books are an indicative second example. Dirt and grime feature often in nineteenth- and early twentieth-century anecdotes concerning children's reading. On a speculative level, "dirty books" may designate uniquely childish reading practices. The dirty marks of children's usages of their books, Benjamin suggests, are apotropaic: "It is good that the patina that has been deposited by unwashed children's hands will keep the book snob at a distance."[101] At the same time, references to "dirty books" expose the pronounced class implications borne by children's reading: disordered or materialized reading might be tolerated, encouraged, or rhapsodized when it takes place within Carroll's nursery filled with "dimpled darlings," but be viewed as evidence of slovenliness and social decay when enacted by working-class children. Thus, slum children were forced to wash their hands before entering David Copperfield's Library, a charitable institution established by John Brett Langstaff in 1922.[102] The creators of children's books might also recognize the different types of child readers in class-based terms. As Trumpener has documented, famed illustrator Randolph Caldecott wrote on November 17, 1883: "A week ago, I received from the Secretary of Free Libraries, Manchester, a volume of my *Picture Books* which had been doing duty in a Boy's *[sic]* Reading Room in a shabby smallhoused, closely-populated district. The book is dreadfully grimy, be-thumbed, greased, torn, tattered, part-mended, and odorous. . . . This is working for the million."[103] Caldecott's list of evidentiary marks of his books' use, registered with patent distaste, forms a counterpoint to Carroll's encomium (published only six years after Caldecott wrote his letter) on the thumbed and dog-eared *Nursery "Alice."* This in turn seems to have influenced children's own responses to their books. Kathleen McDowell writes of a young reader at the New York Public Library who "preferred 'dirty books,' by which he meant books that were quite literally besmirched with dirt. 'I always pick for real dirty ones, then the little spots I get on 'em don't show.'" McDowell surmises that "this boy's hands may have been dirty from industrial work of some kind."[104] These anecdotes represent a response to an expanded reading public: there is a sense that children should have books, but an anxiety over what some of those children will do with them.

This anxiety leads me to introduce an important proviso for this book, one that readers should keep in mind throughout my argument (and that indeed forms an explicit part of my discussion at a number of points): most novelty books cannot offer information about Victorian child readers from a range of backgrounds. They are quintessential luxuries—dispensable items. While some novelty books—mostly those that approached the status of ephemera, such as the panorama—were reasonably priced, others were very expensive. For instance, in 1889, Meggendorfer's mechanical volumes cost seven shillings and sixpence in England—more even than some novels, which by the 1880s had shifted away from the proverbially unaffordable triple-decker model to cheaper republication in single volumes, or even in paperback.[105] (To put this in context, in 1888, *The Nineteenth Century* advised that a clerk's breakfasts, dinners, and teas might cost him seven shillings and eight pence per week.)[106] Sturdy toys, let alone fragile and expensive novelty books, had a limited place in the material culture of working-class childhood in the nineteenth century; by association, it is important to recognize that the readers of the expensive novelty book, whether parsed through in-text constructions or archival traces, would have been middle-class. The very existence of the novelty suggests the sort of childhood memorably described by Viviana Zelizer (in an American context) as "a domesticated, nonproductive world."[107] Like the newly popularized space of the nursery, the novelty book at once constructs and bears witness to the broader trend whereby "one model of the good childhood—the Western model, enacted for and by privileged children" came to hold sway by the beginning of the twentieth century.[108] The novelty book's status as luxury item is linked to its tolerance (albeit circumscribed) of embodied reading and to the class-based assumptions that structured children's reading in the nineteenth century.

Nonetheless, from the evidence left by those privileged children who did acquire novelty books in the nineteenth century, dirty marks and "patina" are constitutive, not incidental. They were the results of the repetitive movements the books solicited. In copies of the Fuller paper doll books, paper doll heads are grubby while the books—with their worthy moral tales—are relatively pristine.[109] The begrimed tab that appears on the double-page opening "My Kittens" in Nister's dissolving-view book *Transformation Pictures and Comical Fixtures* could be read in conjunction with the direction "pull," which has been written by hand on the tab by an older child or by an adult (Figure 1.7).[110] Moreover, the fact that this tab is the only one in the book that is torn evokes a handler who may have too zealously followed the double cue to pull in print and in marginalia. Working with the material evidence of novelty books, the mind wanders: the British Library's copy of *Tale of an Old Sugar Tub,* another of Dean's Surprise Model books, was suggestively caked with powdery dust the last time I called it to the Reading Room.[111] Where had this book been? An extravagant reader might imagine that the book's tales of derring-do, in which Freddy and Jack accidentally set sail in a sugar tub only to be rescued by an old sailor, prompted equally adventurous usages. The book seems to have traveled *with* Freddy and Jack,

FIGURE 1.7. In this copy of *Transformation Pictures and Comical Fixtures* (circa 1891), marginalia is layered with evidence of physical usage: the word *pull* handwritten on a well-thumbed, ripped tab. The Bodleian Libraries, the University of Oxford (2015), Opie EE 32.

becoming coated in sugar on the way—although I was not brave enough to lick it and confirm my suspicions.

For a third case, consider the evidence—scattered, perplexing, and entrancing—of *reconstructions* of movable books from the Opie Collection. Given their haphazard quality, such repairs are unlikely to have taken place at the Bodleian, or indeed in the hands of the volumes' previous private owners.[112] One of the cardboard tabs in *Dean's Moveable Cock Robin* (1857) has been replaced with a strip of paper annotated in flowing script; close inspection of the tab reveals what seems to be a handwritten name and address (Figure 1.8).[113] Part of a French broadsheet newspaper has been pasted onto the back of a page in Dean's mechanical book *The History of How Ned Nimble Built His Cottage,* in order to strengthen it.[114] Attempts have been made to reinforce the Routledge panorama *A Morning Ride mid Country Scenes* (1852) in similar fashion, with paper from an old letter written in a childlike hand, although each panel is now separate, and the panorama has to be put back together with detective work (Figure 1.9).[115]

FIGURE 1.8. A replacement tab has been constructed from scrap paper for the notoriously fragile mechanical book *Dean's Moveable Cock Robin* (1857). The Bodleian Libraries, the University of Oxford (2015), Opie EE 57.

A miscellany of paper doll heads is cataloged under the shelfmark Opie E 32, and a number of the heads look either to have been reshaped by readers or to be publishers' offcuts: one has been cut at an unusually sharp angle below the ear, and another has a very sculpted cheek that produces a haughty effect. Strangest of all, in one movable illustration from the mechanical book *A New Story about Mother Hubbard and Her Dog*, produced by Ward and Lock, Mother Hubbard's body parts seem to have intermingled with those of her dog (Plate 7).[116] Was this an error on the part of the publisher, perhaps a miscoloring of the original part, or a joke by a reader who mended the book in

FIGURE 1.9. The Opie Collection now holds the only copy in the world of the panorama *A Morning Ride mid Country Scenes* (1852), with mending (now failed) of the panels visible. The Bodleian Libraries, the University of Oxford (2015), Opie EE 190.

her own way? Dean's promise to deliver movable books "not liable to get out of order" takes on new meaning in light of such evidence, as child readers and their parents scissorize and remake novelty books when they break down.[117]

Novelty books bear partial witness to Lerer's elegiac reflection on the archival experience of studying children's literature: "To hold one of these books in our modern hands is to realize not that old texts were lost, but that they were so used and handled, pocketed and plucked out, that they must have fallen apart. Worn away by countless children, these books were, quite simply, read to death."[118] Of course, as Sánchez-Eppler points out, in childhood studies "any claim of agency or assertion of desire just has to be hedged around with mediations."[119] Here, I cannot prove definitively that damage to books is the work of children and not adults—parents and caregivers, or later catalogers, scholars, and collectors. And if child readers did indeed inflict the damage documented in this chapter, I cannot state what they were thinking in the process. Nonetheless, a number of factors make such damage significant in the case of the movable book. Theoretically, in books aimed at such small (possibly preliterate) readers, it makes sense that any defacement would occur in nontextual forms. Moreover, in the ways novelty books themselves try to forestall defacement and destruction in text and picture, we find a sort of physical ideal reader, which suggests that author, illustrator, and publisher are wise to the types of nontextual usages that may be visited upon a book, and that may change its meaning dramatically. It remains to consider in depth how individual novelty book formats foster specific modes of childhood reading—the task of the coming chapters, beginning, in chapter 2, with the panorama foldout.

— Chapter Two —

# Against the Wall

## Stories, Spaces, and the Children's Panorama

The making of a children's panorama depends on a technique that is simple—basic, even: folding a sheet of paper back and forth. The panorama picture book is an accordion-pleated strip, usually glued into covers, that can be read in two ways: either as a sequence of separate pages or unfolded into a long, continuous succession of panels (Figure 2.1). In this, panoramas resemble a host of other objects made by folding pieces of paper. Fans fashioned from theater programs to cool theatergoers' faces in warm weather. Cockhat-folded letters, which allowed Victorians to send messages without envelopes. Puzzle purses, which concealed love notes written on early homemade Valentines.[1] The surrealist entertainment *cadavre exquis,* where groups of artists used folded pieces of paper to generate collective artworks—artifacts that, one suspects, mirrored a whole range of earlier, more demotic parlor games.[2] A lot can happen along the fold.

At the same time, children's panoramas embody schisms between book and nonbook objects. Even the word *panorama,* which comes from eighteenth-century painting, evokes a hybrid of book and picture—and, in the case of the children's panorama, toy as well. If the panorama "were not folded, it would be a mural, not a book," the book artist Keith Smith points out. "However, if that mural is stored by rolling, it is a scroll. Is a scroll a book?"[3] Once unfolded, the panorama resembles a scroll, all the

parts of the image and text appearing simultaneously side by side. What implications does the panorama's simultaneity have for the organization of words and pictures? Does the material and symbolic meaning critics have found in the "physical proximity" of the scroll's different parts characterize the panorama, too?[4] And how do readers—specifically, child readers—navigate a book when they can see the whole of it at once?

The midcentury children's panoramas discussed in this chapter provide varied answers to these questions as they seek either to transcend or to embrace the simultaneity of panoramic structure, with models ranging from the temporal logic of a story at one end to the spatial logic of a collection at the other. In every case, panoramas instruct the child in a way of seeing connections and constructing paths through the diverse images in the world. But panoramas also adjust received wisdom about the picture book at an overarching level. While admitting that a few exceptions do exist, commentators on the children's picture book often start by opposing narrative time to pictorial space.[5] Panoramas, by contrast, foreground the fact that pictures take time to parse, just as words do.[6] Whether their pictorial strips are disjointed or continuous, thematically coherent or miscellaneous, panoramas intertwine rather than oppose pictorial space and verbal time. Moreover, while the panorama is a print object in which space is distinctively foregrounded by way of the unusual pictorial format, its physical resemblance to another Victorian object—the wallpaper frieze—allows us to rethink how children's books were used *in* space during the period.

## The Panoramic Century

Victorian children's panoramas appeared within the larger context of the panorama in the long nineteenth century, an era that boasted a dizzying array of panoramic entertainments. First of all, there were the large-scale circular paintings originated by Robert Barker in 1787. Barker's new form of public art entailed a "picture

FIGURE 2.1. All the parts of the long image appear side by side once a panorama such as Aliquis's *Pictorial Humpty Dumpty* (1843) is unfolded. Courtesy of the Lilly Library, Indiana University, Bloomington, Indiana.

of a landscape or other scene . . . arranged on the inside of a cylindrical surface, to be viewed from a central position." Barker aimed to depict a scene "by drawing and painting, and a proper disposition of the whole, to perfect an entire view of any country or situation, as it appears to an observer turning quite round."[7] The invention was highly successful. Some of Barker's own achievements included a panoramic 270-degree view of London from Albion Mill (exhibited from 1791) and a 360-degree depiction of the Grand Fleet at Spithead (exhibited from 1793 in a building prepared to the specifications set out in Barker's patent). Further examples—say, the panorama painting of London at the Colosseum in Regent's Park, which was first exhibited in 1829 but reinvigorated by the Colosseum's new management in 1845—show the form's popularity later in the century.[8]

*Panorama* came to describe entertainments other than paintings, too. There were moving panoramas, such as John Banvard's panoramic scroll of the Mississippi and Missouri Rivers, a gigantic canvas unrolled before spectators so as to give the impression that the scenery in the picture changed. Banvard's moving panorama was exhibited in London in 1848 after a popular American tour, and Charles Dickens himself praised it as "an easy means of travelling, night and day, without any inconvenience from climate, steamboat company, or fatigue, from New Orleans to the Yellow Stone Bluffs."[9] On a smaller scale, many paper pamphlets (often produced in association with public spectacles such as the Great Exhibition or the Lord Mayor's Show) called themselves panoramas, as did the giveaway foldouts issued by periodicals, including the *Pictorial Times* and the *Illustrated London News*.[10] The children's panorama book is a subtype of these pamphlets.

It is because nineteenth-century panoramic objects exhibit such huge variations in scale, materials, and modes of usage that different types of panoramas—tiny paper foldouts, large static paintings, traveling moving pictures—articulate not just panoramic forms but also panoramic *sensibilities.* The word *panorama* (Barker's coinage) quickly became a figure of speech: the *Oxford English Dictionary* parses the subsidiary metaphorical meaning as a "continuously passing scene; a mental vision in which a series of images passes before the mind's eye." For its earliest usage of *panorama* in this sense, the *OED* quotes a letter written from London in May 1813 by Maria Edgeworth: "Be assured that the whole panorama passes before me as a panorama." Edgeworth's phrasing suggests the panorama's irreducibility, as a panorama is like nothing else but a panorama (even when there are many different iterations of panorama). In fact, the word peppers Edgeworth's letters. For example, she uses it again in 1813 to describe the effects of the London season, writing in June that "the brilliant panorama of London is over," and reprises the metaphor in 1822: "Among the great variety of illustrious and foolish people we have seen pass in rapid panoramas before us, some remain for ever fixed in the memory, and some few touch the heart."[11] For Edgeworth, the panorama stands for the metropolis: its speed and abundance. This association arises within the context of individual panoramic shows, which often entailed what Bernard Comment calls "perceptual and representational fantasies" of the city.[12] (Edgeworth saw Barker's panorama of Edinburgh in 1812.)[13]

The panoramic metaphor implied structures as well as subjects, as a second Victorian usage demonstrates. In the July 1859 issue of *Sharpe's London Magazine,* a reviewer uses *panorama* to describe different sorts of fiction: "Thackeray and Dickens succeed mainly because they have *no* plot. Each monthly number, yellow or blue-green, presents its vivid pictures of character and life, amusing in themselves, apart from their connection with the number past and the number to come. Their fictions are like moving panoramas, intended to be seen bit by bit with a striking effect of sunlight or moonlight or storm at regular intervals; while Bulwer's are grand high-art pictures most elaborately arranged."[14] The vivid signature "yellow or blue-green" covers of Thackeray's and Dickens's works absorb the "vivid pictures" of the prose inside them (and the literal "vivid pictures" of any accompanying illustrations) and then in turn conjure up the panoramic entertainment. The panorama is a structural metaphor for this anonymous reviewer, who extrapolates from the form a framework for certain types of fiction: fiction marked by discontinuity between constituent parts of the narrative.

The parallel works in much the same way in a later assessment by Walter Benjamin, who parses the "feuilletonist miscellanies and series of sketches from midcentury" as an "exact counterpart" of the panorama, "not only related . . . in their unscrupulous multiplicity, but technically constructed just like them."[15] In particular, suggests Martin Meisel, panoramic models solve the problem of how to represent modern life in the nineteenth century, as the panorama affords a structure uniquely suited to experiences of rapid change and lack of unification—"a shape transcending the presumed shapelessness of modern life." Moreover, this new panoramic structure privileges space over time: the "range of types and activities" depicted in scenes of public life "would be spatially rather than temporally ordered, so that juxtaposition and proximity would be functions of contemporaneity and without intrinsic narrative value."[16] The time of the story is displaced by the space in which the story takes place.

In the nineteenth century, then, *panorama* became a word with which to think about narrative structure—or rather the lack thereof. Crucially where the children's panorama book is concerned, the metaphorical senses of *panorama* signify a nonnarrative form of entertainment. The panorama as "continuously passing scene" possesses few of the conventional attributes of story as famously defined by Hayden White: while there may sometimes be a "central subject," there is little sense of a "well-marked beginning, middle and end," climactic reversal, or an identifiable, ordering voice.[17] Instead, figurative usages of panorama suggest loose processions in which one thing replaces another without logic or deliberate arrangement. Indeed, even the many travel-themed nineteenth-century panoramas might not proceed in any rigidly determined order. A review of Banvard's panorama of the Mississippi in the *Illustrated London News,* for instance, gives the following account: "Upon a platform in front is seated Mr. Banvard, who explains the localities, as the picture moves, and relieves his narrative with Jonathanisms and jokes, poetry and patter, which delight his audience mightily; and a piano-forte is incidentally invoked, to relieve the narrative monotony."[18] The phrase "relieve the narrative" appears twice, with "monotony" added in the second instance. The reviewer's prose apes the circularity of the entertainment it describes, which, as Richard Altick tells us, looped back on itself: "Instead of rewinding it after every performance, Banvard simply reversed the direction of the trip for the next show."[19] The length of the panoramic scroll dictated the length of Banvard's verbal entertainment, meaning that for every explanation of a beauty spot or bit of local color, there was something incidental to the image, embroideries designed to fill verbal space in accordance with pictorial length and the time it took to unroll the image. Banvard explained the panorama's sights as they unfolded, but he also augmented this sequential relationship between components of the image with nonnarrative verbal forms such as the "Jonathanisms and jokes, poetry and patter" mentioned in the *Illustrated London News.*[20]

Banvard's panorama extracted verbal time from pictorial space, generating a structure in accordance with its image. The number of "Jonathanisms and jokes" needed depended on the length of time the picture took to unspool, and this length of time itself was dictated by the size of the picture—the amount of space it occupied. Indeed, panoramas have always been composite pictorial and verbal entities. Barker, for example, issued "descriptive booklets" in conjunction with his panorama paintings, described by Scott Wilcox as "crude outline print[s] of the painting[s] . . . given gratis to each visitor. Objects of interest were numbered and identified in a key. The booklets, which sold for sixpence, contained not only fuller descriptions of the numbered objects (the keyed prints were included), but also a general historical background, facts on native manners and costumes, and a wealth of interesting anecdotes."[21] The elaborate regulations for the display of panoramic images show how Barker attempted to control his spectators' understanding of the panorama; the augmenting of panoramic images with words to guide or determine the reception of the images was one way to achieve this.[22]

But the words that accompanied panoramas may be ignored by writers on the form. On a practical level, picture and word were often separate, meaning that panoramic texts have been (until recently) difficult to find.[23] Perhaps more significant, however, is that the verbal modes that appear are easily dismissed: they are lists or miscellanies or factual snippets or even just descriptive labels, rather than stories. Where the children's panorama is concerned, this becomes important for two reasons. First, sparse text is a generic characteristic of the format. Katie Trumpener goes so far as to describe panorama books in which text and picture appear separately as "wordless."[24] As Emma Bosch has recently pointed out, however, even so-called wordless picture books usually have titles and colophons—making wordlessness an impression dictated by our sense of which words matter in books, rather than a fact.[25] Second, panoramic structure stands for the fragmented, the discontinuous, the nonnarrative—attributes that are not always associated with children's literature, where *book* and *story* may be used as interchangeable terms ("children's books," "children's stories"). Paying sustained attention to panoramic texts as well as panoramic images accords value to nonnarrative genres in children's literature.

At the same time, though, disregarding the verbal components of panoramic entertainments allows the panorama to stand as synecdoche for modern visuality itself. Panoramas, like many other novelty picture-book formats, evoke protocinematic perception. Their aesthetic seems only a whisker away from what Tom Gunning has famously dubbed the cinema of attraction—early films that aimed less at "telling stories" than at "presenting a series of views to an audience."[26] The interplay between an unfolded strip panorama and its individual panels recalls Gilles Deleuze's gloss on film, in which "instantaneous sections" are "made to pass consecutively."[27] Markman Ellis refers to such links between film and the panorama as the "visual culture reading," in which the panorama stands as "a paradigm for modern mass entertainment both as a technical achievement . . . but also as a watershed event in social history."[28] Ellis notes, however, that such a reading can subsume the historical, cultural, and formal specifics of pre-twentieth-century panoramic entertainments. The remaining sections of this chapter attempt to capture those specifics while paying equal attention to panoramic words and panoramic pictures in the children's novelty.

## Panoramic Sequence, Panoramic Succession

If nineteenth-century panoramic texts for children do not always tell stories, how, then, are they structured? What genres do they adopt? Panoramic examples of two educational genres of children's literature, the alphabet and the history of the monarchy, deploy narrative attributes of sequence and succession, but without creating a story. They also suggest, though, the ways in which novelty formats augment or undermine lessons embedded in picture and word—here, lessons about sequence and succession.

The alphabet is often the child's first sequence. Maurice Rickards and Michael Twyman declare that ABCs can be "a peg on which to hang a succession of related subjects," while Brian Alderson observes that the sole-illustrator alphabet can produce "a unity out of a disparate jumble of unrelated elements," as the illustrator's "singleness of vision . . . imposes on them a thematic coherence."[29] In her work on early American alphabet books, Patricia Crain points out that alphabetic formulas, such as "A is for apple," and their accompanying pictures represent "a purposeful turn away from the alphabet's inherent meaninglessness," a way of structuring the meaning of letters.[30] For the panorama, the alphabet also offers a way of structuring (dividing) a long foldout. In nineteenth-century panoramic alphabets made by such celebrated illustrators as George Cruikshank and Honoré Daumier, as well as others by unknown producers, the alphabet provides a loose, nonnarrative frame for text and pictures that nonetheless has a predetermined—if arbitrary—sequence.[31] Indeed, in the case of the child reader, what the alphabet book teaches is sequence itself, as the child may learn individual letters while at the same time learning the order in which they appear.

Perhaps the most famous nineteenth-century panoramic ABC is Cruikshank's *A Comic Alphabet* (1836).[32] Cruikshank's involvement with foldout illustrations in many different contexts suggests the varied roles the format might play in a publishing career in the period: he produced panoramas as children's books, as components of periodicals such as the *Comic Almanack,* and as humorous parlor entertainments.[33] Rickards and Twyman refer to an alphabet of "related subjects," but the genius of Cruikshank's alphabet is its yoking together of unrelated subjects, or subjects whose relation to one another is unclear. The letter values are as follows:

A Alamode
B Boots
C Chimpanzee
D Dining out
E Equality
F Fashion
G Going
H Holidays
IJ Isaac and John (one panel)
K Kitchen Stuff
L Latitude and Longitude
M Monkies
N Nightmare
O Orpheus
P Pretty-Poll
Q Quadrille
R Racing
S Singing
T Tantalizing

VU Very Unpleasant (one panel)
W Waistcoat
X Xantippe
Y Yawning
Z Zoophyte

A letter might stand for just about anything in the *Comic Alphabet*: a phrase, an object, an animal, a scenario, an abstract concept, the name of a classical figure, an action, or an adjective.[34] Two letters might band together to represent one phrase ("Very Unpleasant" describes the illustration accompanying *U* and *V,* in which a bull chases a portly gentleman) or two characters interacting with one another.[35]

Cruikshank's alphabet aligns panoramic content with panoramic form in its unpredictable choices of subjects for the letters. The panoramic image is typically arranged across a horizontal axis. As such, it eschews other design possibilities for a long, narrow foldout strip—possibilities ranging from the prosaic (a growth chart) to the cosmic (a trip to the moon).[36] Indeed, Cruikshank's panel for *L* plays with this conflict between horizontal and vertical, as an exaggeratedly wide woman and an excessively thin man in evening dress—representatives of latitude and longitude—hold hands. But if the panorama typically depicts objects across the picture plane, rather than up and down it, Cruikshank also takes horizontality as his structuring principle. This works at both a linguistic level, in the haphazard sample of words, and a social one, in the cross section of different types presented across the foldout.[37] *A Comic Alphabet* is a proto-Victorian social panorama, in which down-and-outers, such as the figures for *D,* who eat baked potatoes bought from a street vendor in front of the "Economic Dining Rooms," appear next to well-to-do strollers and revelers. Sometimes the cross section appears within a single letter frame, as in *E,* a satire on social and racial equality in which two men, one white and one exaggeratedly black, walk arm in arm, smoking (Figure 2.2).[38] It is a panorama of town and country, too, juxtaposing urban subjects such as the diners in *D* with rural ones such as the man and bull in *V U* or the zoophyte traveler in *Z,* in his eighteenth-century frock coat, cravat, short breeches, and stockings, using a knife and fork to spear a suspiciously porcine plant.

The cross section is also a cumulative effect occurring as the panorama unfolds, across panels. Meisel's observation about the panorama's spatial rather than temporal organization serves as an apt description of Cruikshank's maneuver. The panorama's leveling quality can both contrast and equalize its subjects, perhaps in the same way as certain real-world spaces—the city, for example. Cruikshank traces the basic sequence offered by the alphabet across the panorama, but the cross section as panoramic form and as social subject renders this alphabet a spatial operation as much as a temporal one. Once the *Comic Alphabet* is unfolded, its motley characters are spatially contiguous, even though each group or figure is associated with only one part of the alphabet's sequence. Moreover, this contiguity of different types combines with a mockery of high society that encourages the child reader to revel in the disruption of social sequences and scripts.

Take the multiple appearances of animals across panels. In *C*, a chimpanzee swings from a branch, reaching out to an aghast gentleman who looks at the chimp through a monocle (Figure 2.3). Numerous cues disturb the seeming opposition between human and animal, spectator and spectacle: the fine gentleman is distinctly simian, the chimp wears a patterned sweater, and there are no bars on the cage. Indeed, the two outstretched hands in the panel—the chimp's extended in friendship or mischief, the gentleman's frozen in shock—suggest that we catch the two just before they touch, in a culminating leveling gesture. This is the first of a number of such scenarios. The *M* panel has monkeys grabbing a gentleman's cane and coattails (the sartorial marks of his superiority) as he jumps in surprise. In the *Comic Alphabet*, the appearances of apes and monkeys work as they do in eighteenth-century literature, where, as Laura Brown has shown, monkeys disrupt not just social conventions but also well-worn narrative arcs, including the marriage plot.[39] Cruikshank also uses parrots in this way, as a young man in buff trousers and blue coat has his finger bitten by a bird in *P*. While these panels show a destabilizing of one hierarchy—the hierarchy between animal and human—they also counter the panels in which humans exploit animals, such as the bearbaiting that illustrates *T*, "Tantalizing." Rather than experiencing the panoramic alphabet as a temporal sequence, the reader confronted by the all-at-onceness of the full foldout is encouraged to jump back and forth across panels, especially when these panels comment on one another by way of thematic parallels.

In the *Comic Alphabet*, there is a division between the lessons presented by the generic content and the lessons implied by the panoramic illustrations. Explicitly, the foldout teaches the alphabet, forming part of the most elementary—the most foundational—educational genre of children's literature. The child reader is taught

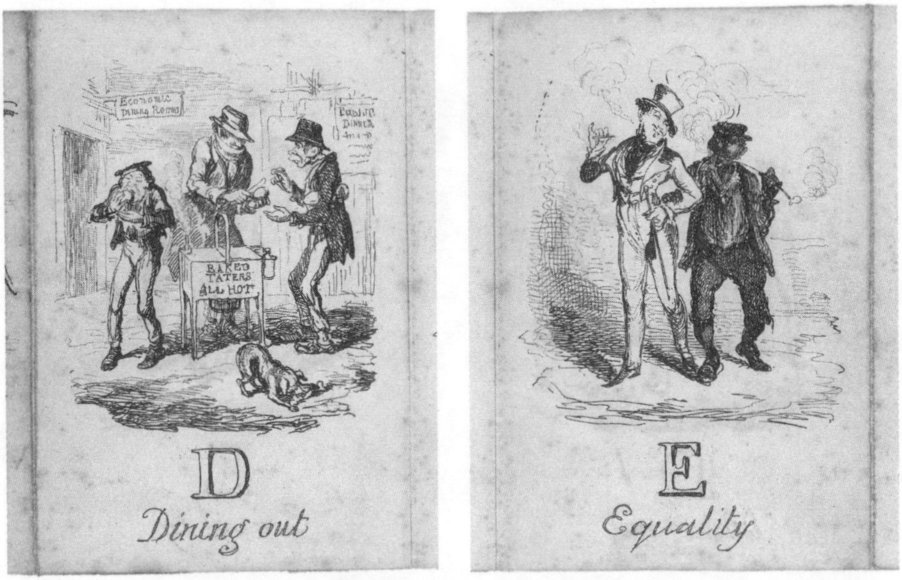


FIGURE 2.2. Both across the panorama and within individual panels, as with the letter *E,* George Cruikshank uses letter forms to juxtapose a variety of social types in his *Comic Alphabet* (1836). Beinecke Rare Book and Manuscript Library, Yale University.

to adhere to this sequence, although it is arbitrary; accepting the naturalness of *A* followed by *B,* on through to *Z,* is part of the lesson. The alphabet is about hierarchy and order. By contrast, the panorama itself is about equivalence, a cue that Cruikshank dramatizes in his satirical, almost carnivalesque, use of the panorama format to taxonomize nineteenth-century types. The few child figures who appear in the images escape such satire, most embedded safely in the *H* panel, where they enjoy a holiday feast, and one seen as a pleased spectator to the monkey grabbing the man in *M.* While even in its costume design Cruikshank's panorama seems to look backward, perhaps to the satires of Joseph Addison and Alexander Pope, Cruikshank turns his satirical lens on adult mores, allying the child with the illustrator as both sit in judgment over conventional hierarchies—judgment enabled or prompted by the panorama format itself.

In its debt to eighteenth-century satire, Cruikshank's *Comic Alphabet* resembles another panorama, one that plays with the conventions of the children's history

FIGURE 2.3. Cruikshank's *C* panel disrupts the hierarchy between man and chimpanzee as part of the panorama's social leveling. Beinecke Rare Book and Manuscript Library, Yale University.

of England. *Alfred Crowquill's Comic History of the Kings and Queens of England from William the Conqueror to the Present Time,* published around 1856 or 1857 by the sometime *Punch* artist Alfred Forrester under his pseudonym, contains illustrations of each monarch (see Plate 1).[40] Looking at *Crowquill's Comic History,* one feature of other Victorian paper panoramas (often miniature moving or peristrephic paper panoramas, which were loaded onto cartridges and viewed using a special device) seems immediately apposite: the focus on processions and parades.[41] Crowquill takes an analogous quasi-ceremonial subject but stages the pageant across history.

Children's histories seek to teach lessons about time—lessons that can be as basic as a list of dates. Conforming to this convention, Crowquill appends a short set of facts to the portrait of each ruler: name, date of birth, date of accession, date of death, and length of reign. John Plunkett interprets *Crowquill's Comic History* as embodying "an unbroken national procession of English and British monarchs" in the format of the panorama itself, and the ordering of the text into date of birth, date of accession, and so on certainly does suggest that the reigns of the monarchs can be read in terms of a series of stable temporal indicators.[42] The temporal relationship, however, is so vastly expanded across the length of the book that the relationship of one figure to another is not quite a narrative. Moreover, through an additional, more substantial section of text in each panel, Crowquill's panorama suggests significant difficulties with reading the British and English monarchs as an unbroken line, or indeed a logical sequence or coherent narrative.

The second piece of text in each panel comprises two rhyming couplets that give a satirical account of the pictured monarch's reign. Crowquill records as many dubious successions as legitimate ones, as many missteps as straightforward progressions: "*Stephen the First,* who had no right, came over from Boulogne"; Richard II "was ousted from his seat, and died, and all was well"; Henry IV "usurped"; and "*Edward the Fourth* came, right or wrong, as had done many more." The fact that the "unbroken procession" from 1066 to 1837 can be retained only with the inclusion of Oliver Cromwell further complicates the timeline, as the text humorously registers:

> Then *Cromwell* came, no King was he; but stern in his intent,
> No statue of him is there at the House of Parliament:
> The partial *few* thus leave him *out,* as he was not a King
> He governed well for seven years, so *we have* put him *in.*

Crowquill's claim to writing a radical history of England's monarchy (in comparison to the "partial *few*") is somewhat weak. Another panorama of royal succession, produced by the firm of Webb and Millington midcentury, also includes Cromwell, changing the format of its text—which otherwise mirrors Crowquill's—slightly: "Reigned" becomes "Ruled," "Began to Reign" becomes "Became Lord Protector."[43] So did many other children's histories at the time, although it was more common to use "The Commonwealth" rather than Cromwell's name as a chapter or section heading.[44] Presumably, this was to avoid any metonymic association between the man himself and the nation, which should remain the preserve of the monarch. Nonetheless, Oliver Cromwell introduces the specter of an alternative historical system, a moment of destabilizing flux in historical time—an undermining of the givenness of royal succession, strengthened by panoramic form, which already upsets chronology in its insistent simultaneity.

There are other challenges to historical time as logical narrative in *Crowquill's Comic History,* too. Sequential markers frequently appear in the text to link panels, and the word *next* often begins the verses, giving the impression of forward motion. These links are in tension with repeated—indeed, almost obsessive—jokes about time. Symbols of time, such as William I's curfew bell, sit next to a coterie of other temporal phrasings and motifs, including the odd assertion that "the temporal and spiritual were swords of equal pride" in the verse for King John and the reference to how Henry IV "quickly went, as nurses say, out like a candle-snuff." As the latter example suggests, many of the panorama's temporal vexations pertain to deaths either premature and rapid or overdue and drawn out. Even the punctuation of these verses produces a morbid effect. An unexpected dash often interrupts plans and schemes, as when Henry III "reigned for fifty years and six, and then—why then he died," or Edward III "did intend—but death popped in, and further works prevented," catapulting the reader into a new panel and new monarch. The short reigns of child monarchs such as Edward V ("His hardly could be called a reign; 'twas but a little shower") and Edward VI ("He reigned six years and five short months, and then he was no more") seem particularly cruel tricks of time. The illustration of Edward VI in a Christ's Hospital uniform underscores the point: living too much, in being brought to the throne at such a young age, has resulted in living too little and dying young. Other monarchs—such as George II, who had "when he died lived too long, and made a pretty mess," and Elizabeth, who, "vain of her charms, an old coquette . . . flirted to the last"—reign for too long.

The final panel showing Victoria contains an appeal to the future in the vocative "oh! placid be your reign" and the optative "long may you reign belov'd and bless'd by all within your land." And yet the overall impression remains that the procession of British monarchs is characterized by instances of time going too fast or too slow, of time's unfairness, and of those who have no right dispatching those who do. Paul Ricoeur once noted that both historians and literary critics assume that "every narrative takes place within an uncriticized temporal framework, within a time that corresponds to the ordinary representation of time as a linear succession of instants."[45] (Ricoeur's choice of the word *succession* shows how powerful a model of sequence and temporal continuity the monarchy can be.) Crowquill combines panoramic form and temporal satire to destabilize history as "uncriticized temporal framework," and by association to mock implicitly the idea of monarchy as progression: the historical catalog may be read as a sequence, but not a smooth or logical one.

Moreover, the juxtaposition of the different reigns within the space of Crowquill's panorama constitutes an inherent questioning of historical time. Once more, what the panorama offers, as a format, is simultaneity rather than succession. As in Cruikshank's *Comic Alphabet,* the format prompts a satirical approach to the presumed educational content of children's history. This panorama teaches children humorous tidbits about the various monarchs rather than facts to be delivered in recitative, such as the ones atop each panel:

> MARY.
> Born in 1516. Began to Reign July 16th, 1553.
> Died December 1st, 1558. Reigned five years.

Much of this information takes the form of jokes about time, jokes that challenge the temporal logic of monarchic succession as well as the need—implicit to the children's history—for child readers to be co-opted into that logic by their books.

### On Horseback and by Train: *A Morning Ride mid Country Scenes*

Panoramic alphabets, panoramic monarchies: these picture books split the foldout strip into individual panels, side by side yet discrete. This division of the panorama leads to disjointed text—a sequence that is more like a list than a story, in line with the panorama's own structural association with disjuncture. Other panoramas, however, combine words and pictures in a narrative manner. In these cases, the panoramic image is often continuous across the foldout and is used to tell a visual story.

The key problem to be negotiated in a continuous panoramic image involves figures that are side by side in the space of the image—in the unfolded panorama—but separated in narrative time. Despite its division into panels, Dean and Son's *Playtime Panorama,* for example, shows a broadly continuous scene across the strip.[46] The book's subject, as the title suggests, is children's leisure activities; depictions of various activities appear across the panorama by season, with a short description at the bottom of each panel. Pastimes range from "Feeding the Ducks" (number one) to the penultimate "Tobogganing," which appears directly before the children move indoors to a cozy nursery. There is a wall at the right of the "Tobogganing" panel, which shows an outdoor snow scene; the viewer passes through the wall into the final panel "Playing with the Kittens" (Figure 2.4). The child viewer takes the same position as the owner of the dollhouse, with walls made transparent and private space opened up to her delectation. This breaking of spatial boundaries in the illustration echoes the larger contours of the panorama: continuity and connection rather than boundedness and enclosure.

Diverse paraphernalia of nineteenth-century childhood fill the nursery in this final panel. In addition to the kittens, there is a pull toy, a book, a Noah's Ark, a doll, and, at the back of the room, a *mise en abyme* reference to the *Playtime Panorama* itself: a panorama book showing animals that stands up as a tiny screen. A board book, the real version can stand up in its concertina form if arranged in a zigzag; in classic panorama manner, it can also be opened and read as a sequence of page openings. Here, to borrow Seth Lerer's evocative formulation, "the book becomes one more item in the furnished room of childhood."[47] The panorama is part of a spatial grouping of objects, presented to the child as a toy rather than as a text to be read. The self-referential game of including the book within the illustration gives the title dual valence: *Playtime Panorama* as a survey of different activities and *Playtime Panorama* as an object that is brought out at playtime along with other toys. Indeed, in the *Playtime Panorama,* the temporal designation *playtime* is inseparable from the spaces where play happens—the nursery, the park, and so on.

Nonetheless, the seasonal progression from summer to winter across panels cues the viewer to perform a temporal operation across the space of the book-image, carrying the core group of children over from scene to scene. This is a fairly familiar technique for visually representing time in the picture book; Maria Nikolajeva's term for it is "simultaneous succession."[48] In conventional picture books, simultaneous succession organizes pictorial space to show time, creating visual codes (such as seasonal imagery) for temporal shifts. But such an arrangement is intrinsic to the panorama, rather than an artistic choice made independent of format. Producing a book as a panorama means that any visual story *must* depict everything side by side. The heightened focus on the space of the panoramic image, an effect of the long, narrow presentation, is inseparable from the heightened importance of time: the unfolding of a visual story, often to match a written narrative, over a continuous image.

FIGURE 2.4. Dean and Son's *Playtime Panorama* (circa 1880–1900) culminates when the children who appear across the continuous image move indoors, with the fold between the final two panels acting as a wall. The Bodleian Libraries, the University of Oxford (2015), Johnson d.2133.

The panorama mentioned in chapter 1, Routledge's *A Morning Ride mid Country Scenes* (1852), is a good place to explore this relationship—that is, the relationship between space, time, and story in the panorama. *A Morning Ride*'s panoramic image folds out from the inside front cover; a fairly long story is presented separately within a small storybook attached to the inside back cover. Introducing its narrative under the rubric "Stories Told in Pictures," *A Morning Ride* contains a continuous panoramic image of a rural landscape. Two boys, named in the text as Edward and Walter, traverse this countryside on horseback. The book uses horizontal space and the social pressures on such a space (and on the children's book) to yield a coherent narrative while taking advantage of the sense of travel across a landscape that a long horizontal strip might encourage. *A Morning Ride* generates a panoramic narrative through a version of what Michel de Certeau calls the travel story as "spatial practice," in which "journeys and actions are marked out by the 'citation' of the places that result from them or authorize them."[49] Here these citations in the text lead the viewer to the panoramic image and its representation of the journey, rather than to real-world places outside the book.

The space of each panel comprises a temporal movement through landscape. Different parts of the picture tell different parts of the story. In the first panel, for instance, Edward and Walter begin their ride in the background of the image, where they are shown coming down an avenue past a group of deer (Figure 2.5). In the foreground, they appear again, having passed the gate out to the road. The various visual landmarks of the boys' journey to visit their cousins across the panorama become verbal plot points—most pleasingly in the case of a marker by the roadside showing how far it is to London (thirty miles), visible in the first panel, which conveys both proximity to and distance from the metropolis. Andrea Henderson argues that eighteenth-century panorama paintings "utilized a system of perspective that presupposed a series of viewpoints along a horizontal line."[50] The text of *A Morning Ride* models this "series of viewpoints" to the viewer like an "I spy" game: "Walter pointed out to Edward a woman milking a cow, and a man ploughing, and a goat and a little kid that were running about in a meadow as playful as kittens."[51] These events appear left foreground, center background, and right foreground, respectively, in panel five, even as the boys have traveled into panel six (Plate 8). The "country lout of a farm-boy" encountered by Edward and Walter is not shown (8); the road the boys travel is at the front of the pictorial panel in which he would have appeared—the "lout" is absent because he effectively occupies the reader-viewer's own position in relation to the vista. The interplay between text and image replaces what Éric de Kuyper and Émile Poppe once called the panorama painting's invitation to see *(voir)* with something more like an invitation to look *(regarder)*, by way of a child encouraged to seek out each sight mentioned.[52]

A connection between the railway and nineteenth-century panoramic modes is well established. *A Morning Ride* appeared only a year or so after Dickens published his rail journey narrative, "A Flight," in *Household Words.* In Alf Seegert's reading, "A Flight" shows the train changing the traveler's perceptions of a journey: a shift "from static diorama—a stable, well-ordered image that invites the inspecting gaze—to moving panorama, an all-encompassing view that avails only glimpses at the finer details as they slide quickly out of view."[53] Seegert's superimposition of the moving panorama onto the train window, which is indebted to Wolfgang Schivelbusch's work on panoramic train travel, connects the train to experiences of transport that were archetypally modern for Victorian travelers.[54] Indeed, as Nicholas Daly notes, modernity can be "represented synecdochically by the train."[55]

It is perhaps no surprise, then, that two trains appear in *A Morning Ride* (see Plate 8). The panorama's use of the train, however, is different from the one outlined above; in *A Morning Ride,* the train serves to "purvey compensatory fantasies" about modernization.[56] The sumptuous landscape that unfolds across this children's panorama performs the same function that Gordon Ray ascribes to certain Victorian illustrated histories of the railway: the panoramic illustration absorbs the spread of the railway into "its surroundings, which remained picturesque despite the intrusion of 'progress.'"[57] The two trains startle the boys' ponies: "a train from London . . . rattling along the railway viaduct, which is built across the valley where the river runs," then "before it was out of sight, another train, going up to London . . . whizzing along" (9–10). Nonetheless, the focus in the panorama is largely on the beauties of the landscape and on the rural vignettes it still affords. Indeed, in its decorative depiction of a particular view, this panorama evokes eighteenth-century prospect engravings, perhaps supporting Altick's idea that the two formats are genealogically related—with *panorama* a cynical renaming intended to increase the prospect engraving's popularity.[58]

*A Morning Ride* is a scale manipulation of the grand panorama's virtual transport to exotic or cosmopolitan settings. Accompanying titles in the same series, such as

FIGURE 2.5. In *A Morning Ride,* background and foreground of the image represent different moments in time. The Bodleian Libraries, the University of Oxford (2015), Opie EE 190.

*A Noon-Day Ramble in the Farm-yard and the Fields* and *An Evening Walk through Lanes and Meadows* (according to advertisements at the back pastedown; neither book is now extant), reinforced this. The panorama provides the child reader (and the adult purchaser) with a pastoral escape, incarnating a wistful, typically Victorian cultural landscape. Trumpener has suggested that the picture book with large-format images in itself "evokes preindustrial spaciousness," an assertion that sheds valuable light on the landscape in and of the panorama, a picturesque view unfolded before the reader.[59] For the owner of the only copy of *A Morning Ride* that survives in a library, such reparative work may have been particularly significant. The Opie Collection copy has the ownership inscription "Eleanor Portal" on the title page, and Eleanor may be Eleanor Jane Portal (circa 1854–1944), one of the children of Wyndham Spencer Portal, created 1st Baronet Portal in 1901 for his services to the London and South Western Railway.[60] This provenance for the book foregrounds the ironic relationship between the panorama picture book's status as nineteenth-century novelty item, a book that is itself a kind of technological wonder, and its depiction of (and possession by) middle-class children idealized as closer to the natural world, or at least in need of "compensatory fantasies" about industrialization.

Early experiments in the novel hang central episodes on mounted journeys. Henry Fielding's *History of Tom Jones* (1749) and Laurence Sterne's *Sentimental Journey through France and Italy* (1768) are two of the more celebrated instances, but the relationship is beautifully self-reflexive in the lesser-known novel *The Adventures of Captain Greenland* (1752), where the narrator remarks: "The number of our pages may serve for Mile-stones, and when he is weary, and has travelled his Day, at the end of our Chapter he may put up his Horse."[61] The journey across a landscape provides a narrative structure for the panoramic mode, as it did for novelistic plotting at the form's inception. The story of a horseback ride told in *A Morning Ride* has a built-in shape; as a journey narrative, it comes furnished with a ready-made beginning, middle, and end. Schivelbusch has shown the railway diminishing "the intensity of travel"—the traveler's sense of the places traveled through—by substituting geographical space for landscape; in the process, he argues, the railway puts an end to the "novel of travels."[62] *A Morning Ride* palliates such effects, endorsing traditional patterns of emplotment and traditional modes of transport, while intrinsically associating such plots (such travels) with the child. The narrative of *A Morning Ride* is paced to match not the rail journey but rather the horseback ride, specifically, the mood of "the morning ride, slowly pacing, full of expectation, your horse as pleased as yourself," as one contemporary treatise phrases it.[63] The inclusion of two rival modes of transport in the panoramic image and its accompanying story is itself a way of engaging with time (progress and speed) as well as foregrounding space (the countryside through which the boys move). Edward and Walter, however, and the children who read *A Morning Ride,* see the train only *from the outside,* in a perspective that does not so much reject the industrial as inoculate it with the rural.

## The Diverted John Gilpin

Many European picture books encourage the reader-viewer to map spatial codes of left and right in an image onto time. As Nikolajeva and Carole Scott point out, the simplest way to use directionality in the picture book is to "arrange the book in a single movement from left to right" in order to convey the progression of the story; they even posit a certain directionality in the picture book's formal unit: a left-hand "secure page" and a right-hand "adventure page" in each page opening.[64] The panorama medium can organize left-to-right movement all the more readily, as it unfolds into one long strip, and a number of Victorian children's panoramas work in this way. The visual plot that occurs across *A Morning Ride,* for instance, has a clear directionality: the main figures in the panorama move steadfastly from left to right across the panorama. But a Victorian panoramic retelling of William Cowper's eighteenth-century ballad "The Diverting History of John Gilpin" introduces another aspect of panoramic technique: the use of directional images to *impose* narrative progression on a text that lacks it.

The tale of a runaway horse and its hapless rider seems to offer the picture book a clear brief for a "single movement from left to right," and the most famous version of this story in the nineteenth century was Cowper's "John Gilpin." The ballad, in which a London draper's journey to meet his wife and family at an inn is stymied by his out-of-control horse, was first published anonymously in the *Public Advertiser* in 1782 and then revised for publication in Cowper's *The Task* (1785).[65] Between these versions, the ballad "became the most popular poem in England," according to Charles Ryskamp.[66] The limited critical mentions of "John Gilpin" tend to equate the poem's scenario with a forward-moving, fast-paced narrative. "In ballads, traditionally, there is a break-neck gallop," says Geoffrey Hartman, giving "John Gilpin" as well as poems by Gottfried August Bürger and Johann Wolfgang von Goethe as instances of this trend.[67] For Tony Voss, Gilpin's "nightmare headlong gallop" is an identifiable "Romantic topos" signifying "the journey of life."[68] Although neither critic spells it out, both Hartman and Voss—like Fielding and Sterne—view the horseback ride as a narrative trope suited to the ballad's generic status as a narrative poem.

"John Gilpin," however, left countless traces in popular visual culture over the long nineteenth century, many of which flout left-to-right conventions of pictorial narratives. The first print illustration of the ballad, which appeared as a folding frontispiece to *The Wit's Magazine* in July 1784, was Samuel Collings's "Gilpin Going Farther Than He Intended."[69] Collings shows Gilpin speeding from right to left past the Bell at Edmonton, Gilpin's destination. A second example: Gilpin appears on a number of lottery sheets in the John Johnson Collection of Printed Ephemera at the Bodleian. (These flat sheets organize little illustrations in a grid; their purpose is uncertain, although Andrea Immel has documented their advertisement alongside sheets for decoupage.)[70] On the lottery sheets, Gilpin is grouped along with a number of other horses, horsemen, and riding scenarios; Gilpin moves right to left across the cell, tilting backward, his nag's rib cage visible in humorous counterpoint to his own prominent gut.[71] A set of late Victorian scraps (pictorial ephemera designed to be cut out and pasted into a scrapbook) of the story likewise shows no clear cues for direction, though it derives a moral from the ride that is absent from the ballad: "Gilpin makes up his mind that he will never ride again!"[72] One Victorian John Gilpin toy-book hybrid comprised "a large wall-chart on which a text of the poem is printed, with a border of crude wood-cut illustrations showing a horse and rider in a considerable variety of postures" packaged together with a mechanical toy that could be manipulated to imitate the woodcuts.[73] Across these examples, John Gilpin serves as a character type, one of Stuart Tave's amiable humorists: an emissary of "that vein of Victorian culture which cherished evidences of some men's innocence in a wicked world, to which it responded with a gentle smile and affectionate chuckle."[74] The translation of the story into nonnarrative print forms—the miscellaneous lottery sheet and scrap, the wall chart with tie-in toy—confirms that a narrative shape was not what "John Gilpin" gave to eighteenth- and nineteenth-century popular culture.

Storybook adaptations of "John Gilpin" also presented unpredictable visual narratives. Rejecting neat formulas for how picture books represent stories—begone, adventure and secure pages!—Alderson gives as his example the most famous Victorian picture-book version of the John Gilpin tale. Randolph Caldecott's *Diverting History of John Gilpin,* first published by Routledge in 1878, observes few conventional rules of left-to-right progression; as Alderson puts it, "The north-bound road to Ware is found leading promiscuously from left to right, from right to left, and straight down the center of the page."[75] In fact, it is in the book's pièces de résistance, Caldecott's two full-color pictorial page openings, that a right-to-left progression is most pronounced. The image from *John Gilpin* emblazoned on the Randolph Caldecott Medal, the American Library Association's annual prize for the year's best picture book, also runs right to left.

There is, however, an alternative to reading these pictures and picture books as eschewing left-to-right directional conventions for visual narratives. In fact, these varied representations of John Gilpin recognize aspects of narrative structure neglected both by scholarly pronouncements on direction in visual stories and by readings of the ballad's momentum. The problem here is the bias toward narrative straight lines and (in scholarship concerning the picture book) toward thinking about how pictures might represent such lines. Images might equally query left-to-right directionality in order to represent less straightforward, less rollicking story lines. Peter Brooks opposes the straight-line narrative, plotted along "the shortest distance from beginning to end," to the narrative arabesque constituted by the "arbitrary, transgressive, gratuitous line of narrative"—the narrative of "deviance, detour."[76] In the case of "John Gilpin," we can add a third term to Brooks's list: diversion.

"The Diverting History of John Gilpin" fulfills the promise of its title in two senses: in its famed charms and in the structure of its story. The poem's subtitle, common to both the original and the revised texts, is "Shewing How He Went Farther Than He Intended and Came Home Safe Again." At the very beginning of "John Gilpin," the reader learns that the narrative journey met by the character will differ from the one he expected. The joke of the poem is in the repeated frustration or diversion of progress and forward movement. (Compare also Leigh Hunt's remarks on Cowper, in which the poet is placed in a position analogous to that of the ballad's diverted hero: "He was alone, not because he led the way, but because he was left on the road side.")[77] In "John Gilpin," there is the false start occasioned by the draper's customers:

> John Gilpin at his horse's side
> Seized fast the flowing main,
> And up he got in haste to ride,
> But soon came down again. (346)

There is the reconfiguration of Gilpin's supposed destination, the Bell, to a halfway marker, which delights the balladic narrator—the horse's second flight "brings me to / The middle of my song"—and a similar move in Ware (353, 355–56). At the end of the verse, in the penultimate stanza, the toll-men's belief that Gilpin "rode a race" is ironically validated:

> And so he did and won it too,
> For he got first to town,
> Nor stopp'd 'till where he had got up
> He did again get down. (358)

The earlier version of the poem for the *Public Advertiser* makes the blocked narrative energies yet more apparent: "Nor stopp'd till where he *first* got up / He did again get down."[78] Thanks to the temporal marker "first," the final stanza evokes the poem's opening, while the rhyme structure further implies a returning, circular energy as opposed to a forward rush.

The panorama picture book *Cowper's Diverting History of John Gilpin,* produced by Read and Company and illustrated by George Cruikshank's nephew, Percy Cruikshank, depicts a number of these stopped narrative moments.[79] For example, in the delays to Gilpin's departure on horseback, characters face each other across relatively unadorned space in the center of the panels, left and right neutralized (Figure 2.6). Another panel shows Gilpin's horse rearing up, facing the left-hand side of the panel. At the eventual end of his journey, still mounted on his horse, which faces right, Gilpin leans backward slightly, while the maid Betty stands in the doorway of the draper's shop, facing left and presenting a visual barrier to the continuation of the story. The panorama also, however, uses left and right to bring the diverting narrative of John Gilpin from arabesque to straight line. Cruikshank's panorama is much more orthodox in its plotting of left and right than, say, Caldecott's version. Although each section of the concertina is illustrated as a discrete scene, Gilpin's horse tends to travel left to right across panels. Scenes do not continue over the fold, except for one attempt to simulate continuity: Gilpin's runaway horse emerges from the fold of panel nine, only half visible, although the image has not in fact continued from the previous panel (Figure 2.7). In the case of Percy Cruikshank's *John Gilpin,* then, it is the image and not the text that is best equipped to depict, or perhaps even force, a sense of temporal progression. The picture does not so much take time as *make* time.

If "John Gilpin" were read aloud or recited to children, its stops and starts might be the source of greatest pleasure. Each time the story (and the journey) begins, it quickly halts; each time a stop is expected, the story-journey continues. The child reader who looked closely at Cruikshank's illustrations might expect movement, only to have that expectation frustrated as the narrative once again founders. Narrative humor combines with the comedy inherent to Gilpin's caricatured figure and the exhausted figure of his horse (surely another of the story's key attractions for children). Moreover, even though Cruikshank illustrates each panel of the visual story as a discrete scene, retaining the way conventional picture books encode time in the turning of pages and the spatial separation of one picture from another, the simultaneity of

FIGURE 2.6. Percy Cruikshank's *Diverting History of John Gilpin,* produced around 1850, manipulates left-to-right orientation: as John Gilpin is delayed, he either faces right or is stopped by another character. The Bodleian Libraries, the University of Oxford (2015), Opie EE 60.

FIGURE 2.7. Cruikshank fakes a continuous scene by showing John Gilpin's horse bursting out of a fold. The Bodleian Libraries, the University of Oxford (2015), Opie EE 60.

the panorama foldout is de facto a means of conveying diversion and narrative frustrations. The story unfolds into a spatially continuous artifact, one that could be read as a loop if the ends were joined. In this, it is a perfect illustration of Gilpin's journey itself, as well as a fitting reminder of the alternative visual stories that children's panoramas proffer.

## Panoramic Papers

Thus far, I have charted the panorama picture book in terms of a number of temporal properties: sequence, succession, journeying, and diversion. But many Victorian children's panoramas are organized according to other criteria; their written texts and images have no self-contained temporal axis, no necessary order. Such refusals of narrative link not to the panorama's content but to its shape. Children's panoramas adopt the form in which many posters have reached their audiences: as foldouts, "graphic highlights detachable for purposes of exhibition in the home."[80] The connection between the panorama and the poster is speculative: no panoramas I have examined provide evidence of such usage—they lack holes in their corners, for example, that might indicate that they were pinned to walls. Nonetheless, the link is an irresistible one; even Alderson and Felix de Marez Oyens abandon bibliographic caution in their tome *Be Merry and Wise* (2006) by suggesting that a nineteenth-century panoramic music primer, unfolded to its full length, "would have looked charming on the walls of the nursery music room."[81] Speculatively unbinding the panorama can open up neglected angles on children's use of print in the nineteenth century—specifically, the fact that middle-class children encountered print on the walls of their nurseries as well as in their own hands or the hands of parents and caregivers. Such potential uses of the children's panorama in social space in turn affect panoramic texts: the panorama as nursery decoration, as opposed to handheld book, does not demand reading, let alone sequence or narrative.

The most obvious connection between children's print culture and the decoration of nursery space is the design and printing of special nursery wallpapers in the nineteenth century. The Victoria and Albert Museum holds a number of examples. At midcentury, for instance, the firm of F. Scott and Son adapted William Collins's immensely successful painting *Happy as a King* (1836), showing children swinging on a gate, into a blue-and-sepia-toned wallpaper; the design historian E. A. Entwisle classifies this as a "cheap machine-printed nursery paper."[82] This wallpaper takes children as its subject, and while its original inspiration would seem to come from an oil painting, the genealogy is complicated by the fact that Collins's painting was converted into a print quickly after its initial exhibition, appearing as one of the engravings in the third part of *Findens' Royal Gallery of British Art* (1839), for instance.[83] In a yet more direct correspondence between the print culture of childhood and nursery walls, pictures by children's illustrators including Kate Greenaway and Walter Crane appeared on wallpapers, sometimes with matching friezes, in the second half of the century. Greenaway's "The Months" paper and frieze were produced by David Walker, while Crane's designs included "The Sleeping Beauty" and "Mistress Mary" for Jeffrey and Company.[84] Storybook wallpapers suggest the links between books and other objects in the child's world. Indeed, overt representation of storybook characters was what made nursery papers "for children." With the prince and princess figures removed, Crane's "Sleeping Beauty" design was repurposed as a non-nursery-specific paper, "Briar Rose."[85]

Viewing images made by Greenaway or Crane on the walls of a room spatializes the children's picture book. At the same time, both the purpose and the aesthetic of nursery papers differed from those of their source material: instead of using pictures to tell or accompany stories, printed wallpaper is oriented toward circuitousness and repetition, as the panels of all but the most expensive papers reprise motifs. (Queen Victoria's own chinoiserie wallpaper from the Royal Pavilion in Brighton, which does not contain one repeated bird, butterfly, or flower across its hand-painted round, is a notable exception.) The Crane and Greenaway nursery papers may work to convert books and stories into this repetitive schema. For example, the Greenaway paper "The Months," made in 1893, uses pictures taken from Greenaway's Almanacks, released between 1883 and 1895 by Routledge.[86] The translation from book to wallpaper heightens a governing condition of the almanac: its cyclical nature. Instead of one year's almanac being replaced with the next, the pattern begins again with the same set of components as the panels are spliced together: the May Queen, gathering apples, celebrating the harvest, lanterns in November; the May Queen, gathering apples, celebrating the harvest, lanterns in November. (The superimposition of the matching frieze called "The Seasons" would have further consolidated the effect.)

Nonetheless, pictorial nursery papers seem made *to be read*—to be fitted into the plots of the books and stories that originated them. But how? The small and portable objects produced in association with children's books from the eighteenth century onward, such as the tie-in toy, facilitate acting out and continuation of the story in the book. By contrast, wallpaper signals no such purpose. In fact, wallpaper seems to imply a passive child imposed upon—indeed, literally surrounded—by adult decisions. One of the most famous wallpapers in nineteenth-century fiction—ranked somewhere between the titular paper in Charlotte Perkins Gilman's short story (itself a nursery paper) and the outmoded *papiers panoramiques* adorning the walls in Honoré de Balzac's 1835 novel *Le Père Goriot* (Old Goriot)—relates to such childhood experiences.[87] In Charles Dickens's *Hard Times* (1854), the first stage of the famous war between child and adult, fancy and reason, revolves around wallpaper. Sissy Jupe and a number of her classmates believe that wallpaper and carpets could be adorned with horses or flowers; it is the duty of the "third gentleman" at Mr. Gradgrind's school to contradict them: "You never meet with quadrupeds going up and down walls; you must not have quadrupeds represented upon walls."[88] As Lesley Hoskins has noted, this scene parodies Victorian design principles forbidding pictorial wallpapers, along with one deviser of such principles, Henry Cole (founding director of the South Kensington Museum, later renamed the Victoria and Albert Museum, and sometime children's author under the pseudonym Felix Summerly).[89] At base, the scene concerns children and material culture, and the way that lived space, education, and print intersect in the child's world—the expectation that printed wallpapers encode lessons is what unites the school inspector with Dickens himself, even if the lessons the two seek to teach are different. This didactic logic finds its reverse image in the child's extraordinary destruction of his nursery in Maurice Ravel's lyric fantasy *L'Enfant et les sortilèges* (The child and the spells), first performed in 1925 but with a libretto written by Colette years earlier; at one point, shepherds and shepherdesses torn from a printed wallpaper mourn their own strange designs: "We'll no longer graze our green sheep on the mauve grass!"[90]

Nursery papers institutionalized the connection between children's books and children's walls at the production stage, but print became fodder for nursery decoration after the fact as well. Thackeray offers his readers such print practices at work in little Rawdon's nursery in *Vanity Fair*: "Rawdon bought the boy plenty of picture-books, and crammed his nursery with toys. Its walls were covered with pictures pasted up by the father's own hand, and purchased by him for ready money. When he was off duty with Mrs. Rawdon in the Park, he would sit up here, passing hours with the boy; who rode on his chest, who pulled his great mustachios as if they were driving-reins, and spent days with him in indefatigable gambols."[91] The makeshift friezes on the walls symbolize Rawdon's mode of fatherhood—at once slipshod and tender—in like manner to the events relayed immediately afterward, in which Rawdon tosses Rawdy up and accidentally smashes his head on the ceiling, then saves the boy from Becky's wrath by urging him not to cry.

Rawdy's picture books, and the pictures pasted on the walls of his room, give a snapshot of print culture as consumed or bought "for ready money," but also as used. The idea of Victorians pasting pictures up on walls might now seem surprising. As David McKitterick observes, however, the period often saw "the original intentions of publishers . . . forgotten as printed matter was reused and rearranged in scrapbooks, as extra-illustration in other books, as lining paper, as wallpaper, as paper patterns for dressmaking, or simply as wrapping"; these practices are characteristic enough to appear in McKitterick's introduction to the history of the Victorian book.[92] While McKitterick assumes that such usages involve disobeying the publishers' intentions, in the case of child consumers, they might be allowed. In *Vanity Fair,* the pasted-up pictures signify not just the affective freight of printed objects in the child's world but also the special dispensations framing nineteenth-century children's relationships with print matter, as a few examples can show. In the preface to his famous, expensive multivolume children's encyclopedia, which was published between 1790 and 1830, F. J. Bertuch requests that children be allowed to use the book like a toy, to leaf through it at any time, to extra-illustrate it, and even—with permission—to cut the pictures out and paste them on pieces of cardboard.[93] The pictures on the pages of Bertuch's encyclopedia appear in serried rows, creating a visual analogy for a frieze and a visual invitation to paste the pictures not onto card but around a room.

Design experts and household guides of the period also counsel such usages. *Cassell's Household Guide* hints that children might mount and varnish pictures of animals and domestic scenes on cardboard, and then display them in the nursery "for ornamental purposes."[94] While in *Cassell's* the printed pictures remain discrete images to be displayed in a rough-and-ready child's gallery, the design guru Robert W. Edis makes it the child's prerogative to cut out pictures and paste them onto walls. In his 1880 Cantor Lectures at the Royal Society of Arts in London (published the following year as *Decoration and Furniture of Town Houses*), Edis asks, "Nowadays, when really good illustrations are generally, and not as an exception, to be found in so many of our monthly and weekly publications, why not, instead of destroying them, cut them out, or, better still, let the little ones do so, and paper them over the whole of the lower portion of the walls?" He goes on to suggest specifically that these illustrations might be used as a frieze: "A band of colour might be made by buying some of the Christmas books,—which Mr. H. S. Marks, R.A., Miss Kate Greenaway, and Mr. Walter Crane have so charmingly and artistically illustrated,—and by pasting the scenes in regular order and procession, as a kind of frieze under the upper band of distemper, varnished over to protect from dirt." Edis further suggests various subjects for such friezes (chiefly fairy tales); such usages coexist with nursery paper designs, which he also mentions.[95]

Edis's *Decoration and Furniture of Town Houses* extends the culture surrounding nineteenth-century print practices such as scrapbooking, whereby, as Ellen Gruber Garvey points out, children might be praised for "creating valuable works from waste paper."[96] The child's radical interaction with print affects not just the print object itself but also nursery space, as some of the scarce material evidence of such practices can show. Karen Sánchez-Eppler draws attention to the pictures pasted on the nursery doors at the Evergreens. These decorations, which were taken from children's periodicals and books, show a group of children who cut out and pasted up images in much the way that Edis envisaged. Moreover, as Sánchez-Eppler points out, the children's wall collages "[sever] picture from word with often striking results," as, for example, an incidental image of performing dogs is the sole element pasted up from a maudlin moral tale.[97] Even when children were permitted by parents to repurpose their printed materials, the way they did so might adjust or even disobey the generic and narrative scripts embedded in these texts.

Why might the panorama be a printed object especially suited to these sorts of uses? A number of midcentury panoramas produced by the Leeds publisher Webb and Millington can demonstrate why. Extant Webb and Millington panoramas for children include the *Panorama of Kings and Queens* mentioned above, a panoramic alphabet, and a sea panorama; animals characterize most titles in the series, including the *Panoramic Keepsake, Panoramic Museum, Panorama of Horses,* and an indestructible panorama titled *Beasts*.[98] The copy of the *Keepsake* held in the Baldwin Library of Historical Children's Literature at the University of Florida can serve as a basic exemplar of the format.[99] The publication comprises a long panoramic foldout with images pasted onto brown paper boards, each of which is embellished with an elaborate border and typographical flourishes around the title. The foldout consists of a series of numbered panels with decorative borders, mostly showing different animals; the only text is a caption at the bottom of each panel identifying what is pictured (Plate 9).

The first feature of the *Panoramic Keepsake* that suggests it might have been pasted up on walls is its low price of one shilling.[100] In the 1880s, the unflocked but colored version of Crane's frieze "The Peacock Garden" sold for three shillings and sixpence per yard (thirty-six inches).[101] Utilizing Webb and Millington panoramas as friezes would have been economical by comparison: where the *Beasts* indestructible panorama was concerned, for example, a twenty-eight-inch foldout cost sixpence. The very practice of touting the length of panoramas in advertising materials signals the panorama's allegiance to nonbook materials such as wallpaper and wall friezes; for instance, Dean and Son sold panoramas by the foot, with panoramas measuring six feet, six inches in length costing a shilling and sixpence.[102]

A second, related point is the panorama's ephemerality. As Timothy Young has noted, libraries classify ephemera based on function. The influential descriptor of ephemera from the *Art and Architecture Thesaurus* reads: "Everyday items manufactured for a specific, limited use, and usually intended to be discarded thereafter, especially printed matter on paper."[103] Equally, though, format helps to define works as ephemera, as Young's bottom-line classification "nonbook material"—discussed in the Introduction with reference to the harlequinade—shows.[104] Panorama foldouts fit both criteria: they often function as souvenirs of particular occasions, and they adopt an unusual format, one bordering on the "nonbook" despite their typically appearing within covers. It is these features that lead to the panorama's inclusion in Rickards and Twyman's *Encyclopedia of Ephemera.* The panorama's ephemerality returns us to Edis, and to the counterintuitive balancing of destruction and conservation in children's print culture. Edis contrasts the preservative activity of pasting up pictures with the disposability and destruction of print in many households. This disposability is inseparable from the governing conditions of Victorian print culture—that is, the proverbial fair-weather favor met by ephemera, periodicals, and even seasonal books. (Recall that Edis mentions Greenaway and Crane's "Christmas books" as likely objects for cutting up.) Destroying the panorama in order to paste it up on the wall becomes, then, a way of preserving the ephemeral. This process is in action at the Evergreens, where, as Sánchez-Eppler notes, many of the images on the doors come from children's periodicals, rather than from books.[105]

Third, though, a reader might paste the *Panoramic Keepsake* up on a wall because of the book's approach to text. Excluding the title and publication information, the *Panoramic Keepsake* has just eighteen words. The naturalistic hand-colored illustrations suggest an educational function, encouraging children to recognize animals and, to a lesser extent, character types and objects. If the *Panoramic Keepsake* is a primer designed to teach the child specific words and their meanings, extra text may only confuse the lesson. At the same time, sparse text and bold images mean that the *Panoramic Keepsake* could be readily pasted on the wall without losing its intrinsic appeal. Even nursery papers contained small amounts of text, as in Crane's "Mistress Mary" frieze, which repeats the nursery rhyme in blue letters at the top of the design.

Finally, thinking about the panorama as a protofrieze can help illuminate the organization of whatever text it does contain. The *Panoramic Keepsake,* like many other Webb and Millington panoramas, does not suggest any sort of internal sequence. While the *Panorama of Horses* has a narrow theme, most of the publisher's animal panoramas do not: the *Keepsake* ranges from domestic animals (dog, canary) to farm animals (horse, cow, goat, ass) to exotic birds (hoopoe). The principle of the Noah's Ark, the intensely popular Victorian toy that housed pairs of miniature animals, seems to rub off on these materials. At the same time, the panorama even seems to extend by analogy the definition of animal by way of its few nonanimal illustrations, expressly, "Sweep," "Greenlander," and "Beggar," which equate social or ethnic categories with different species. The logic of the panorama is not that of a story, but that of a collection. The firm's *Panoramic Museum,* which also features carefully framed images of animals, evokes the museum as Foucauldian heterotopia of time: "A place of all times that is itself outside time and protected from its erosion . . . a kind of perpetual and indefinite accumulation of time in a place that will not move."[106] Like the Victorian museum, these panoramas organize their content thematically rather than sequentially—annexing time to space in the process, and suggesting their fitness, perhaps, as objects to be pasted up on nursery walls.

This chapter has been a first exercise in applying fine-grained analysis to the forms of novelty picture books for children, in giving speculative attention to the impacts of those forms on picture-book texts as well as to what those forms suggest about children's possible usages of their books. In the case of the phantom panorama as frieze, the form gives clues that the material evidence left over from Victorian nurseries does not, as the palimpsest of paper upon paper—itself a metaphor for researching the intersections between children's print and material cultures—may obscure salient evidence. We almost never know what appeared on Victorian children's walls, although material objects can help us here, too. The records of decoration absent from nurseries themselves are found in the miniature decoration of dollhouses. When thirty-year-old Amy Miles made herself a dollhouse in 1890, she re-created her childhood nursery and equipped it not just with pictures and toys but also with a tiny animal frieze—a Jack Russell terrier chasing chickens round and round the walls.[107]

— Chapter Three —

# The Movable Book in 3-D

Their eyes are not concerned with three-dimensionality;
this they perceive through their sense of touch.
—*Walter Benjamin, "A Child's View of Color"*

Reading is an exercise that depends on focusing one's eyes in a certain way—keeping them on the surface of the page, not looking into or behind the text. By association, books often seem outright inimical to depth; for instance, a conceptualization of the book in two dimensions is so widespread that, as Roger Stoddard observes, even bibliographers record only the measurements of the page when cataloging. "The book's third dimension," writes Stoddard, "its thickness, is never included in statistics."[1] Number of pages, the sole regularly conveyed measurement that might reflect such information, substitutes the page once more for the book. Illustrated books can, however, disrupt this particular point of view, tasking readers, in David Bland's words, "to reconcile the flatness of the text with the depth of the picture" as they move through word and image.[2]

If illustration can bring the book into 3-D, the book's traditional allegiance to flatness is further disrupted by the movable format discussed in this chapter. *Pop-up* is the familiar contemporary term for what the ArchBook collective describes as "a three-dimensional paper construction found in books."[3] The pop-up is a book in which a sequence of cutout layers affixed to the page makes a three-dimensional image (Figure 3.1). The antiquarian book dealer Michael Dawson gives a clear summary of hinge projection, the most elementary pop-up technique: "As the pages open, parts of the picture representing the middle distance and foreground separate themselves from the background by means of pasted-down paper tabs or threads, standing proud to form a miniature tableau which, when viewed from the front, gives a heightened sense of perspective."[4] The pop-up book's illusion of three-dimensionality is at once visual and tactile: reliant on an image that uses established visual rules for representing depth, but also offering actual three-dimensionality produced by the child reader's physical manipulation of the book. In this, it offers an alternative aesthetic—something like the sensory transfer, the illusion of three-dimensionality experienced through touch, that Benjamin associates with the child.

The pop-up invites its child readers to marvel at, draw pleasure from, and scrutinize the ways in which surface and depth are bound up together. In this chapter, the pop-up book's negotiation of pictorial surface and depth is examined alongside parallel strategies in three other nineteenth-century visual modes. The first section explores the overlaps between pop-up pictures and flat pictures, while subsequent sections consider surface and depth in the theater and in the stereoscope. Throughout, the discussion concerns how the nineteenth-century preoccupation with regulating perspective and depth of field plays out within these modes—both reinforcing and troubling conceptions of children's literature as a controlling apparatus.

The pop-up format changes the reader's relationship to the book as an object, to its surfaces and its dimensions, as well as to its visual and verbal components. Ultimately, in intertwining surface, depth, and three-dimensionality, the pop-up encourages larger perspectival play from the child reader: turning the book upside down, opening and closing it, examining the mechanics by which it creates its illusion. One of the pop-up's precursors was the three-dimensional diorama called a peepshow, another term for which was *perspective box*.[5] Pop-ups are perspective books, revealing properties often abstracted from the reading experience, even though the book—unlike the surface of the page, which stands as its synecdoche—is always a three-dimensional object.

FIGURE 3.1. The pop-up's cutout layers spring into three dimensions when the book is opened by means of hinge projection—as in this example from *Peeps into Fairyland* (circa 1896)—or when a tab is pulled. Reproduced by kind permission of the Syndics of Cambridge University Library (1896.14.15).

## Pop-Up History

Today, the pop-up often serves as a representative figure for all children's movable books. The editorial preamble to Geoff Fox's essay on twentieth-century movables in a scholarly collection, for example, states, "Most of us are familiar with at least one kind of movable book—the pop-up."[6] The pop-up's emblematic popularity is at least in part due to the nature of its formal innovations, which contrast with those of the panoramas discussed in chapter 2. The panorama relies on a basic paper technique—concertina folding—that was widely utilized in both book and nonbook items before being redeployed in children's publishing. By contrast, the pop-up book is more complex: it is enabled historically by the development of strong papers and cards, and materially by the insertion of mechanical devices into the book. As such, the pop-up is the first "true" movable picture book discussed in this volume, both because of its formal conceit—parts of the page move when a tab is pulled, or more simply when the page is turned—and because of its association with particular moments in the history of the book.

Here, I use the word *pop-up* for convenience. There was no consensus of terminology for naming the pop-up book in the nineteenth century, although a brief examination of the nomenclature demonstrates some of the format's potential and associations. In the nineteenth century, peepshows were packaged between covers as telescopic or tunnel views that unfolded into three-dimensional scenes. While these items were not expressly aimed at children, extant examples show children using them (Figure 3.2). Pop-up books might also call attention to the links between their formal properties and those of the peepshow, as in Nister's *Our Peepshow.* Other makers, though, used bibliographic terminology to showcase different properties. Dean and Son released pop-up books at midcentury under the rubric New Scenic Books, touting the pop-up's potential to realize a scene (if not a story or characters) more fully.[7] By the end of the century, the same firm released its Surprise Model series; the name Surprise Model foreshadows solidity as well as the spontaneity later implied by *pop-up.* Reviews, meanwhile, picked out relief as the format's key feature, referring to "figures that stand up" or pictorial pages that "stand out as the book is opened."[8] The proliferation of different types of pop-ups has today resulted in taxonomic fervor, as collectors and scholars distinguish among countless techniques and mechanisms: pull-ups, grotto effects, and multiple types of hinge projection can all be carefully enumerated and defined.[9]

This is not to say that pop-up techniques were used only in books in the Victorian period. Wider trends in paper products are an important context for the children's pop-up book, especially in view of the fact that prolific fin de siècle publishers of children's movables, such as Nister and Raphael Tuck, also manufactured greeting cards. Novelty cards were a growth industry quick to deploy paper engineering techniques. Pop-up Christmas cards were popular by the 1880s, and when the women's magazine *Hearth and Home* published an article on Nister's factory in 1897, the manufacture

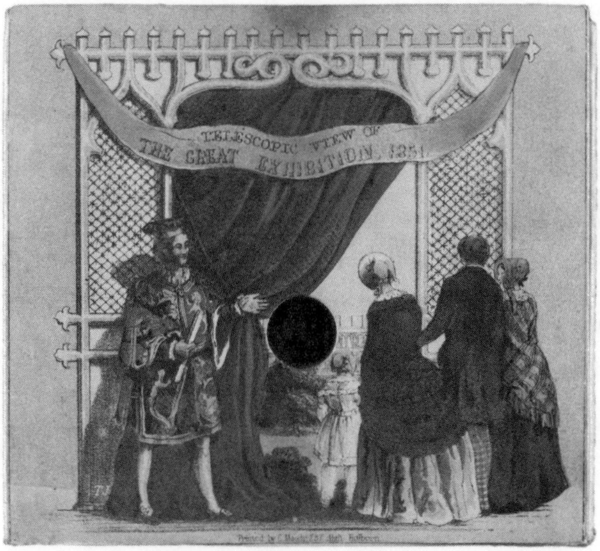


FIGURE 3.2. Nineteenth-century paper peepshows, such as Lane's *Telescopic View of the Interior of the Great Industrial Exhibition* (1851), often seem aimed at a mixed-age audience. Avery Architectural and Fine Arts Library, Columbia University in the City of New York.

of pop-up cards by female workers in particular was celebrated: "We especially noticed the deft way in which they constructed pretty little cardboard Swiss châlet cards with a Christmas greeting on the floor within, and which are made to fold up to go in an envelope. Verily, of ingenuity of the designers there is no end!"[10] As with hand-colored illustrations (discussed in the Introduction), the material inventiveness of the pop-up book could impart romance even to the conditions of its production.

Movable books and other print media were synergistic in the nineteenth century: chromolithographed images might be produced in both pop-up and flat forms by the same firm. For instance, six Raphael Tuck scrap images became illustrations for the pop-up book *Fun at the Circus* (or vice versa; dates are uncertain), with only minor changes (Figure 3.3).[11] *Fun at the Circus* was part of Tuck's Combined Expanding Toy and Painting Book Series, the phrase *Expanding Toy* conveying the pop-up technique: *Fun at the Circus* achieves a rudimentary three-dimensionality by mounting the cut-out image of a clown on a cardboard spring that can either lie flat against or push up from the page. The use of the same image for a scrap and for a pop-up is evidence of the interweaving of children's publishing with other popular nineteenth-century print paradigms, such as scrapbooking and greeting cards. It also hints at the increasing commercial and ideological separation of children's literature and domestic activities from entertainments that were coded male and cosmopolitan, even as the appearance of the image as both book illustration and scrap places the professional publisher on the same conceptual level as another figure in this chain of circulation: the person who pastes a scrap into an album and makes a different sort of book.

But while the connection between paper ephemera and the pop-up is important, it is what happens to the image when it is made movable and incorporated into a book that is significant. *Fun at the Circus* foregrounds the presence of spectators through the flat backdrop printed on the page behind the clown. The book's words and images offer its child audience the experience of being at the circus, an organized piece of entertainment with a succession of performers and an audience, rather than a stand-alone iconography of the circus, as in the scraps. The apotheosis of this trend is Meggendorfer's spectacular pop-up *Internationaler Circus* (International circus), first published in 1887, in which, to quote Margaret Higonnet, "The mechanical animation of the page played into the circus themes of stylized entertainment and surprising antitheses, achieved through juxtaposing human with animal performers and dancers with clowns."[12] The whole book folds out into a semicircular space like an amphitheater, or even a full circle, able to be viewed from above. Meggendorfer's book gives a sense of spatial plenitude and expansiveness, as the ranks of spectators in the stalls recede into the distance toward the top of each page. (As Maurice Sendak once admired, "The crowd serves only as background, but Meggendorfer has gone to the trouble of characterizing everybody.")[13] The focus of such a pop-up, and of *Fun at the Circus,* is being entertained, is spectatorship itself.

The fascination with acts of looking constitutive of the picture book is yet more important to the pop-up. For instance, a trompe l'oeil effect present in both versions of the Tuck image, with the clown's head breaking through a round screen, is heightened by the pop-up's trickery, its substitutive rendering of depth whereby physical or material distance augments illusionistic visual cues: the drawing of ripped and torn paper around the clown's head, say. While trompe l'oeil is, as Lindsay Smith argues, a device associated with the "self-centred role of the artist," the heightening of that effect through a manipulation of the page grants the reader agency over the image and over perspective itself.[14] While the intersections between the pop-up book and other branches of Victorian print are significant, then, there is a fundamental difference between (on the one hand) a static image and a pop-up one, and (on the other hand) a pop-up card and a pop-up book.

FIGURE 3.3. Raphael Tuck produced images including this one as pop-up illustrations in a children's book, *Fun at the Circus* (circa 1892), and as a set of die-cut scraps. Baldwin Library of Historical Children's Literature, Special and Area Studies Collections, George A. Smathers Libraries, University of Florida, Gainesville / The Bodleian Libraries, the University of Oxford (2009), John Johnson Collection Scraps 10 (33b).

## Surface and Depth in the Pop-Up: Two Scenes

When Dean's New Scenic Books claim the pop-up's purview as that of the scene, they summon associations with setting and landscape, leitmotifs that run through nineteenth-century pop-ups. The pop-ups discussed in this section, produced by Raphael Tuck circa 1896 in a number of formats—at the end of books titled *Country Life* and *Seaside Pleasures,* and as part of a combinatory volume called *Summer Surprises*—confirm the pop-up's scenic bias not just in their titles but also in attendant advertising patter promising a "6 page diorama" or "6 tier color litho dimensional scene."[15] (For ease of expression, I refer to the *Country Life* pop-up and the *Seaside Pleasures* pop-up throughout this chapter.) Each pop-up is of the floating-layer type, in which flat cutout scenes are layered atop one another and linked together at the sides with paper concertina folding.[16] The pop-up's unique three-dimensionality can be illuminated by putting *Country Life* and *Seaside Pleasures* in dialogue with conventional, flat Victorian pictures (especially landscape paintings and prints). More broadly, these titles allow an initial exploration of the ways in which pop-up surfaces and depths interact.

As its proverbial title suggests, *Country Life*—in good company with other nineteenth-century titles, such as *Scenes and Occupations of Country Life* (1844), *English Country Life* (circa 1870), and *Old Country Life* (1890)—traverses well-worn territory.[17] Ruskin's critique of "the common idea of a picturesque village" is an apt introduction to the pop-up piece: "pretty bow-windows, or red roofs, or rocky steps of entrance to the rustic doors, or quaint gables."[18] Each layer of cutouts—there are five, the backdrop pasted on the inside back cover making six as advertised—contains an assortment of human figures, animals, and scenic elements both architectural and natural (Plate 10). Part of the pleasure of looking at such a pop-up is in shifting attention from the whole to individual elements, which are often highly detailed. A girl in the front layer has a pink ostrich feather in her hat. A farmer with old-fashioned whiskers and smock, chasing a runaway horse, is an archaic presence in the fourth layer. A boy in a sailor suit looks askance toward the viewer from the second layer. At the rear, the background resembles a nondescript landscape print: the sky streaked with pink, a path winding into the distance, clumps of trees, and a distant windmill.

So far, so conventional. The entire pop-up image embodies a Wordsworthian landscape ideal, in which the "interposition of green meadows, trees, and cottages, and a sparkling stream" variegates the pleasant prospect, or (more scathingly) "the Victorian village picture" at its nadir: "A picture-postcard affair, full of ancient thatched cottages, hollyhocks, and little girls in white bonnets."[19] Indeed, the scene's lack of specificity demonstrates the persistence of the picturesque in the mass market for print, which existed even while the Victorian landscape painting proper (as Andrew Hemingway points out) renounced the picturesque's "generalized signs for trees and locale" in favor of a more naturalistic, topographical mode.[20] More important, the image aims to educate the child in an appreciation of picturesque convention, as a child figure at the front looks into the scene in order to sketch it. *Country Life* underscores the ways in which the countryside might look like a picture and be looked at as a picture by a child. This gesture makes self-referential the general importance of framing to the picturesque: in Alison Byerly's words, "A picturesque scene does not have to be physically painted on a canvas—it need only be 'framed' by an appreciative spectator."[21] The child viewer should recognize this scene as picturesque, as a picture, via her avatar; the little artist frames the scene, just as much as the grove of trees at left of the top panel or the wood-slatted wall at right, both of which form a physical frame.

The instructive visual register of the pop-up in *Country Life* recalls some models of Victorian art education: the ones that, as Victoria Ford Smith puts it, envisioned the child "as an inept artist striving toward adult mastery."[22] While adult-defined artistic standards were often technical, here they are aesthetic, linked to an appreciation of the rural landscape and a conversion of that landscape into pictorial form. The accompanying text further bolsters the consensus:

> Don't you love the country, Children, don't you revel in the flowers?
> Can't you listen to the birdies singing songs, for hours and hours?
> Is there anything that's prettier than little lambs at play?
> Is there anything smells sweeter than the clover and the hay?
> Than, the cottages all covered with the jasmine and the rose,
> And the pretty purling streamlet that through the green meadow flows?

This series of questions, taken from the titular poem "Country Life," draws child readers into a particular, and inescapable, attitude toward the countryside—an aestheticized sensory appreciation of its charms. The rhetorical question turns out to be an exhortation: not so much "Is there anything?" as "There is nothing." *Country Life* amplifies this harmony of opinion across the volume as well as within individual poems, as "Country Joys" ("If you leave the pleasant country you'll long to be there again") leads to "Busy Bees" and "The Little Gardener." As in the panorama *A Morning Ride mid Country Scenes,* the association between child, picture book, and countryside is ironic: the rural is the child's provenance, even as the novelty picture book that brings it to her is a technologized, bourgeois artifact.

But these prompts to childish appreciation of the country scene coexist with the pop-up's unique perspectival requirements. In most pop-up books, the layers of the image are arranged so that the individual elements of each single panel are visible in the whole both when it is lying flat and when it is folded out or popped up. This is a quirk of the pop-up's construction, the process called nesting by which the pop-up begins with its individual layers "arranged together onto a flat piece of paper."[23] (The image rests in this way when the book is closed.) By extension, the disposition of the pop-up's multiple layers organizes the composite image: the eye is drawn to the space between figures and to the background landscape and horizon line between the different components. The pop-up thus melds conventional cues for reading depth in a picture (light, shade, geometric and atmospheric perspective) with the pop-up technique, which brings physical depth (actual distance between the layers of the illustration) into the book.

The flat components of the pop-up image (its surfaces) crucially realize depth. As the concept of nesting would suggest, the pop-up organizes depth as a sequence of surfaces. But focusing too closely on any one surface detail of the image (the young girl with the feather, say, or the farmer in his smock) may diminish the perception of depth, which is best achieved when the eye traverses the pop-up picture in a different way: traveling into it, rather than being caught by its individual details. The art historian Charles Harrison identifies a "strange and distinctive form of scepticism about appearances that is set in play when the allure of imaginative depth meets resistance from the vividness of decorated surface"—an idea that is relevant to the pop-up, and to a pop-up such as the one in *Country Life* in particular, where the encouraged juvenile appreciation of the entire scene and its depth of field "meets resistance" from a sequence of gorgeous surfaces and their recalcitrantly appealing details.[24] Surface and depth, in other words, exist in tension.

Such resistant surfaces originate in part from the technological developments that make pop-ups such as *Country Life* possible. Like many other children's books, pop-ups rely on a beguiling and decorative use of color. They are, moreover, inseparable from the refinement and popularization of chromolithography at the end of the nineteenth century, as demonstrated by the involvement of chromolithographic printers, including Tuck and Nister, with children's pop-ups. Raphael Tuck, the eponymous head of *Country Life*'s publisher, established his London firm in 1866, but the business came to the height of its powers along with chromolithography. (Tuck was awarded a royal warrant as publisher to Queen Victoria in 1893.)[25] The colors of children's books are their most obvious surface attribute, and color printing in general is intimately involved with the rise of children's literature—to give two famous examples, Edmund Evans's mastery of color wood engraving as applied to Routledge's toy books from the mid-1860s and the use of three-color, halftone printing for Beatrix Potter's "little books" at the turn of the twentieth century (also printed by Evans's firm).[26] In fact, the association between color printing and children's literature is so axiomatic as to be dismissed by two historians of printing as follows: "The burst of inspiration which colour facilitated in children's books in the latter part of the [nineteenth] century is too well known to require comment."[27] Other dismissals of colorful children's books imply that color's status as a superficial property makes the children's books that exult in it equally superficial, as when Alderson calls color "a delusive quality" in Victorian picture books, which "by its prominence . . . distracted attention from what the illustrator was able, or was not able, to express in line," or when the twentieth-century illustrator Edward Ardizzone refers disparagingly to the idea that "the work of an amateur or inexperienced artist is suitable for books for little children, provided they have a certain spurious brightness of colour."[28] Some children's books, both critic and practitioner suggest, emphasize colorful surfaces to make up for a figurative lack of depth.

Alternatively, the dependence on color in children's books might be considered a distinctive aesthetic attribute. Compare the privileging of line and draftsmanship over color with Benjamin's jubilant exploration of the same subject: "This resplendent, self-sufficient world of colors is the exclusive preserve of children's books. When in paintings the colors, the transparent or glowing motley of tones, interfere with the design, they come perilously close to effects for their own sake. But in the pictures in children's books, the object depicted and the independence of the graphic design usually exclude any synthesis of color and drawing."[29] As in his "three-dimensionality perceived through touch," Benjamin fantasizes an oppositional definition of children's aesthetics: while decorative surfaces might interfere with a proper appreciation of paintings, the children's book is a location where color and drawing need not be synthesized perfectly. Michael Taussig points out that, instead of pitting color against line, Benjamin prizes their "mischievous interaction," a space where "color, image, and word manifest a mysterious unity more present or more obvious in primers than in adults' books."[30] The luxuriant pleasures offered by colorful children's books implicitly contrast, too, with the aesthetic lessons that even novelty books such as *Country Life* seek to provide to the child.

The second key development in the surface of children's books is in the paper from which they were made. Machine-made paper is a nineteenth-century innovation marked by two key features: smoothness and lack of visible fibers. Indeed, there were anxieties over these attributes of the new papers. In 1829, John Murray criticized machine-made paper for using pulp "ground to the finest possible consistency, and . . . void of fibrous materials," which resulted in weakness, while at the end of the century William Morris rued the "thick, smooth, sham-fine papers on which respectable books are printed."[31] The coated papers first employed and patented in 1827 are the smoothest of all.[32] Pop-up images are typically made from coated card for durability; the coating renders them glossy and in the process produces certain distinctive surface effects. "Glossy paper gives colors a glistening clarity," Nodelman remarks, "but it is distancing, an overall sheen that attracts attention to the surface of a picture and therefore makes it more difficult for us to focus on specific objects depicted."[33] Significantly, where pop-up images are concerned, rich colors and glossy pages win the viewer over to the surface in a book where depth is at stake.

The interplay between the smooth and colorful surfaces of each pop-up layer and the pop-up's constitutive concern with depth effects is dynamic. As Kate Flint has noted in her discussion of Victorian picture making:

> Depth is, by its nature, resistant to visibility. It is never spread out before our eyes, but appears to them only in foreshortened form—that is, if what we wish to see is not quickly obscured by impenetrable density of matter. When we conceive of depth, figure it in our mind's eye, it becomes tacitly equated with breadth seen from the side: depth made visible by, as it were, turning it on its axis. We thus perform a sort of mental acrobatics when we envisage depth, which severs imaginary perception from any actual possible positioning as a spectator.[34]

Flint draws her point from Maurice Merleau-Ponty, who begins his analysis of the subject in *The Phenomenology of Perception* (1945) by stating that "traditional ideas of perception are at one in denying that depth is visible." This is due to the fact that "depth cannot be seen because it is not spread out before our eyes, but appears to them only in foreshortened form," and hence "what I call depth is in reality a juxtaposition of points, making it comparable to breadth. I am simply badly placed to see it. I should see it if I were in the position of a spectator looking on from the side, who can take in at a glance the series of objects spread out in front of me, whereas for me they conceal each other."[35]

Even as its scenes are conventionalized and tacitly didactic, the pop-up book presents both depth and breadth to the viewer through the form of the book itself. This can be simply demonstrated through the juxtaposition of two views taken from a facsimile of the second pop-up book for discussion, Tuck's *Seaside Pleasures.* The first displays the book's pop-up image as it appears front on (Figure 3.4).[36] In the composition of the illustration, perspective is achieved through apparent size and convergence, the two properties that Merleau-Ponty identifies as archetypal to the way we perceive depth.[37] The viewer reads depth into the image not just through the pop-up technique but also by noting, for example, that the children in the foreground are larger, hence closer to the front of the scene. The considerable empty space between the figures draws the eye to the horizon line, which is midground and splits attention between the picturesque sea-and-skyscape background and the lively figure groups. The background could be a seaside postcard; indeed, the entire image might be a postcard that has taken coastal scenery as well as droll human vignettes as its subject. An explanatory caption present in the original, "Fun on the Silver Sands," even resembles the postcard's short promotional text, its linking of location, pastime, and feeling.

Alternatively, the entire image can be read as a Victorian social landscape. Paintings such as William Powell Frith's *Ramsgate Sands (Life at the Seaside),* produced between 1851 and 1854, represent a tradition of seaside resort pictures where "landscape was only ever a secondary or incidental feature, and the main emphasis was on what was implied to be the characteristic behaviour of the visitors" (Figure 3.5).[38] *Ramsgate Sands* and the *Seaside Pleasures* pop-up share a setting; a sprawling, triangulated figure grouping; the mix of pursuits depicted; specific human and animal figures, such as black minstrels (notably changed into white musicians without

FIGURE 3.4. The layered pop-up scene stands to attention in a twentieth-century facsimile of *Seaside Pleasures* (originally published around 1896). Author's collection. Photograph by Stuart Robinson.

makeup in the facsimile), parents, children, and donkeys; and jokes about looking—effected in the pop-up through the children with their backs to the viewer who gaze into the image, and in Frith's work by figures looking out, including two little girls, one of whom holds a telescope. Sustained attention to the illusion of depth may be a further shared attribute; in an otherwise ambivalent review, Ruskin praised the "drawing of the distant figures" in one of Frith's paintings in a similar vein, *The Derby Day* (1856–58), as "especially dexterous and admirable."[39] By placing the viewer on the beach, however, rather than in the waves, the Tuck image comprises a picturesque seascape complete with steamboat, as well as a social landscape.

Of course, though, as the pop-up book springs into three dimensions, the nested image extends out so that the illusion of depth in the picture becomes actual spatial distance. A second view of *Seaside Pleasures,* taken from above, reveals the mechanics

FIGURE 3.5. William Powell Frith's *Ramsgate Sands (Life at the Seaside),* completed between 1851 and 1854, presents the seaside as a site of leisure, pleasure, and visual games with the viewer. Royal Collection Trust / copyright Her Majesty Queen Elizabeth II 2018.

of the pop-up image's depth: the illusion requires a physical transformation of the book (Figure 3.6). What might a child reader do after transforming the pop-up scene? The book cries out to be looked at from above, to have its tricks of perspective and depth investigated. Merleau-Ponty anatomizes the adoption of a different perspective in relation to an image thus: "In order to treat depth as breadth viewed in profile . . . the subject must leave his place, abandon his point of view on the world, and think himself into a sort of ubiquity."[40] The two views of the pop-up physicalize Merleau-Ponty's operation. The child reader of *Seaside Pleasures* embodies a perspectival ubiquity, able to investigate the image's construction—to take a new view on depth—by turning the book around. Such effects change the ways in which the pop-up images are read: visual games in the pictures, such as the child artist who appreciates the picturesque scene in *Country Life* and the children who direct their gazes into the pop-up in *Seaside Pleasures,* encourage perspectival games with the book itself. Part of the fun of the three-dimensional movable is in looking at it from the top or the side, to see how the illusion of depth is created—a gesture that allows the child to control, quite literally, her own perspective on book and image.

FIGURE 3.6. This second perspective on the seaside pop-up is from the vantage point of an aerial viewer, who can look between the layers and see how the image creates its illusion. Author's collection. Photograph by Stuart Robinson.

## Staging the Pop-Up

When the pop-up creates the illusion of depth using a series of flat layers, it recalls a second Victorian visual entertainment: the theater. Many early movable books and other children's printed ephemera took inspiration from the theater.[41] For instance, as mentioned in the Introduction, the first movable books for children were harlequinades. The toy theater or juvenile drama, in which flat sheets of cutout characters were combined with miniature theaters and short scripts for children to act out, is a further example of nineteenth-century theatrical ephemera produced for children.[42]

This section analyzes connections between theatrical picture making and the pop-up book, considering formal resemblances alongside shared subjects and structures, and explicit references—particularly as they relate to depth, perspective, and three-dimensional effects. The pop-up's theatricality can also make a perhaps unexpected contribution to recent criticism that uses nineteenth-century children's involvement with the theater as audience members and performers to rethink models of childhood in the period.

The pop-up's ways of framing a scene, its trade secrets, are theatrical. In Dean's New Scenic Books, the pop-up images obscure the text when folded down; when a ribbon threaded through each panel of a pop-up image is pulled, the three separate layers spring up to stand at right angles to the page, allowing the text to be read and the three-dimensional picture to be examined. An illustration from the first book in the series, *Little Red Riding Hood,* is typical (Plate 11).[43] The characters stand in the front layer of the pop-up, carefully arranged in stagy postures: Little Red gingerly puts her hand to her throat, while the wolf raises one foot from the ground in a familiar attitude of movement from the picture book. ("A quick glance through any group of typical picture books might suggest that the entire population of the known universe spends most of its time with one foot in the air," as Nodelman quips.)[44] The girl's apprehensive posture anticipates the end of this grisly iteration of the tale, which follows Charles Perrault in consigning the heroine to the wolf's jaws. Stock scenic elements—here trees, elsewhere rose bushes—form the midground. The third layer depicts a river and moon bridge, but the scene is not detailed in its cutout contours, aping the painted backdrop of the theater. At points of greater dramatic import, as in the final page opening, the action shifts ground: the overturned furniture in the front panel forms only a low barrier to the scene of the woodcutters attacking the wolf in midground and background. Indeed, the setting of such action further into depth evokes a dramaturgical limitation: the necessity of having difficult-to-stage scenes, such as deaths and battles, somewhat obscured. Lines printed on each page of the New Scenic Books, visible in ripped copies and copies where the original assembler took little care, show where the parts of the pop-up should be pasted. These lines and the cutouts pasted onto them recall classical set design, with its wings and flats slotted into grooves in the floor, an arrangement that prevailed in nineteenth-century theaters until the introduction of free-plantation scenery in 1881.[45] In the series title alone, while *scenic* means picturesque it also suggests scenery in a theatrical context; the publication of Dean's *Little Red Riding Hood* in French by Guérin-Müller, a firm known for movable books, under the rubric *livre théâtrale* (theatrical book) cements the point.

In addition to formal resemblances to the theater, the pop-up often incorporates theatrical subject matter. Dean's four New Scenic Books include some of the most popular mid-nineteenth-century subjects for comic, spectacular, and pantomime performances: fairy tales ("Cinderella," "Little Red Riding Hood," "Aladdin") and retellings of a smaller roster of familiar narratives, such as that of Robinson Crusoe (produced in the theater since the eighteenth century).[46] In pop-ups as in other branches of nineteenth-century children's literature, fairy-tale subjects were immensely popular; an immediate context for these is the pantomime's syncretic blending of fairy-tale traditions. The fairy itself was also key source material for popular entertainments. While the importance of fairies (and the fairy tale) to children's movable picture books is discussed substantially in the next chapter, for the moment it is worth noting the association of fairies with the theater. "Fairies were everywhere in nineteenth-century culture," says Nicola Bown, "in the nursery, certainly, but also in the parlour or drawing room, on the stage and on the walls of annual exhibitions."[47] Diane Purkiss argues that, contrary to the present-day association of Victorian fairies with poetry, the visual arts, and children's literature, "for many Victorians, particularly early Victorians, fairies would have conjured up a vision of theatrical splendour."[48] Although certain genres, including pantomime and the extravaganza, were especially associated with the fairy, Tracy Davis has documented fairies "in productions from every decade and in every genre."[49] Fairies were, then, *theatrical* creatures for the Victorians, and their appearance in the pop-up is also theatricalized.

The six pop-up pieces in Nister's *Peeps into Fairyland* offer a succession of exquisite fairyland scenes: a "Procession of Nursery Rhymes," a snow queen's palace, a fairy lake, "The Queen of the Bird Fairies," and the Babes in the Wood surrounded by fairy spirits (Figure 3.7; see also Figure 3.1). The only one of the pop-up pieces not to contain fairies is nevertheless from a fairy tale: an image illustrating a version of the story of Jack and the beanstalk, where Jack is depicted running away from the magical land of the giant. This list of fairy settings recalls modes of spectacular drama: their construction as "an anthology of scenic possibilities," to borrow Stephen Orgel's formulation.[50] *Peeps into Fairyland* as a sequence of stories about travels into fairyland gives each pop-up as a set change, much in the way that, say, the production of *The Sleeping Beauty and the Beast* mounted at the Theatre Royal, Drury Lane, on Boxing Day 1900 gave audiences a Fairy Parliament in a wooded glade, a Royal Aviary, a Tangled Forest, and an Enchanted Crystal Garden in the Beast's grounds.[51]

The fairyland pop-ups recall late Victorian theatrical sets in their appearance. The pop-up grotto effect, a "scenic decoration that forms an elaborate border to the page," mimics the effect of stage scenery in its framing of a central, staged composition and its creation of depth that is depth in flatness.[52] The grotto has been printed in different colorways in order to evoke different landscapes across *Peeps into Fairyland*: cherry blossoms or snowy branches in the same book. The grotto effect is the visual and technical equivalent of a piece of stock scenery in the theater; the process by which a publisher created a movable book, often using predevised parts, resembled the process of a theater manager fashioning a new production out of old trappings, something so common in the period that ticket prices were raised when a theater acquired new scenery.[53] Fairy transformations composed scenes around a "central pedestal" that elevated "the brightest and most glittering spirit or fairy queen," and pop-up scenes such as "A Visit to the Snow Queen's Palace," where the queen presides from atop a giant snowball, imitate this formal arrangement.[54] Moreover, just as the perspective of the theatergoer necessitates an elevated central figure, the pop-up demands it, too, because of the disposition of layers: we need to be able to see all the characters, even though the spectacle of the paper engineering depends on a crowded stage and layers of action, scene, and character.

Spectacle is a generic feature of what Meisel calls a "cluster of related forms," expressly, "pantomime, fairy-play, and extravaganza."[55] This grouping bears clear links to *Peeps into Fairyland* in terms of subject matter and compositional strategies; there are also structural parallels, though. Instead of appearing at the end, as the pop-ups do in Tuck's *Country Life* and *Seaside Pleasures,* the pop-up scenes in *Peeps into Fairyland* are interspersed throughout, typically falling at the end of each story. As such, the pop-up realizes aspects of nineteenth-century dramatic plotting as conceived by Meisel:

> In the new dramaturgy, the unit is intransitive; it is in fact an achieved moment of stasis, a picture. The play creates a series of such pictures, some of them offering a culminating symbolic summary of represented events, while others substitute an arrested

FIGURE 3.7. In *Peeps into Fairyland,* the "Procession of Nursery Rhymes" pop-up evokes the theater through its conventional subject matter (fairy extravaganza) and its woodland frame, which imitates stage scenery. Reproduced by kind permission of the Syndics of Cambridge University Library (1896.14.15).

> situation for action and reaction. Each picture, dissolving, leads not into consequent activity, but to a new infusion and distribution of elements from which a new picture will be assembled or revealed. The form is serial discontinuity, like that of the magic lantern, or the so-called "Dissolving Views."[56]

Meisel's chosen analogues for theatrical storytelling in the nineteenth century are the magic-lantern effects called dissolving views, which give their name to the format of movable book at the heart of chapter 4, but the comparison is just as appropriate to the pop-up. Each individual story in *Peeps into Fairyland* crystallizes in the pop-up

PLATE 1. *Alfred Crowquill's Comic History of the Kings and Queens of England,* produced around 1856 or 1857, is a foldout history, with each king or queen occupying one panel of the panorama. Courtesy of the Lilly Library, Indiana University, Bloomington, Indiana.

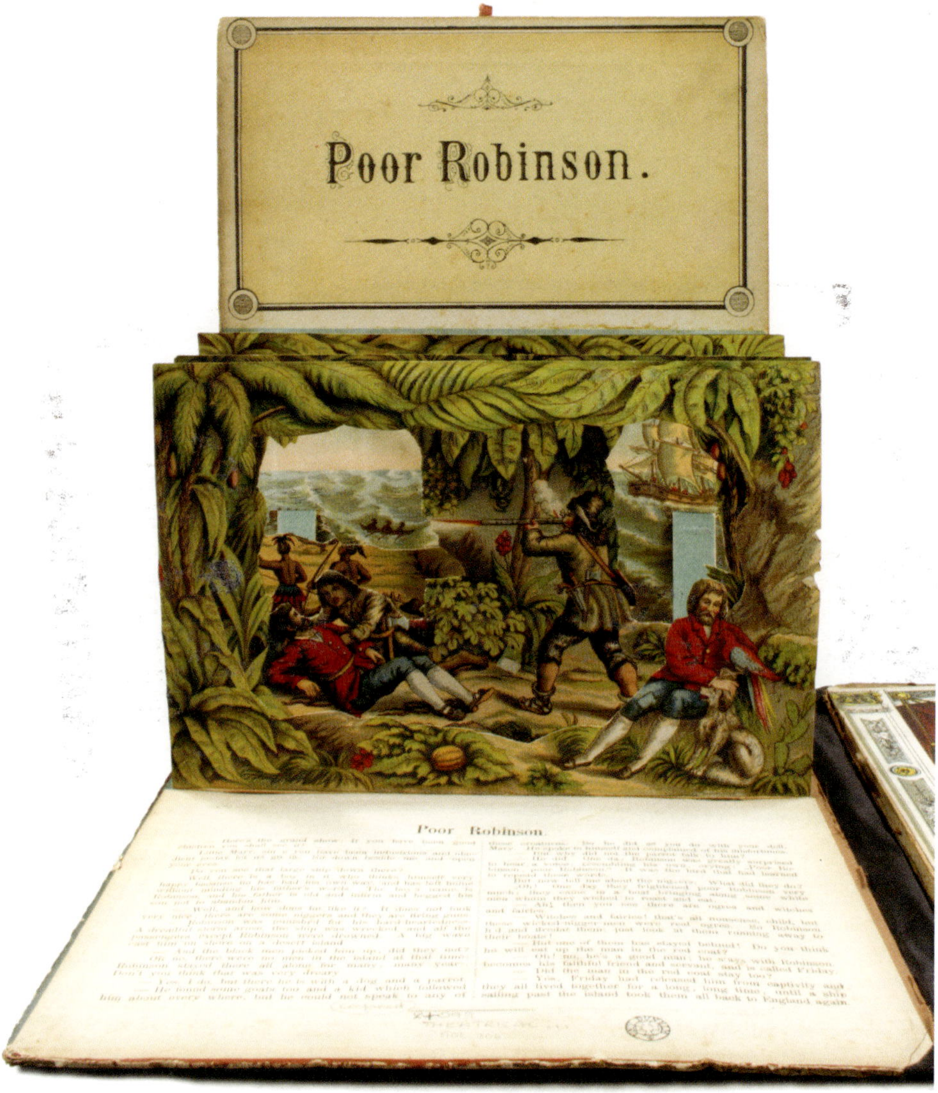


PLATE 2. Nineteenth-century pop-up books often deliberately evoked the theater, as is the case with the *Theatrical Picture-Book* (1882), which documents a child's trip to a production of the story of Robinson Crusoe. Reproduced by permission of Durham University Library.

PLATE 3. In one of the publisher Ernest Nister's signature dissolving views, from *Come and Go* (circa 1890), three cherubic children move from a snowy doorstep to a snug fireside. The Metropolitan Museum of Art, New York, gift of Lincoln Kirstein, 1970.

PLATE 4. The outstanding movements in Lothar Meggendorfer's mechanical books, including the straining angler in *Always Jolly!* (circa 1891), are famous. Courtesy of the Lilly Library, Indiana University, Bloomington, Indiana.

PLATE 5. The parade of torn mechanical figures in one movable book from the Opie Collection, *This Is the House That Jack Built* (a Dean and Son title released around 1860), includes this mutilated cat. The Bodleian Libraries, the University of Oxford (2015), Opie EE 117.

PLATE 6. The title page of the Opie Collection copy of Dean and Son's pop-up *A Visit to the Country* (1891) has been colored in. The Bodleian Libraries, the University of Oxford (2015), Opie EE 300.

PLATE 7. What looks to be part of Mother Hubbard's blue-sleeved arm has been placed where her dog's right foreleg should be in a mended copy of Sarah Catherine Martin's *A New Story about Mother Hubbard and Her Dog,* produced between 1854 and 1861. The Bodleian Libraries, the University of Oxford (2015), Opie EE 198.

PLATE 8. The long panoramic illustration in *A Morning Ride mid Country Scenes* (1852) works like an "I spy" game: the text points the child reader to various landmarks and figures in the image. The Bodleian Libraries, the University of Oxford (2015), Opie EE 190.

PLATE 9. Like many nursery friezes, Webb and Millington's *Panoramic Keepsake* (circa 1855) largely focuses on animals across its length. Baldwin Library of Historical Children's Literature, Special and Area Studies Collections, George A. Smathers Libraries, University of Florida, Gainesville.

PLATE 10. *Country Life* (circa 1896), produced by Raphael Tuck, gives a picturesque rural scene in pop-up form, framed by the child artist in the top layer. The Bodleian Libraries, the University of Oxford (2015), Opie EE 59.

PLATE 11. The pop-up illustrations in Dean and Son's *Little Red Riding Hood* (circa 1856) are theatrical both in the characters' static poses and in the use of scenic elements as framing devices. Courtesy of the Lilly Library, Indiana University, Bloomington, Indiana.

PLATE 12. In the movable pictures in *Something New for Little Folk,* published by Ernest Nister around 1899, kaleidoscopic swirls of color change into representational images (and back again). Courtesy of the Lilly Library, Indiana University, Bloomington, Indiana.

PLATE 13. Seasonal dissolves, such as this early example from *Dean's New Book of Dissolving Views* (circa 1861), allow the two-part movable image to represent the progress of the year. Courtesy of the Bill Douglas Cinema Museum, University of Exeter.

PLATE 14. One mechanical figure in Lothar Meggendorfer's *Aus dem Leben* (From life), produced around 1890, rocks her baby from side to side when the tab is pulled. Bayerische Staatsbibliothek München, Res/4 81.11737, fol. [5]r, "An der Wiege."

PLATE 15. Each page of *Les Excentriques* (The eccentrics), a French mechanical book by Pierre Delcourt produced around 1900, presents an over-the-top character such as this English tourist. The Rare Book and Manuscript Library, University of Illinois at Urbana-Champaign.

PLATE 16. In Lothar Meggendorfer's final illustration in the mechanical book released around 1890 in Britain as *Comic Actors,* in Germany as *Lustiges Automaten-Theater,* and in France as *Les Héritiers de Monsieur Babylas,* a white child attempts to wash her black nurse white. Staatsbibliothek zu Berlin.

image, its "achieved moment of stasis," which occurs only to be displaced by the next story and the next pop-up picture.

The constitution of Nister volumes, including *Peeps into Fairyland,* as anthologies is a further structural resemblance to the nineteenth-century theater and its preference for "variety, vividness, and memorability" over narrative unity.[57] Different stories within a given volume are by different authors. (Hildegard Krahé, the German scholar and collector of children's books, documents that this was a specifically English feature of Nister books: the standard formats for German texts involved single authors composing whole texts, rather than groups of authors.)[58] In this anthology mode, the unification of the book reverts to the publisher and its shaping of generic parameters for the book, largely via the pop-up pieces, as the black-and-white illustrations accompanying the stories are also by multiple hands. The conditions of production of the Nister book may, then, be summarized using Michael Booth's characterization of the Victorian pantomime, in which "the author could be a relatively unimportant partner."[59] The mixed constitution of *Peeps into Fairyland* does not attempt to weave a continuous narrative but instead revels in the diverse effects produced by the book's authors, illustrators, designers, printers, and assemblers.

When critics mount defenses of the movable book, these typically relate to its interactivity. This is the case when Higonnet finds "points of entry" in the morphological variations of the movable book, when Reid-Walsh anatomizes the interactive design of various mechanical books but ultimately critiques their substitution of "pleasurable activity" for true agency, and when Carothers invokes "mental participation" arising from the "physical manipulation" demanded by movables.[60] Theatrical ephemera for children may be introduced to such arguments. In particular, the juvenile theater seems—in its assembly model, its demand for interactive play, and its imprint on great Victorians, including Charles Dickens and Robert Louis Stevenson—a model of creative interactivity par excellence.

The static nature of pop-up spectacle in a work such as *Peeps into Fairyland,* in which the movable parts are ultimately received as a tableau, seems to render such arguments inapplicable. But explicitly theatrical pop-ups can introduce alternative (if equivocal) viewpoints on such questions of agency, once more through the guiding principle of perspective. The simple title of the *Theatrical Picture-Book,* produced in 1883 in Germany, belies sophisticated stage business in the cover image: a trompe l'oeil playbill, surrounded by flourishes and figures, with a central image of a curtained stage.[61] The text relays the plot of each production, framed in the voice of an adult taking a child to the theater. In the Bodleian's copy, a robust pop-up image is mounted on recto and verso of the page opening, presenting a double bill: the stories of Robinson Crusoe and of Puss in Boots. Each plane of the pop-up shows a different scene from the respective play, so the successive temporal arrangement of the text is displaced onto the simultaneous presentation of the pop-up: narrative mapped into depth, in comparison to narrative plotted across a picture plane, as in the panorama (see Plate 2).

A number of scholars have recently explored children's involvement in the nineteenth-century theater. This might involve acting work—as, for instance, with the Marsh Troupe of child actors, whose publicity, as Shauna Vey points out in her study of the ensemble, touted the diminutive size and tender age of the performers.[62] More commonly, though, well-off children might *attend* the theater at this time. Marah Gubar notes that, despite the relative neglect of the subject, "young people were so omnipresent as intended and actual audience members . . . that virtually all forms of popular theater from this era—including melodramas, minstrel shows, and vaudeville—can profitably be considered children's theater." For Gubar, who traces a range of child stereotypes (from comfortably angelic to discomfortingly rough-and-tumble), the American stage exhibits "a profound ambivalence about the bourgeois ideology of childhood innocence and vulnerability" and an associated challenge to constructions of children as lacking in agency.[63]

In one important sense, the *Theatrical Picture-Book* enhances this challenge. The theater could present little opportunity for spectators (especially children) to investigate just how its effects were produced. Gubar seems to confirm this point indirectly in her study of children's responses to theatrical productions when she quotes from letters written by child fans of *Peter Pan,* who tell of attempting, but failing, in their home theatricals to reproduce the flying effect so beloved in the original production: "I have been trying to fly like you all day."[64] By contrast, the pop-up's three-dimensionality through touch puts spectacular and theatrical effects into the child's hands. The pop-up image is a temporal artifact in which meaning is made gradually and cumulatively. Just as the pop-up book can always be viewed from above, there is also always a becoming-scene as the reader produces the three dimensions of the pop-up, either directly, by the pulling of a tab or ribbon, or indirectly, by the opening of the book. Playing games with the three-dimensional image (opening the book a little and then shutting it up—studying the movable image in various stages of dishabille, as it were) is familiar to every reader of the pop-up. In this, the pop-up resembles a theatrical production where stage business is not masked by a curtain, but rather takes place before the reader's eyes, like the transformation scene unfurled beautifully in front of the viewer.

But what the format implies, the text may contradict. Orgel characterizes spectacular theater as "a machine for controlling the visual experience of the spectator," whereby the rules of perspective entirely shape the viewer's experience.[65] The *Theatrical Picture-Book*'s establishment of control as a key motive in the text seems germane to this conception: the text models a figurative perspective on events for the child reader to match the pop-up's guiding of perspective. For example, attending the theater is a reward for obedience: the first line reads, "Here's the grand show; if you have been good children you shall see it!" The text assumes a child audience for theatrical productions that is heavily supervised, and that requires adult mediation of the spectacle. This mediation occurs at the level of basic protocol, as when the adult addresses the child spectator: "Now, Mary, the show is going to begin, let us listen attentively!" Good behavior lets the child visit the theater in the first place, but it must continue while she watches the play, too.

It also occurs, though, in terms of the process of interpreting the production, as can be demonstrated through "Poor Robinson," the version of the Robinson Crusoe story narrated in the *Theatrical Picture-Book.* The textual structure is catechistic, as the child asks the adult about various occurrences on the stage; in the following exchange, she takes specific interest in Robinson's interactions with the cannibal visitors to the island. "But now," says Mary:

> Tell me about the niggers. What did they do?
>
> "Oh! One day they frightened poor Robinson very much; they came in a boat bringing along some white men whom they wished to roast and eat.
>
> —Ah! then you see there are ogres and witches and fairies.
>
> —Witches and fairies! that's all nonsense, child, but these wicked-nigger-men were real ogres. So Robinson hid and [illegible] them: just look at them running away to their boats!

The fictional production dramatizes the exact moment at which Crusoe "becomes the fully-fledged colonial adventurer, self-composed, ready for action," to recall Peter

Hulme's assessment: the moment when he defines himself against the cannibals.[66] The exchange between child and adult theatergoers consolidates this viewpoint, as the adult rejects the child's perspective on the cannibals as demonic creatures while reinscribing them as nonhuman others ("real ogres"). It also makes the exchange much more triumphal than it appears in Daniel Defoe's text, where the cannibals may run away but their appearance causes considerable soul-searching for Robinson.

The question-and-answer exchange between Mary and her adult interlocutor, which imposes a clear set of values on the play's narrative, corresponds to the controlled perspective the pop-up offers. The image emphasizes Robinson's triumph in the face of the cannibals' panicked rush, as every part of the cutout guides the viewer's perspective to the central figure: Robinson with his gun. Looking at the pop-up book demonstrates the regulation of perspective itself as a maneuver involved with agency in theatrical pop-up books, designed to control the child's reception of a performance.

## Stereoscopy and the Minor Depths of the Pop-Up

While landscape painting and theatrical tableaux were crucial visual modes for surface and depth effects, the quintessential Victorian entertainment that generated images with a heightened illusion of three dimensions was the stereoscope. In his influential discussion in *Techniques of the Observer* (1990), Jonathan Crary argues that the stereoscope's techniques for representing three-dimensionality are "essentially different from anything in painting or photography." He continues: "We are given an insistent sense of 'in front of' and 'in back of' that seems to organize the image as a sequence of receding planes. And in fact the fundamental organization of the stereoscopic image is *planar.* We perceive individual elements as flat, cutout forms arrayed either nearer or further from us."[67] There are many parallels between Crary's assessment of the stereoscopic image and the techniques of the pop-up book. Crary's flagship assertion that "the fundamental organization of the stereoscopic image is planar" could have been written as a description of the pop-up: the pop-up always organizes depth as a series of planes, a series of flat layers. One cannot write about a pop-up without relying heavily on language that positions the individual planes as "'in front of' and 'in back of.'" Indeed, it seems that Crary might have the pop-up in mind when he uses the word *cutout.*

Crary's intermedia comparisons of stereoscopic photography with other sorts of photography and with painting have Victorian precedents: both defenders and critics of the stereoscope structured their arguments around existing art forms. In the second edition of his manual for young would-be draftsmen, *The Elements of Drawing* (both the first and second editions were published in 1857), Ruskin includes an appendix of illustrative notes. One of these has the author "sorry to find a notion, current among artists, that they can, in some degree, imitate in a picture the effect of the stereoscope, by confusion of lines." This misapprehension leads to an impossible painting: "You might just as well try to paint St. Paul's at once from both ends of London Bridge as to realise any stereoscopic effect in a picture."[68] Ruskin's discussion of the stereoscope is part of an attempt to explain perspective, and the proliferation of his text around this subject (ostensibly excluded from *The Elements of Drawing*) suggests that this is a difficult task.[69] The note on the "stereoscopic effect in a picture" is a note to another note, while Ruskin's follow-up to *Elements of Drawing*, titled *The Elements of Perspective* (1859), further expands on the topic. In this specific case, though, Ruskin's note reflects anxiety over cross-pollination between new and old pictorial forms. He is anxious that painters and draftsmen might come (in David Trotter's phrase) to "think stereoscopically."[70]

The stereoscope's inventors approached the problem from the opposite direction: they sought to demonstrate that the technology would produce images in line with traditional pictorial modes. Charles Wheatstone, the developer of telegraphy, invented the stereoscope in 1838. While Wheatstone stressed the exceptionality of his research in the subtitle of the article that introduced stereoscopic principles to the world ("On Some Remarkable, and Hitherto Unobserved, Phenomena of Binocular Vision"), he also identified Leonardo da Vinci as an early explorer of associated principles and concluded his initial discussion with a reference to painting.[71] Wheatstone's stereoscope, which utilized mirrors to achieve the three-dimensional effect, was supplanted in 1849 by David Brewster's improved version, which replaced the mirrors with lenses. Brewster discusses the machine at length in *The Stereoscope: Its History, Theory, and Construction* (1856), giving summaries of traditional artistic craft that are even more technical than those of Wheatstone: the artist "produces apparent solidity, and difference of distance from the eye, by light and shade, by the diminished size of known objects as regulated by the principles of geometrical perspective, and by those variations in distinctness and colour which constitute what has been called aerial perspective." Brewster also gives an account of an artist producing a study of a sculpture from a stereoscopic photograph, or stereograph, and reassures painters outright that the stereoscope will not usurp painting.[72] The proponents of the stereoscope, then, thought about this new visual technology using existing models in a cultural circuit that complicated Ruskin's "stereoscopic effect in a picture" by envisioning conventional pictorial effects in a stereoscope, so to speak. This point can be proved in action by the many stereographs that ape the visual modes just explored—showing picturesque landscapes or elaborately staged tableaux.

Brewster's improvements to the stereoscope were aesthetic as well as technological: he discouraged large stereoscopic images, which were favored by Wheatstone, and instead miniaturized the stereo camera, its component cards (which he reduced to three inches square), and the stereoscopic viewer. This led, Rudolf Kingslake suggests, to the stereoscope's becoming an intimate technology for conveying three-dimensionality. The nature of the stereographs available reflects such intimacy: pornographic views were a subtype, for example.[73] John Waldsmith's 2002 collectors' guide to stereographs, however, contains only a page and a half of views classified as "Risqué and Nudes," in contrast to four pages of listings under the subheading "Children."[74] This may be because erotic views were censored, or because modern collectors wish to distance themselves from them. Equally, though, it may be because, as Trotter asserts of the stereoscope's hyperreality, "the duller the image viewed, the more profound the enthrallment."[75] Alongside the thrilling subjects of stereoscopic views—pornographic scenes, or, say, the travel cards that allowed viewers using handheld stereoscopes to "experience the sensation of cradling . . . immensity in their palms," to quote Sheenagh Pietrobruno, or the horrific phantasmagorias—mundane, dull, and domestic views proliferated.[76]

Both surviving photo cards and their marketing support this point. Take *One O'clock: Children at Table,* an 1860s stereograph by James Elliott held at the Victoria and Albert Museum.[77] The image shows three children, a woman, and a dog around a table for tea. The details of decor and arrangement (such as the cane chairs and the painting on the wall) suggest a comfortable home. Except for the dunce at the back, with her highly colored striped dress, the scene looks unposed; in particular, one child appears to be caught midaction while drinking from a cup raised by her mother or nurse. The scene opens out details of middle-class domestic life that could have been experienced by most families wealthy enough to own a stereoscope. Indeed, even within this, the subject itself is a routine one, representing not a celebratory scene but instead the average progress of the day, marked by meals at regular times. Where *One O'clock* survived, it would seem that multiple comparable examples were lost. For instance, a catalog of stereographs from the London Stereoscopic Company, often bound along with Brewster's treatise, classifies a number of views as "Miscellaneous Subjects of the 'Wilkie' character, very popular." Not only does the advertisement use conventional picture making to legitimate stereoscopic views, but it also allies stereographs with David Wilkie as a painter of rustic scenes (rather than as a history painter, one of his other areas of expertise). The titles of the "Wilkie" views, such as *Baby Asleep in Cot, No. 2*, *Piece of Coral (Very Striking)*, and *Child Seen through Anti-Macassar*, once more evoke a parlor entertainment devoted to representing the home itself *en abyme*.[78] *Child Seen through Anti-Macassar* even co-opts a formal gimmick that spectacularly heightens depth, resembling those of Victorian phantasmagoric stereographs (as well as 3-D horror films today), but to a sentimental rather than sensational effect. Depth is deliberately exaggerated only to achieve the humblest of effects: to show a child peering out from underneath a bit of household drapery.

These minor depths of the stereograph mirror Victorian pop-up books that detail the life of the child, which exist in parallel with glamorous subjects such as the circus, the seaside, the fairy realm, and the stage spectacular. *The Robins at Home* juxtaposes a circus attraction with such domestic entertainments as ice skating, farmyard chores, a game of blindman's buff, and fishing. The convex pop-up technique in Dean's Surprise Model series may be used to produce dramatic effects, such as a train curving across the page opening (see Figure 1.6). Equally, though, it might present the gentler curve of a dovecote seen on a family trip to the country. Sometimes, glamour and the mundane combine. One of the pop-up scenes in *Our Peepshow* shows children playing in and around a makeshift tepee (Figure 3.8). The scene visualizes something of what Rayna Green has identified as the appeal of "playing Indian" for white children across the game's long history: the permission to "'run wild,' whooping, hollering, behaving in a completely unorthodox manner."[79] (Observe the boy at front, with his tomahawk tucked into his belt at a rakish angle, and the girl who comfortably holds her toy rifle at right.) But the children's play is also rendered commonplace, mundane even, by the illustrator's focus on nursery decor, including animal pictures on the walls, and the objects the children use to make the tepee—a stack of books, left unread, holds a cloth over a table to make the tent. Indeed, the effect of two children peeking out from the tent recalls the lost stereograph *Child Seen through Anti-Macassar*. The mild tenor of these genre scenes is matched by the slightness of the relief, the humbleness of the 3-D effect produced by the pop-up pieces.

The analogy between stereoscope and pop-up inheres to the body. At first, the stereoscope was a representational marvel, as multiple commentators have pointed out. Smith writes: "The discontinuity that the stereoscope creates between cause and effect (two images seen with two eyes become one composite image) means that the stereoscopic image calls attention to itself as mediated in a manner different from any previous optical instrument and to a much greater degree."[80] The way in which the stereoscope flaunted its mediatedness was in turn related to touch: Crary positions the stereoscope as a "quintessentially nineteenth-century" visual technology because of its construction of "tangibility (or relief) . . . solely through an organization of *optical* cues (and the amalgamation of the observer into a component of the apparatus)."[81] Laura Burd Schiavo elaborates on a parallel point: "By inducing the illusion of solidity with only binocular *cues,* and prompting the experience of solidity where no depth actually existed, the stereoscope called into doubt the alleged subordination of vision to touch, an assumption predicated on the belief in a self-present world 'out there.'"[82] As Trotter evocatively reflects, stereoscopic images give "the feeling that one could reach out and touch them, or be touched by them"—even though one cannot.[83]

But as Schiavo has shown, the stereoscope's problematization of the relationship between vision and the material world on the one hand and fresh emphasis on the body's imperfect capacity to confirm what is seen on the other was not borne out when the technology shifted from scientific instrument to parlor entertainment. Instead, the producers of the parlor stereoscope marketed it as a technology for viewing highly accurate representations, insisting on "stereoscopic representations as transparent, reflective, wholly reliable transcriptions of retinal images, themselves unfailing equivalents to the external world they signified."[84] While Schiavo does not connect this shift to what is depicted, the prevalence of the dull and the domestic in parlor stereographs is an aesthetic choice that brings stereoscopic subjects in line with this reabsorbed model of stereoscopic visuality. Where supernatural or spectacular views dramatize models of unreliable or impossible vision, the mundane stereograph becomes proxy for the real itself.

The pop-up book augments this further. *Our Peepshow* and the Surprise Model book *A Visit to the Country* present 3-D scenes that ape stereoscopic illusionism but

FIGURE 3.8. Rather than employing 3-D to thrill, pop-up images may show humble depth effects associated with children's play, as in this example from *Our Peepshow* (circa 1897). Copyright the British Library Board, Nister.d.123.

rationalize such illusions through the child reader's body. The pop-up's literalness—so distinctive from the figurative modes of touch associated with Aloïs Riegl's haptic, which influences both Crary and Trotter—brings depth of field firmly back into the material world, and the body's relationship to that world, as the child manipulates the page. Comfortingly, touch can confirm what the eye sees, even as an illusion is mounted. At the same time, mundane pop-ups define what a "real" childhood is. The child's world should be filled with material comforts—pictures on the walls, abundant books, costumes for make-believe play, dolls and other toys—as it is in pop-up images, where these objects are so solid you can touch them. The three-dimensional solidity of the book itself, restored to the child by the illusionary pop-up, comes to symbolize nothing less than the rightness of the middle-class childhood itself.

## — Chapter Four —

# Ernest Nister Christopher Columbus

## The Tale of a Dissolving-View Book

No account of Victorian movable books for children could leave out Ernest Nister (1842–1909), color printer and publisher extraordinaire whose eponymous publishing house produced more than one hundred titles in an ingenious array of formats. The business began when Nister acquired a small Nuremberg chromolithography concern in 1877. The firm became successful enough by 1888 to expand operations to London and secure a deal with the American publisher E. P. Dutton to distribute Nister productions stateside.[1] The company actively developed new printing techniques and book designs, as in its trademarking of, among others, the innovative three-color process and star-shaped movable piece discussed in the Introduction.[2] Indeed, the firm was so successful that it served as an exemplar of German industrial prowess to the British government. While the British Department of Science and Art's initial reasons for visiting the publishing company were chilly—motivated by "the effects of German competition [which] have recently been prominently brought into notice"—Nister's works won over the department's representatives. They praised the publisher's large, richly decorated buildings along with its cutting-edge modes of production in a report that also included numerous technical details of the embossing and stamping, folding, binding, and printing—on steam-driven as well as hand-operated presses—taking place. As the report's authors noted, in 1896 Nister employed almost a thousand people, including 140 lithographic artists, producing work in Germany for English-language markets (as well as German-language children's books).[3] By 1909, Nister's publications were seen by at least one American reviewer as epitomizing "the best of the lithographer's art," the firm's productions "famous the world over for richness of design and color."[4]

This précis of Nister's firm draws on fairly conventional sources in book-historical research: handbooks for collectors of works produced by particular publishers (in this case, Julia and Frederick Hunt's *Peeps into Nisterland*) and general primers on printing, such as Geoffrey Wakeman and Gavin Bridson's *Guide to Nineteenth Century Colour Printers.* Governmental reports constitute a further genre in which details about printing and production can be found, as do the book review sections of contemporary periodicals; Nister's pursuit of the Christmas market meant that its children's movables were often given holiday notices. More unusually, though, Nister's books rehearse the stories of their own composition, illustration, publishing, printing, distribution, and reading: a child's history of novelty picture books, composed in doggerel verse and accompanied by lavish movable color plates. These fantasies of the novelty book make the industrial heroic, the mechanized organic, the ephemeral or gimmicky enduring. At the same time, a central trend in Nister's productions asks the child to convert the unrelated into the related. Nister was best known for its dissolving-view books, in which one picture transforms into another by means of a system of interlocking paper slats (Figure 4.1). While some image pairings are straightforward, Nister's repurposing of pictures across publications (presumably to save money) means that dissolves may be randomly juxtaposed. In such cases, the firm's signature format asks the child reader to "write" the connections between different parts of the picture book. This chapter, then, lets the Nister movable tell its own history, using its fantasies and elisions to illuminate novelty publishing for children—its producers, purchasers, and readers—at the end of the nineteenth century.

## Origins: Nister's Family Romances of the Movable Book

The stories that Nister dissolving views tell about themselves might involve how the book came into being, or who the publisher is, or who the author is, or how the publisher relates to the author and illustrator. They might caricature the book's producers as farmers (and hence make the book seem more natural) or use fairies to render the

FIGURE 4.1. The patterns made midtransformation in dissolving-view books are often striking, as in this snowflake-shaped example from Ernest Nister's *All the Way Round Pictures* (circa 1899). Reproduced by kind permission of the Syndics of Cambridge University Library (1911.10.113).

creation of the chromolithographed children's book magical. In many cases, these tales resemble Sigmund Freud's concept of the family romance: they retell the book's origins in "the fulfilment of wishes and . . . correction of actual life."[5] Indeed, my choice of the term *family romance* to frame this section perhaps demonstrates the infectious nature of the obsession with families in nineteenth-century children's publishing, as in the grand tradition of familial banners and titles—*Aunt Judy's Magazine, Father Tuck's Annual, Our Children,* and so on—which Brian Alderson and Andrea Immel characterize as presenting the book or periodical as the locus of an "idealised Victorian family circle presided over by an elder sister . . . who could tell stories ranging from domestic tales to the Kunstmärchen, as well as devise an endless variety of entertainments educational and recreational."[6] Such marketing devices render children's publishing intimate, domestic, and collaborative. While the latter state of affairs does occur in the nineteenth century, as Victoria Ford Smith has recently shown in her book *Between Generations* (2017), in Nister's case such patter constitutes not reality but instead a family romance for the book itself.

Even in children's literature, where publisher control over texts can be pronounced, Nister's case remains singular, as any superficial inspection of a Nister book can reveal. The line illustrations in Nister's books (which appear alongside colored illustrations, often movable, and the printed text) were reproduced so that "the artist's signature was lost with the cropping of a picture from a larger form," as Hildegarde Krahé notes—not just cropped, but subsumed underneath the printed signature of Nister himself, which "found its space somewhere on the work no matter what the reproduction and design constraints were."[7] The dominance of the printer-publisher is visible on almost every page in Nister children's books—a matter of house style, as Nister's signature takes precedence over artists' marks.

Omitting the name of the designer and the crayon worker who drew on the chromolithographic stone was in fact fairly typical of nineteenth-century chromolithographers (although not of monochrome lithographers).[8] But the words and pictures in Nister books dramatize the publisher and printer's dominance in other ways, too. While there is a strong tradition of authorial self-insertion in literature for adults, the practice is less common in books for children. Still less widespread in either context is the insertion of the *publisher* into the narrative—a repeated trope in Nister titles. Take a poem attributed to Nister's London publishing director Robert E. Mack that appears in the dissolving-view book *More Pleasant Surprises for Chicks of All Sizes.*[9] "A Puzzle" accompanies a fairly typical vertical dissolve movable piece in which a picture of a girl feeding an apple to a white pony turns into a picture of a girl riding a brown pony. Mack's verses, though, are notable for giving a step-by-step account of writing children's books for Nister. First of all, the publisher comes to the writer with a particular commission for a poem: Nister specifies the age and sex of the protagonist (an eight-year-old girl) and the names of her two ponies (Nell and Kate) before adding, "Now hurry up with these precious verses." (In classic Nister fashion, Mack rhymes this line with "His manner terse is.") Nister's demands bamboozle the writer: he can see only one pony in the picture, though "Nister clearly said there were two." Eventually the versifier "pull[s] the string" and gets the joke, as the picture of the white pony dissolves into the picture of the brown. But even after working out the puzzle the author remains equivocal; the poem concludes:

> But which is Nell, and which is Kate,
> And which is the dear little girl of eight,
> And whether she's walking or whether she's riding,
> Is not a matter that I'm deciding.
> In such a matter I have no voice,
> You pay your money and take your choice.

The "pleasant surprise" of the book's title, the novel technology devised by the publisher, is this verse's subject. The process of book publication involves an author being set the task by a publisher—and grumpily at that—to produce text for a particular and preexisting set of movable illustrations. Only the publisher is in on the secret of the book, as the author's final declaration of voicelessness shows. (In Verity Hunt's words, the author is "at the bottom of a hierarchy of production of meaning here.")[10] Underscoring this situation, one of the black-and-white line illustrations accompanying the text shows Nister himself holding out toward the viewer a book titled *Nister's Annual 1894* (Figure 4.2).

"A Puzzle" recalls Leah Price's distinction between the "idealist" tenor of fiction about children and the "materialist" one of children's literature: "Coyness about the book trade in fiction *about* children contrasts sharply with its prominence in fiction *for* them."[11] In showing that the movable book is produced by multiple hands, and acknowledging the publisher's control, Mack's poem is materialist in the way that Price posits. Other examples from within this volume and beyond provide, however, a fantasized point of origin for the book rather than an unblinking exposure of its publisher. Nister is Aladdin in *Here and There,* for instance, his lamp producing the "transformation pictures" promised in the book's subtitle, and a Pied Piper of

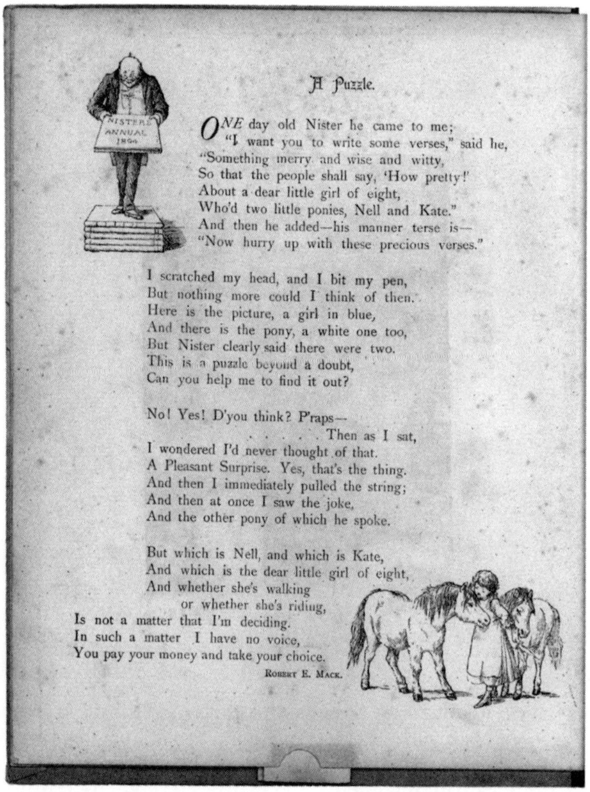

A Puzzle.

ONE day old Nister he came to me;
"I want you to write some verses," said he,
"Something merry and wise and witty,
So that the people shall say, 'How pretty!'
About a dear little girl of eight,
Who'd two little ponies, Nell and Kate."
And then he added—his manner terse is—
"Now hurry up with these precious verses."

I scratched my head, and I bit my pen,
But nothing more could I think of then.
Here is the picture, a girl in blue,
And there is the pony, a white one too,
But Nister clearly said there were two.
This is a puzzle beyond a doubt,
Can you help me to find it out?

No! Yes! D'you think? P'raps—
. . . . . . Then as I sat,
I wondered I'd never thought of that.
A Pleasant Surprise. Yes, that's the thing.
And then I immediately pulled the string;
And then at once I saw the joke,
And the other pony of which he spoke.

But which is Nell, and which is Kate,
And which is the dear little girl of eight,
And whether she's walking
or whether she's riding,
Is not a matter that I'm deciding.
In such a matter I have no voice,
You pay your money and take your choice.

ROBERT E. MACK.



FIGURE 4.2. Ernest Nister frequently appears in the books released by his eponymous publishing house, as in the illustration at top left of this page from *More Pleasant Surprises for Chicks of All Sizes* (circa 1893). Courtesy of the Strong, Rochester, New York.

Hamelin figure who entices children from all around the globe (from all around the universe, in fact, once we read the fine print) into a cavern and reads them "pretty picture-books" at another point in *More Pleasant Surprises.*[12] When Nister appears as "Ernest Nister Christopher / Columbus" in Clifton Bingham's untitled final verse to the same book, the heroic and the commonplace mix. Nister "vowed he'd make a stir / And take a trip in a great big ship / And sail to Storybook Land in her." While "Storybook Land" is fantastical, the resulting state of affairs reflects contemporary publishing fact: "Every week, from across the sea, / Most wonderful ships are taking trips / As full of books as they can be." Nister's transatlantic agreement with Dutton (potentially noted in the choice of Columbus as model), as well as the transport of the firm's books from Germany, where they were printed, to England, maps onto the fairy tale of Storybook Land. Across these examples, the publisher himself becomes the book's hero, likened to mythic figures, and the production of movable books is aligned with heroic feats. Indeed, it seems that reviewers pick up these epic parallels, as when Nister is called "that Nestor among the makers of pictured books for children" in the *Literary World,* an American weekly, in November 1896.[13]

Mister Nister's appearances furthermore involve explanations of how movable books are produced. In *Pleasant Surprises,* Nister, the "magic-picture man," grows books on "Story-Farm." The first page opening contains several floating line illustrations, variously captioned. "Going to Sow the Seed" shows Nister with a bag labeled "BOOK SEED" over his shoulder and a flock of children clamoring around him. In "Sowing the Seed," the seeds falling from his hands are letters. Nister waters small books on stalks with cans marked "WATERCOLOUR" and "FLOWING VERSE" in the third picture, while "Sunny Smiles" depicts Nister looking up at a grinning sun. The final image, "A Magnificent Crop," has Nister presenting fully grown books on stalks to the viewer. The untitled verse on the facing page explains that children demand "more books! more books!" leading Nister to "[sow] it all complete, / With alphabets by bushels, and pictures fair and sweet." He waters these crops with poetry drawn from "the muse's fountain," and the poem concludes: "If you like his picture-books, and if you love him true, / He'll sow some more in Story-Farm, and give them all to you." Like young spectators clapping to save Tinker Bell at a performance of *Peter Pan,* children seem to control the continuation of the story here: their emotion is directly elicited, and they are made to feel powerful. The child's approbation or love of both Nister himself *and* his books is necessary for continued growth. Moreover, the making of the book is organic: the "growth" imagined in conjunction with the Nister book is not economic, just as the undertones of the Pied Piper story—a tale of adults exploiting children—go unremarked.

Other titles heighten the family romance by making the Nister book's creation magical. In *The Fairies' Playtime,* the volume at hand has been prepared by fairies under the guidance of the Queen Fairy, who suggests that her subjects "make something" for children. As the fairies create "such a beautiful book," even the volume's title is given a magical backstory: "hard work" transforms into "play." Doggerel, the form that Nister poems take, is itself fitting in this context: the little, cute, whimsical qualities of Victorian and Edwardian fairies seem well represented by irregular comic verses.[14] The Queen Fairy's cottage printing industry is perhaps not as strange as the source of a book in another magical origin story, from *Something New for Little*

*Folk*: the child is encouraged to believe that the material book, instead of being composed of paper, card, and cloth, has been made—again by fairies—from butterfly wings and rainbows. (Pleasingly, *rainbow printing* is a term for the most common form of chromolithographic selective inking.)[15] Its verses, too, were purportedly written by the Man in the Moon rather than by Mr. Clifton Bingham of Broadwater Down, Tunbridge Wells: professional author, frequent Nister contributor, and lyricist of sentimental ditties including "Love's Old Sweet Song"—popular enough some fifty years after its release to warrant inclusion in James Joyce's *Ulysses* (1922) as one of the songs Molly Bloom will sing at Blazes Boylan's upcoming recital, and then as a sort of refrain running through Leopold Bloom's thoughts.[16] F. E. Weatherly, another prolific writer of Nister dissolving views, was perhaps an even more successful lyricist.[17] The magical fantasies of publishing and writing children's movables take on significance, then, in proportion to the commercialism of Nister's actual publishing model, which included a network of prolific, jobbing authors spanning not just Bingham and Weatherly but also other figures both obscure (such as Helen Marion Burnside, who wrote four hundred verses a year for twenty years after a childhood illness left her deaf) and celebrated (such as E. Nesbit, who wrote her most famous books for children at the same time she was composing abundant poetry, drama, romance novels, and ghost stories).[18]

The fairy origin story is worth exploring in greater depth. As I have suggested in chapter 3, the figure of the fairy is often related to the theater in the nineteenth century, and the fairy godmothers who are imagined producing Nister dissolving-view books add a further dimension to this connection. Nister often used the phrase *transformation pictures* to describe the dissolving-view format, thus summoning the earlier Victorian pantomime trick of the transformation scene, in which a spectacular magical transformation—often involving fairies—took place onstage before the theatergoer's eyes.[19] For instance, the pantomime *Hop 'o My Thumb and His Eleven Brothers,* designed by the originator of the transformation scene (William Beverley) and staged for the Christmas season in 1864–65, "saw the clouds disperse to display the glories of the sun, while fairies floated up and down before the rays."[20] The dissolving-view book's gimmick, in which one image becomes another by way of moving slats, echoes—in a one-dimensional, miniaturized, private, and temporally telescoped way—the public splendor of the transformation scene. But the transformation scene and the dissolving-view book share another attribute, too: their somewhat troubled relationship to the technology that allows the transformation. Behind-the-scenes images of nineteenth-century transformation machinery can demonstrate this; in one example, the star trap used to catapult performers onto the stage sits awkwardly with the stage fairies who crowd around it—not to mention with the workman who operates the lever.[21] As Diane Purkiss observes, the transformation scene and its fairies are inseparable from the mechanics of their production: "The more romantic [they] appear, that is, the more 'authentic' they look, the more they can hardly help celebrating and advertising the advanced technology that creates them." The rural and romanticized associations of the fairy in Victorian culture seem incommensurate with the grubby mechanics of the theater—and yet are ensured by these mechanics.[22] Movable books are subject to like vicissitudes. The movable technology and chromolithographic vividness facilitate the book's representation of magic, while a fantasy of fairy figures creating the book's effects palliates this same technologization.

A parallel equation takes place in "Fairy Land: Mrs. Allingham and Kate Greenaway," Ruskin's lecture on children's literature in *The Art of England* (1884). The critic's thoughts quickly turn to the morality of recently honed technologies of artistic production. Discussing advances in visual media, Ruskin notes: "Having then the colour-print, the magic-lantern, the electric-light, and the—to any row of ciphers—magnifying lens, it becomes surely very interesting to consider what we may most wisely represent to children by means so potent, so dazzling, and, if we will, so faithful."[23] As Katie Trumpener remarks in her discussion of this lecture, Ruskin's response to the technologies of pictorial reproduction overlaps with his concern about the impacts of machines more generally in children's lives. For Ruskin, "the brightly illustrated children's book gave a new generation of children unparalleled means of viewing, investigating, and imagining the world around them—but also . . . changed that world irrevocably, threatening Britain's architectural, social and moral fabric."[24] The fairy and the fairy tale soothe Ruskin's initial concerns regarding apt subjects for new visual technologies; fairies rewrite the origins of the Nister book in a similarly "reparative way" (to quote Nicola Bown's formulation of the nineteenth-century fairy's power).[25]

Moreover, the idea of fairies creating books inverts the scenario that took England by storm around the time of World War I: that of the Cottingley fairies. The fairies photographed by Elsie Wright and Frances Griffiths in Cottingley, Yorkshire, in 1917 proved to be paper cutouts from a volume titled *Princess Mary's Gift Book* (1914).[26] In this case, then, a book created fairies—from such modest materials as cardboard—rather than the other way around. Attitudes toward the photographic mechanism that equally generated these magical beings were vexed. Purkiss argues that contemporary coverage of the Cottingley fairies never mentioned Elsie Wright's career as a photographic technician, "less because it pointed to photographic fakery than because it linked Elsie uneasily with an adult world of work, an industrial world of colour plates and chemicals."[27] Carol Mavor, by contrast, believes that the technology is part of the magic at Cottingley. For Mavor, the "romanticism of the magical and alchemical qualities of photography as a medium" is implicit in the story of Frances, Elsie, and the fairies: "In 1900, a Brownie was both a fairy and a camera."[28] Purkiss's and Mavor's viewpoints contrast, but they do not necessarily contradict one another, representing as they do the complex relationships among magic, technology, ideals of childhood, and the book—relationships echoed in Nister dissolving views.

The Nister movables' involvement in, or knowledge of, mechanical production must be reconciled with their status as books for children. These books' origins, their beginnings in urban industry and mechanical innovation, not to mention professional authorship, are often recast in self-conscious "histories of the book."[29] Such recurring family romances rewrite the book's provenance while ensuring the achievement of ancillary goals: maintaining the sense of brand that outright references to Mister Nister produce, for instance, or glamorizing said brand's production of new formats. At the same time, it is the technologies of these books—their dissolving-view gimmicks—that dictate their appeal.

### Book Gifts: Nister's Dissolving Views and Their Readers

Like most other novelty books, Nister's movables often offer guidance—some tacit, some explicit—for their own use, and the advice continues the books' stories about themselves. In particular, dissolving views present themselves as books *to be given* to children. Thinking about Nister movables as gift books, and tracing evidence of whether they were used as such, exposes how different fantasies of the book worked on their purchasers (mostly adults) and readers (mostly children). In the case of the widespread injunctions to reread, these instructions form part of the movable's attempts to ensure good treatment (and hence a long life) from its child readers—as well as an expansion of the discussion of the instructive registers of the novelty book as mounted in chapter 1.

A key vogue for book giving in Victorian juvenile publishing is the reward book: volumes given to children "as rewards or prizes to mark an achievement, and to reinforce a lesson or set of values in the process," to adopt Kimberley Reynolds's definition.[30] In some cases, Nister dissolving-view books present themselves as intended for (or at least compatible with) this practice. For example, *Pleasant Surprises* is the self-proclaimed "book of all books [and] prize of all prizes," this play for the reward market appearing on the title page, while the fairies' rainbow-colored book is for children to "treasure and prize." The Nister dissolves in the Opie Collection, however, display no evidence that they were given to mark particular successes. There are no bookplates from schools, for example, or inscriptions indicating prize giving. This may be because both the format and the text of the Nister dissolving view did not fit with prevailing wisdom on books suitable as rewards. In *What Books to Lend,* for instance, Charlotte Mary Yonge advocates recreational reading and unimpeded access to materials designed for this purpose from libraries, but expresses quite a different opinion regarding prize books for children:

> There is very little call for improving books in the lending library, in proportion to those meant for recreation; but I would urge that they be used for prizes. At present, the usual habit is to choose gay outsides and pretty pictures, with little heed to the contents, but it should be remembered that the lent book is ephemeral, read in a week and passed on, while the prize remains, is exhibited to relatives and friends, is read over and over, becomes a resource in illness, and forms part of the possession to be handed on to the next generation. Therefore after the infant period, the reward book should generally be of some worthiness, either religious, improving, or at least standard fiction.[31]

Yonge insists that, despite the fact that the practice of giving a book as a reward evokes (to recall Price) some of the things that Victorian readers did with books other than reading them, the prize book should also be *read by* the child. This leads in turn to particular material requirements: although colorful, attractive books with little edifying content (such as Nister dissolving views) may be permissible in the "infant period," a category that includes children under five or six years old in Yonge's usage, they are undesirable as prize books once children begin attending school or Sunday school in earnest.

There is much proof, though, that Nister books were both produced and used as gift books—reward books' less sober cousins. For instance, their composition, featuring short poems (as in many of the Nister pop-ups discussed in chapter 3), is typical of the format. Indeed, one of the few characteristics shared by the gift books popular earlier in the nineteenth century and the chromolithographed ones that superseded them by the fin de siècle is the tendency to use poetry as, in Richard Maxwell's words, "the servant of illustration."[32] Maxwell's formulation evokes Yonge's objections to certain types of books being given as rewards, but it also perfectly fits the verses of Nister's books, many of which were composed by their writers in response to the pictures. (This happened with earlier gift books, too, such as *Home Thoughts and Home Scenes,* from 1865, which saw a number of poets compose verses in relation to a series of preexisting illustrations, as Lorraine Janzen Kooistra has explored in detail.)[33]

Moving beyond the general principle of poetry in service to pictures, individual dissolving-view books attempted to woo key markets for the gift book. Take the title *Pleasant Surprises,* produced around the beginning of World War I.[34] The book's colorful cover image depicts Santa Claus in a smart office filled with toys; he is speaking on a telephone, and in the background, through a glass window, elves can be seen hauling full sacks. Numerous small details, such as a desk calendar open to December 24, reinforce the Yuletide atmosphere, while a snowy landscape frames the central image of the office. *Pleasant Surprises* is, then, not just a gift book but also a Christmas book. The movable mechanism is of the double-disc dissolve type, meaning that each movable page opening contains not one but two sets of dissolve pictures. Every page opening is branded with Christmas imagery: the dissolve images are framed with unfurling green ribbon bows and sprigs of holly, part of a grid of three central fixed images between the dissolves (Figure 4.3). One of these panels shows Santa holding a doll and a toy train, ready to give to children.

References to Christmas in Nister point to key Victorian trends in the observance of this holiday. Regardless of the degree to which the Victorian Christmas comprised invented traditions and patterns of celebration (a familiar argument), certainly the size of the market for Christmas goods changed in the period: the first

FIGURE 4.3. *Pleasant Surprises* (circa 1914) uses the dissolving-view format to multiply Christmas imagery and motifs, including ribbon bunches, plentiful holly, and Santa Claus. The Bodleian Libraries, the University of Oxford (2015), Opie EE 39.

advertisements for toys designed specifically for Christmas appeared in the 1850s, and such products became big business by the 1880s. The origin of Christmas toys was of concern; indeed, in the 1890s the predominance of German toys at Christmastime caused twofold strife in what the historian Mark Connelly refers to as the "Made in Germany" debate.[35] Worries over Germany's economic dominance of the Christmas market are visible in reviews of Nister books, as when the *Morning Post* concludes an otherwise favorable notice for the firm's novelties: "It is regrettable that the publishers should have found it necessary to go to Bavaria to have their productions printed."[36] Concerns about manufacturing were interwoven with concerns about a possible German aesthetic dominance over English Christmas celebrations. New nineteenth-century English habits of decoration aped German traditions, as when Prince Albert popularized the Christmas tree in England by way of a much-reprinted image of the royal family around their tree at Windsor Castle.[37] In Nister books, the heavy snow across landscapes might be considered more typical of the German climate than of the English, and its aestheticized reproduction likewise more fitting for a German Christmas narrative. Less speculatively, the use of a Santa Claus figure to hide the commercial origins of Christmas toys, which Gary Cross associates with "the modern embrace of abundance in a new consumer culture," fits with Nister's fantasized origins for its books.[38]

As Cindy Dickinson points out, however, attention paid to gift books as art objects can neglect a central question: "What made them appropriate as gifts?"[39] In the case of the Nister book, with its self-conscious appeals to its readers, the poems themselves model patterns of gift giving. In the fantastical origin stories discussed in the preceding section, for instance, adult figures often give the books to child readers; ideally, this internal pattern of book giving will be reproduced externally, as books come to observe particular occasions. The many presentation inscriptions in Nister dissolving views not only demonstrate the success of the company's holiday- and gift-book marketing but also provide information about the social customs of giving books to children. In some cases, as M. O. Grenby has shown in *The Child Reader,* inscriptions can offer "a sociological profile of book-owners," including gender, age, and social class.[40] Individual copies of movable books in the Opie Collection sometimes perform this work: for example, Augusta Perigal (1863–1943), the tenth child in her family, was given the French lift-the-flap book *Les Aventures de Robinson Crusoë* (The adventures of Robinson Crusoe) by her sisters Gertrude and Mary, who were, respectively, two and four years older than her.[41] Not only does the inscription help the reader to find incidental information about Augusta and her relatives—for example, her uncle was the stockbroker and amateur mathematician Henry Perigal, who posed an elegant proof of the Pythagorean theorem now known as Perigal's dissection—but it also gives a picture of the logic underpinning the present. The fact that the book is in French is significant, because Augusta's father, Frederick, published reminiscences of the family in 1887 under the title *Some Account of the Perigal Family,* including substantial passages in French from eighteenth-century family letters and documenting the family's "intimacy with many Huguenot families unto the present time." Augusta's younger sister was named Adèle, the *e grave* lovingly rendered in the family tree at the end of Frederick Perigal's *Account.*[42] Augusta Perigal's movable *Robinson Crusoë,* then, was not just a token of sisterly affection but also a material link to her heritage. Perhaps her sisters gave it to her when she began to learn French.

The information that can be gleaned from Nister dissolving-view books in the Opie Collection, however, is less comprehensive. Usually only the names of the donor and the recipient are given, along with the occasion of the gift; in some cases a date is also included. Some examples: "Many Happy Returns of your Birthday / Love & best wishes to Lucy from Rose J. Bywater," in *Transformation Pictures and Comical Fixtures*; "For Peggy / with love & all Good wishes for Christmas & the New Year / from / Mary Teresa [Mundell?]," in *The Children's Wonderland*; "George. / With Reginald's love," in *Here and There.*[43] Even when first and last names are provided, I have not been able to trace any of the donors or recipients of these dissolving-view books definitively. The one exception to this dearth of information is an inscription in a copy of *Something New,* which, rather than providing demographic information, gives a snapshot of creative book use and exchange. The inscription, written in a lovely hand, reads, "To Dear Harry / with much love / from his Cousin Grace / Xmas 1899."[44] Around her message, Cousin Grace has drawn a smiling star and swirling clouds, which reillustrate the stars and clouds that appear in the title-page image of fairies. Cousin Grace's doodle embodies the donor's participation in creating a permanent artwork, which is then passed on to the child, in an effect reminiscent of the one Clare Pettitt ascribes to the Victorian serial assembled "part by part" by readers: "The boundary between the artwork and its consumers became less distinct."[45] The stars and clouds also dismantle any unthinking distinction between print and manuscript, handwritten picture and words foreshadowing or underscoring the printed pictures and words that follow. Hence any account of the Nister book is in part one given externally by the readers who wrote in these gift books, responding to the books' textual and paratextual positioning of themselves.

The gift-book marketing of Nister dissolving views places the novelty in dialogue with the permanent—recall Yonge's "ephemeral" borrowed book, not fit to remind the child of any particular lessons or to mark any particular occasion. As such, Nister dissolves can be read through the lens of what Nathalie op de Beeck calls the picture book as ready-made antique. As op de Beeck writes: "Every picture book is a ready-made antique, because its significance encompasses past, present, and future. Picture books are not only material goods for immediate enjoyment; they function also as manufactured antiques with nostalgia and sentiment built in."[46] The Nister book sets itself up as a gift book—something that will endure—just as its material format suggests that it is made for "immediate," and perhaps even transient, enjoyment. The relative's or friend's choice to buy one of these brightly colored, expensive titles, and to write on the endpapers to commemorate the occasion of the gift, palliates other aspects of the book's makeup: its reliance on the dissolving-view gimmick, its involvement with a developing lucrative market for Christmas books for children, and so forth. In their self-realization as gifts, and the evidence that they were bought and used as such, these books thus resemble their fictional autobiographies, in which the Nister brand subsumes its writers and illustrators, and magical fantasy overlays chromolithographic innovation.

The relationship between ephemerality and permanence is foregrounded in one final aspect of the Nister book's self-image: instructions to reread, which stake a claim for the book's enduring value as opposed to its ephemerality or novelty. Nister dissolving-view books often ritualize the act of reading, and in particular the ending of each book may be ceremonially marked. The last poem in *Transformation Pictures,* for example, tells the reader: "The pretty book is done; / You've found each hidden picture / And looked at every one." Both the movable technology ("hidden picture") and an ideal reader's engagement with that technology ("found" implying an active and intelligent discovery of the device, and "every one" valorizing a steady and studied attention in reading) are carefully demarcated. The poem continues, "And when you close the volume, / You've looked the pages through," foregrounding the reader's physical progress through the book—looking at all the pages and, finally, after this verse, closing the volume. Each of the child's acts as she read the book is revisited in a sequence of rites: the rite of page turning, the rite of closing the finished volume, and of course the Nister rite of publisher-worship ("Say 'thank you' to the kind folks / Who *made* them all for you").

But the child reader may—indeed, should—avert the book's ending. Hence, although the final poem of *Playtime Surprises* is emphatically titled "The End," it introduces the motif of rereading. A child reader dismayed at finishing the stories is instructed to "turn the book o'er," while the last lines state: "If you read it through twice, oh! / 'Twill seem twice as nice, oh!— / I'm certain it will when you try." In the adjacent line illustration, a child sits on three sheets of paper: one marked "beginning," one marked "middle," and one marked "end." (She points to the last one.) A clever child can forestall the book's ending and avoid the potential sadness of finishing the book not by fussing or crying but by reading it twice. *All the Way Round Pictures* materializes the problem of ending the book and the solution of rereading: "This is one end when you've finished it quite— / The other is where you begin it."[47] Rather than being a category of story, the end is a physical part of the book; rather than moving toward its terminus in a linear fashion, *All the Way Round Pictures,* as its circular title would suggest, is cyclical, its end only the precursor of its (re-)beginning. Indeed, author Maud Carlton's play with the book's two ends sketches in miniature the features of children's literature that I address in this volume: the mutually constitutive interactions among material form, narrative structure, and reader use in novelty books for children.

Instructions to reread in Nister movable books relate to these books' status as occasional books, but rereading holds wider significance, too, representing as it may a childish mode of reading. Susan Stewart explores the idea of "graduating" from a book when we finish it.[48] Encouraging a repetitive engagement with Nister books contests the graduation model of reading, its associations with age, temporal progress, and movement away from childish things; it also evokes rereading as a peculiarly childish habit. Roland Barthes notes that rereading, a practice that challenges prevailing norms of consumption, is "tolerated only in certain marginal categories of readers (children, old people, and professors)," and as Deborah Thacker has argued, relating Barthes's arguments to children's literature, rereading may be "an exercise in re-writing, or taking possession of a text in an active and open way, as part of the process by which the reader forms a relationship with the author and the author's voice."[49] In this, it resembles Nister's demand—anatomized in the next section—that the reader write the likeness between the two parts of a dissolving picture.

## Connecting the Dissolve

Perhaps the most substantial story that the Nister dissolve tells about itself is the story of the two pictures—the relationship between the first and second parts of each dissolving view. The movable piece and the two images it contains are the governing conceit of the book as a whole, referenced in titles such as *Transformation Pictures* and lines of verse such as "each, you'll find / Has another behind" in *Playtime Surprises.* How is the connection between the two parts of the dissolve established or explained? Does this take place in the written text accompanying each illustration, or is the child reader asked to draw her own conclusions from the pictures themselves? These questions are particularly significant because the relationship between pictures is not organic: the Nister firm habitually reused images from publication to publication, and the poems were written to accompany the (perhaps arbitrary) pairings contained in the movable pieces.

The dissolving-view book must first alert the child reader to the very existence of two pictures rather than only the one visible before the book is manipulated. The introductory verses here take on a further role: in addition to reflecting on the production of the book (Nister on Story-Farm), they orient the reader to the book's form. The guidance can be explicit—"Each one, when you pull it rightly, / Chang[es] into something new" in *Transformation Pictures*—or even imperative, as when *Pleasant Surprises* instructs, "Put down one picture another arises." At other points, the introductory poem adopts vaguer language so as to alert the child to the book's special qualities while preserving the mystery of what those qualities are, as in the eponymous opening verse of *The Children's Wonderland,* which simply states that the child reader's eyes "will open in surprise" at what she finds between the covers. In all of these cases, the written text shapes the child reader's basic understanding of the book: the fact that the dissolve's essential nature is hidden, because the reader sees one picture when there are really two.

In a further effort to govern the child reader's understanding of the movable pieces, Nister books often include short verses, which act as captions, on dissolve images (see Plate 3 and Figure 4.3). As Barthes observes in "Rhetoric of the Image," captions have a dual function, at once answering "the question: *what is it?*" and broadly dictating the *"correct level of perception"* (what should be noticed about an image).[50] Rather than giving a direction as to the way the pictures work—their hidden transformations—Nister captions work in this way when they describe the content of the two parts to a dissolve: "Pull the cord and Summer goes, / Giving place to Winter's snows" in *Pleasant Surprises,* for example. The two-line form of these verse captions, and their equal division between the subjects of the first and second pictures, works as a sort of calligram representing the two-part image. If the couplet "It's fun to run hard on a snowy day; / And fun with your toys at home to play," in *Pleasant Surprises,* is a description of what the reader should expect, then it confirms that there is not just one image on the page. In part, including these short verses suggests that the dissolve's makers are unsure about the way the different parts of the book will relate, an unease that arises from the composite nature of the Nister book: it combines movable illustrations, static illustrations, and caption verses, but also longer verses, which extend the story of what is going on in the dissolve by narrating the relationship between its two halves. These words complete or bridge a gap between pictures that is both literal (produced by the mechanism) and figurative (produced by the sometimes odd picture combinations).

The word *dissolve* summons visual entertainments other than the picture book, and these can be used to consider the relationship between the two halves of each Nister dissolve. Although Nister usually refers to its multiple-view movable effects as *transformation pictures,* the use of the word *dissolve* to describe this format was current in the nineteenth century: the earliest example of the dissolve format seems to be *Dean's New Book of Dissolving Views,* published around 1861.[51] In using the term *dissolving view,* Dean and Son linked its book to the magic lantern. As Joss Marsh explains, a dissolve was a particular type of magic-lantern projection: "Light was slowly stopped down on one lens and one image and brought up on another, with perfect registration, so that the second image slowly—almost magically—replaced the first on the illuminated screen."[52] The dissolving view was invented by the magic-lantern maker Henry Langdon Childe in 1807 and perfected in 1818.[53] Childe continued to improve on his innovation into the century, exhibiting, for example, what Deac Rossell describes as "lanterns capable of subtly blending one image into another, or producing a variety of effects from snow and rain to lightning and billowing smoke" at the Royal Polytechnic Institute in London in the early 1840s.[54]

The later cinematic dissolve takes its name from the dissolving-view projection, and dissolving-view books create effects that resemble cinematic dissolves in a number of ways. This means that film studies can provide a useful classificatory framework for thinking about Nister dissolving-view books. A straightforward example occurs in the kaleidoscopic-disc dissolve, where the dissolve entails one representational picture and one kaleidoscopic pattern of abstract color. (The term *kaleidoscopic* was used to describe the effect at the time the books were published.)[55] The Nister books *Something New* and *Wonderland Pictures* are both of this type, with multicolor stripes—red with black and blue with orange, both accented by white—and ombré color blocking giving way to a picture of, say, a child and a peacock (Plate 12).[56] A few poems seem to allude to the colored patterns. For instance, part of insisting on a magical provenance for *Something New* is making chromolithographic bursts of color themselves fantastical: "The Star Fairies some of their bright colours lent." More typically, though, the accompanying verses do not even mention the gorgeous colors, let alone narrate the relationship between parts. In fact, the kaleidoscopic transformation exemplifies a feature of the cinematic dissolve: the role that "the path itself" plays, whereby, as Christian Metz points out, "the device doesn't simply plot out some relationship between two segments on the level of the signified, it combines their signifiers physically."[57] The kaleidoscopic-disc dissolve makes the moment or process of transformation its subject—the child reader is encouraged to take a sensuous pleasure in the abstract pattern and its entrancing bright colors, rather than to think about the relationship between those colors and the accompanying words or representational pictures.

In particular, though, models for analyzing the cinematic dissolve can help to parse the relationship between the two parts of the Nister dissolving-view image when both halves are representational. The cinematic dissolve most obviously functions "to link jumps in space and time," as Torben Grodal observes.[58] There are, however, additional ways in which filmmakers use dissolves. Metz draws upon Roman Jakobson's famous account of metaphor (associated with similarity, selection, and substitution) on the one hand and metonym (signifying contiguity, combination, and sequence) on the other.[59] Metz writes of cinematic dissolves: "Their metaphorical or metonymic character (sometimes their *double* character, which does not mean hybrid or indiscernible) . . . depends on the relation between the two images in question. . . . The relation is metaphorical if one of the two images is extra-diegetic, metonymic if they are both aspects of the same action (or the same space, etc.), and double if one of these aspects resembles the other, or is compared to it, or connotes it in some sense, etc."[60] Dissolving-view picture books also raise this question of "the relation between the two images," which can be imagined according to the (metaphoric) association between something within the action and something outside it, the (metonymic) linking of different moments in time and space, or a double relationship, often but not always comparing the first and second images.

Many dissolves work metonymically, forming a simple visual sequence. In *Transformation Pictures,* one image shows two dogs (wearing children's clothing) about to uncork a bottle of lemonade; pull the cardboard tab, and a second image shows the bottle overflowing (Figure 4.4). The relationship between pictures is cause

FIGURE 4.4. One dissolving-view illustration from *Transformation Pictures and Comical Fixtures* (circa 1891) plots logical consequences, so that the second image shows what happens when a bottle of lemonade is uncorked. The Bodleian Libraries, the University of Oxford (2015), Opie EE 32.

and effect, clear to a visually literate reader from the two pictorial halves of the dissolve alone, and the connection between pictures is temporal—a small plot, as the two halves of the dissolve show successive moments in time. Nonetheless, the text does expand on this story at length (perhaps for very young readers developing their understanding of how pictures tell stories). Taking two chronologically in-order events from a familiar story is a related strategy: an image of a cat ushering kittens out of the family home, where a pie steams on the table, gives way to a happy cat family sitting down to dinner in *The Children's Wonderland.* The accompanying adaptation of the folk song "Three Little Kittens," though not in the standard wording and with the added element of a caption, further encourages or even enables a sequential reading of the dissolving pictures.[61]

Other books, other sequences: the seasons figure as two halves of a dissolving view in a number of titles, including *Pleasant Surprises,* with its rhyming of "Summer goes" and "Winter's snows," and *Dean's New Book of Dissolving Views* (Plate 13).[62] While the seasons are the explicit point of comparison in the latter, the images proliferate oppositions—between the exotic palace and the stark mountainside, but also, the verse suggests, between warm weather and human kindness.

> Where SUMMER almost rules the year,
> Man's grandest palaces appear:
> Where WINTER reigns 'mid Alpine snows,
> Man's heart with warm affection glows.

This Dean and Son book includes a day-and-night dissolve as a further variation on the theme. The contrast between seasons or between times of day, the natural temporal progression from one to another, is well suited to a dissolving picture; indeed, as Maria Nikolajeva and Carole Scott suggest, images of seasonal change are a common means by which "the flow of time can be expressed visually" in the picture book.[63] At the same time, as noted in the Introduction, the Dean book's explicit nod to the dissolving view in its title, and its inclusion of summer–winter and day–night transformations (two of magic-lantern originator Childe's renowned effects), shows the cross-pollination of the dissolving-view projection with the book.[64] Although the effect is not celebratory in Dean's dissolve, winter scenes can also signal the status of individual books as Christmas objects and the text's sustained focus on arranging its pictures according to the festive theme.

In the dissolves discussed so far, the relationship between images is, to borrow Mieke Bal's definition of sequence, based in a "logical concept."[65] The succession of images traces a narrative arc that is predictable as part of either a rational cohort of possibilities (everybody knows that day turns into night) or a preestablished familiar story (everybody knows the song about the three little kittens). One topic leads to another, and the two moments in each picture seem either to touch in time or to occur more broadly in succession. In part, temporal dissolves seem to socialize the child into the predictability of these sequences, encouraging pleasure in knowing what comes next, an investment that becomes more potent when the book is read aloud repeatedly. Moreover, this rapid-fire, two-part sequence of pictures is in fact the only narrative sequence the book offers its young readers; like the pop-ups discussed in chapter 3, Nister dissolving-view books in English usually offer collections of short pieces by a variety of authors rather than a single continuous story. The subject matter and tone within a book can be diverse, disparate even: the role of animals within any one volume, for example, may comprise animals as pets, as wild creatures encountered outdoors, and as talking characters in their own stories. There is great unevenness in the lengths of pieces as well, from the two-line caption verses on dissolve pages to longer verses. The temporalized link between pictures, then, becomes the book's chief claim to any sequence at all.

But other relationships between the two halves of dissolve images encourage the child reader to compare two things or substitute one thing for another, rather than to place two things in sequence. For example, the first dissolve in *Playtime Surprises* is an image of a dog watching over a small girl, followed by an image of puppies tearing brightly colored ribbons. The connection between pictures is, then, thematically oriented around a child and her pets. This occurs across verses as well as within them: in *Pleasant Surprises,* children serve tea to their kittens and dolls, feel irritated by younger siblings, extol the relative merits of cats and dogs, encounter and appraise other children during a trip to the park, and ride trains. The double-disc dissolve format mentioned above, which has not one but two dissolving pictures embedded in each page, allows multiple depictions of these naturalistic variations on the child's life, as activities are substituted for one another. Here, the child reader is asked which she prefers, cats or dogs, and what she would rather do, go to the park or hold a tea party. The dissolve pictures are not wedded to sequence or cause and effect; instead their relation is one of similarity, of likeness, of substitutability. Moreover, the comparison and similarity is supposed to work outside as well as within the book, as the child reader might be expected to compare her brothers and sisters, pets, and favorite activities to those represented in the movable book.

## Forced Connections and the Fairy Tale as Childhood Property

But what about the means of production for these dissolving picture books? As Higonnet observes of movable books more generally, "The very form . . . turns its segments into transposable parts, like a game of lego."[66] Colored images in particular are frequently reused across Nister books. The methods of reuse vary: static color plates from earlier titles may become one half of a dissolve, as when *Pleasant Surprises* recycles Harriett M. Bennett's illustration for the picture book *Queen of the Meadow* (1888), or images may be used in more than one movable format—a picture of fairies shifting from pop-up in *Peeps into Fairyland* to dissolving-view disc in *Little Folk's Peep Show.*[67] Some dissolve images are simply used twice, but in different combinations. The dissolving view's texts are composed in accordance with those images. This means that (to recall Christian Metz's idea of the "hybrid" dissolve) *forced* comparisons between the two parts of the dissolve are frequent. This is especially true in the large number of Fairyland dissolving views, which encourage the child reader to draw comparisons between characters, stories, and objects, and in which a corollary of the sometimes nonsensical connections is children's freedom to play with their common property: fairy tales themselves.

In Nister dissolving-view books, *Fairyland* means not only a place where magical beings live but also a heterogeneous imaginative space where characters from different fairy tales interact. (Both meanings relate back to the Victorian theater, particularly the pantomime, with its jocular mixture of folkloric subjects.) In dissolving-view books, two of these characters typically feature as the two halves of a picture. Also called Nursery-Tale Land, Nursery Rhyme Land, Wonderland, and Storybook Land in Nister titles, these settings have an economic function. They facilitate Nister's recycling of images across movable books, as in a dissolve image of Cinderella that appears in both *The Fairies' Playtime* and *Little Folk's Peep Show* (see Figure 4.5). Fairy-tale pictures act as what Richard Altick calls convertible subjects in these books, as in nineteenth-century illustration, whereby "a generalized design of a fortification could be used interchangeably for the walls of Troy or a castle in a medieval romance."[68] This makes the ways in which a connection between characters is established (usually in the text) all the more interesting, because the pairing of images is random and challenges the patterns of similarity or at least comparison that we might expect.

In the verses, the heterogeneous Fairyland space may be self-conscious, as in the fairy-tale exposé, which initiates the reader into the "real" story behind a fairy tale. In *Transformation Pictures,* the poem "How It Happened" gives the reason for the disappearance of Bo Peep's sheep—they were scandalized by a kiss she received from Little Boy Blue—while a fictional fairy-tale gossip rag provides similar information in "The Wonderland Mail," a set of verses in *The Children's Wonderland.* Other Fairyland inhabitants become involved in detective work about their neighbors. In *The Fairies' Playtime* retelling of "The Three Bears," the bear family comes home from market to find the house in disarray. The girl in the story is not Goldilocks, however, but Little Red Riding Hood, who witnessed the bears returning home and "said to herself, as she tripped down the vale: / 'Oh, I know who did it—for I've read the tale!'" Even fairy-tale heroines are familiar with the trajectories of different tales: their predictability, ubiquity even, is the point. Moreover, the book encourages the child reader to adopt a similar attitude: to be familiar with fairy tales but also adept at disrupting their established scripts.

Nister's Fairyland dissolves, however, do not always illuminate (or even relate to) the tongue-in-cheek goings-on of the poems. In fact, the status of the second tale is often uncertain. Does the dissolve blend two fairy-tale plots, or does it allow one story to make an external comment on the other? In the "Giants" page opening in *The Fairies' Playtime,* for example, the relationship between the parts of the book varies depending on whether the reader focuses on text, static pictures, or movable pictures. In the verse, Puss in Boots sets off to kill giants only to find that "his comrade Jack" has dispatched them all. Alongside the verse, a line illustration shows Jack and Puss formally greeting each other in a visual scenario that complements the poem's Fairyland setting: as the verse suggests, these disparate characters occupy the same space. By contrast, the dissolve pictures show Puss brandishing his sword and talking to his master—a winsome child in eighteenth-century dress—and Jack climbing a beanstalk. The dissolves are drawn from the original tales, not the sequel given in the Nister book; they show events and moments that are not depicted in the text. The Fairyland conceit goes unrepresented by the movable piece.

Despite the discrepancy between the logic of the verse, which is reinforced by the line illustration, and the dissolve pictures in "Giants," there is a metaphoric connection between Jack and Puss: both stories, whether they are versions of the originals or this fanciful Nister expansion on them, involve the same fantastic being subjected to the same treatment. Puss and Jack are like each other, just as the giants of the stories (and the title of the poem) are alike; the dissolve pictures are paired because of similarities between the two depicted characters. The beauty of Cinderella and the fine lady of "Ride a Cock Horse to Banbury Cross," two pictorial subjects in *Little Folk's Peep Show,* is likewise a clear link—one concretized in the verse's title, "A Pretty Maid." The comparison between characters becomes a sort of child's guide to folklore and motif, as the child reader can compare different fairy tales in terms of narrative pattern, character features, and so forth.

The connection between characters can also be ridiculous, though, as when *The Fairies' Playtime* pairs Old Mother Hubbard and Cinderella. Once again the dissolving pictures show episodes from the original stories (Figure 4.5). Old Mother Hubbard is pictured with her famous dancing dog and cat, the image conflating the ninth and tenth stanzas of Sarah Catherine Martin's *Comic Adventures of Old Mother Hubbard and Her Dog* (1805), the first printed version of the rhyme: the dog feeding Mother Hubbard's cat and the dog dancing a jig.[69] The dissolve picture of Cinderella shows the girl in her finery, surrounded by a smoky cloud as the Fairy Godmother raises her wand and the pumpkin-coach waits. The cloud seems to operate as a sort of thought bubble, with Cinderella reflecting on her own story here, though from how long ago we cannot tell. Is she still within the early chain of events (her fine pink dress outside a ball setting might suggest otherwise), or is this a depiction of her life after the fairy tale ends?

The accompanying verse "The End of the Story" places the child in the period *after* happily ever after. Following a brief account of the two characters' stories, the narrator offers, "I'll tell you now exactly how / Their stories were completed." Cinderella, after her wedding, "recollected she'd once read / Poor Mother Hubbard's story." While the self-conscious depiction of reading a fairy tale within a fairy tale is itself of interest, the outlandish result of Cinderella's reading is remarkable:

> She made her come and live at Court,
> With servants five and twenty;
> So Mother Hubbard's happy now—
> Her dog gets bones in plenty!

The static black-and-white illustration accompanying this verse shows Old Mother Hubbard curtsying before Cinderella, pictured with her dog and a box labeled "LUGGAGE MRS HUBBARD" (see Figure 4.5). As if to reinforce the unsuitability of these characters as companions for one another, illustrator E. Stuart Hardy depicts Cinderella and Mother Hubbard as denizens of different eras. Cinderella is a medieval princess in an ermine-trimmed robe with a chaplet and veil; Mother Hubbard is the apron-wearing, hook-nosed matron shared across versions of the rhyme (and

FIGURE 4.5. Nister's habit of reusing illustrations means that fairy-tale characters sometimes find themselves unlikely partners in a dissolve, as in *The Fairies' Playtime* (circa 1896). The Bodleian Libraries, the University of Oxford (2012), Opie EE 28.

indeed forebears to it, such as "Dame Trot"). While the dissolving pictures depict the characters in their own tales and adopt visual styles compatible with these tales—knockabout comical hijinks for Old Mother Hubbard and her pets, gauzily hued reverie for Cinderella—the black-and-white illustration foregrounds the unusualness of the relationship, so that the new story becomes a reading of the original tales. The text confirms that the relationship between the two images is metaphoric; however, the comparison between the images seems unconvincing. The awkward grouping of the fairy-tale pictures is retrofitted to outlandish or implausible narrative connections.

The dissolving-view format makes a lack of connection between the two pictures, and by extension the fairy tales they contain, impossible: two characters or stories become physically linked, and it is the job of the versifier and of the child reader to justify those links. In fact, the Fairyland dissolving view reproduces a late Victorian and Edwardian childhood empire of the fairy tale, a sense of the fairy tale as children's common property—the links between fairy tales are justified in no small part because every tale *belongs to the child.* Such a feeling was gaining sway in the 1890s: at the same time Nister was producing his dissolving-view books, the folklorist Andrew Lang released his immensely successful series of Colored Fairy Books, which span from the original *Blue Fairy Book* in 1889 to *The Lilac Fairy Book* in 1910. Much of the nineteenth-century vogue for fairy tales involved the publication of collections by single authors or compilers. Lang himself wrote an introduction to a collection of stories by the Brothers Grimm—the two-volume *Grimm's Household Tales,* translated by Margaret Hunt and published in 1884—and edited Charles Perrault's stories in 1888.[70] The Colored Fairy Books, in contrast, mix stories from a variety of sources. Stories in *The Blue Fairy Book,* for instance, come from Charles Perrault, Madame Leprince de Beaumont, Henri Carnoy, Jean Nicolaides's *Traditions populaires de l'Asie Mineure* (Popular traditions of Asia Minor), and Jonathan Swift's *Gulliver's Travels,* to choose a few examples at random.[71] Lang documents the sources for each assiduously in the early prefaces, along with the fact that certain folklorists objected to his catholic tastes: "In the Yellow Fairy Book, and the rest, there are many tales by persons who are neither savages nor rustics, such as Madame d'Aulnoy and Hans Christian Andersen. The Folk Lore Society, or its president, say that *their* tales are not so true as the rest, and should not be published with the rest. But *we* say that all the stories which are pleasant to read are quite true enough for us."[72]

As Molly Clark Hillard has shown, Lang positioned himself as "simultaneously editor, compiler, superintendent, translator, and adaptor, yet also guardian and owner of the material in the Colored Fairy Books."[73] In addition to this overarching authority, Lang sets up the very rationale for the books as the fact that fairy tales—no matter where they come from—are the child's global birthright. He explores this idea succinctly in *The Pink Fairy Book* (1897)—"All people in the world tell nursery tales to their children"—and rephrases it at greater length in *The Brown Fairy Book* (1904): "All people, black, white, brown, red, and yellow, are like each other when they tell stories; for these are meant for children, who like the same sort of thing, whether they go to school and wear clothes, or, on the other hand, wear skins of beasts, or even nothing at all, and live on grubs and lizards and hawks and crows and serpents, like the little Australian blacks."[74] Fairy tales belong to the child, their universality trumping even the racist counterpoint between well-clothed and schooled white children and indigenous Australian children supposedly subsisting "on grubs and lizards." Fairy tales are childhood's common property.

The child's ownership of the fairy tale can in turn enable critical engagement in what Hillard calls Lang's ideal of the "endlessly renewable resource" of the fairy tale.[75] In fact, this operates once more as a sort of child's own structuralism, where the child's task when encountering a Colored Fairy Book is to think about the principles of combination of character or motif within and across volumes: "A certain number of incidents are shaken into many varying combinations, like the fragments of coloured glass in the kaleidoscope. Probably the possible combinations, like possible musical combinations, are not unlimited in number, but children may be less sensitive in the matter of fairies than Mr. John Stuart Mill was as regards music," Lang writes in *The Grey Fairy Book* (1900).[76] Nister's dissolving-view pieces mimic this logic both formally (recall the kaleidoscopic dissolves, which break the picture down into a whirl of color and then reassemble it) and in terms of the responsibility they imply for the child reader. Fairy tales can be repackaged by Nister's authors and writers in part because the fairy tale is children's to do with what they will—the power transfers from intended reader to publisher, as critically engaged child readers recognize the similarity, connection, or dissimilarity between Jack the Giant Killer and Puss in Boots, or between Old Mother Hubbard and Cinderella.

The textual acrobatics of verses such as "The End of the Story" opportunistically pair pictures of two fairy-tale characters and then craft a poem around these pictures, most probably in order to ensure profitability. At the same time, though, the absurdity of the connections is a source of pleasure in Nister's movables, as the child can mix and remix fairy tales at will. In *S/Z* (1970), Barthes makes a celebrated distinction between the writerly text, that which "can be written (rewritten) today," and the readerly one, in which "reading is nothing more than a *referendum*."[77] In Nister's dissolves, the book's meaning may be constructed by the child reader rather than by the adult writer, as the reader may enjoy the sometimes absurd connections between the two halves of the dissolve. Moreover, this relates to the alteration of familiar dynamics among readers, purchasers, writers, illustrators, publishers, and printers of these books. An offshoot of the Nister book's depiction of its own conditions of production and existence, the wild connections between fairy tales and their characters restore the imaginative possibilities of story to the child reader, while the unrelated dissolve pictures invite the retelling or reliving of the original stories.

## — Chapter Five —

# Going through the Motions

## Lothar Meggendorfer and the Mechanical Book

If Ernest Nister today stands as a canny impresario of the nineteenth-century novelty book—a representative, perhaps, of novelty for novelty's sake—another German creator, the illustrator and paper engineer Lothar Meggendorfer (1847–1925), is by contrast the movable book's most celebrated auteur. Even as early movable books languished in obscurity, Meggendorfer was discussed alongside Hans Christian Andersen and Beatrix Potter by no less a luminary of children's literature than Maurice Sendak.[1] The Movable Book Society, founded by Ann Montanaro, gives its supreme prize for paper engineering in his name.[2] Facsimile editions of Meggendorfer titles have been produced to cater to modern-day fans.[3] In a further compliment to his work, the children's literature scholars Michelle Ann Abate and Amanda Brian have recently written about Meggendorfer's books without treating their unusual formats first and foremost.[4] Meggendorfer can stand on his own as an author-illustrator of picture books *tout court,* rather than only as an author-illustrator of movable picture books.

Meggendorfer was a master of the mechanical or tab-pull book, in which figures on the page move when the reader pulls a tab. The format combines elements of the mechanical toy and the puppet, and these two material analogies offer a key to the format's preoccupations and its intended effects on the child reader. The repetitive movements of the mechanical book, which resemble those of the mechanical toy, lead to a hyperawareness of time in word and image. Time becomes a crucial concern for the books' mechanical actors in ways that relate both to representation and lifelikeness, or its lack, and to labor. Meanwhile, as other critics, including Brian and Margaret Higonnet, have documented, Meggendorfer's books rely on caricatured depictions of a range of types—professional, subcultural, national, and racial.[5] Meggendorfer's caricaturist sensibilities in turn confirm the resemblances between mechanical books and puppetry. Across Meggendorfer's caricatures of "different people" (a direct translation of the title of one of his German-language picture books), the physical power of child readers—assumed by both word and image to be white and middle-class—over the mechanical figures, which they can manipulate at will, metaphoricizes their problematic position of power over the representations the books contain.[6] At the same time, though, mechanical movement threatens to implicate, or even overpower, the reader—child readers become mechanized as they operate the books. Meggendorfer's creations were released in a number of languages, not typically as translations of original German texts but often as new responses to the mechanical illustrations, so at times in this chapter I adopt a comparative methodology—using English, French, and German texts to explore the varied approaches to the illustrations' mechanical movement. While I discuss many different Meggendorfer titles, I focus in particular on the sequence of illustrations released around 1890 in English as *Comic Actors,* in German as *Lustiges Automaten-Theater* (Merry machine theater), and in French as *Les Héritiers de Monsieur Babylas* (The heirs to Mr. Babylas).[7] Throughout, I provide literal translations of Meggendorfer titles in preference to systematically giving the titles of the English versions. This is because the individual titles offer important cues sometimes lost as the books transform across languages—as when *Lustiges Automaten-Theater,* with its privileging of the mechanical or even automatic, becomes *Comic Actors.*

## Like Clockwork: Timing the Mechanical Book and Toy

The seventh movable figure in *Curious Creatures,* Meggendorfer's large-format illustrated bestiary, is a tree frog (Figure 5.1). The only parts of the frog printed on the page are its feet. Otherwise, the frog is fully articulated and jointed: at the ankles, at the hind-leg flexor, at the base of the torso, and at the foreleg. The rivets holding the frog's individual parts to the page can be multipurpose, as when the rivet at its shoulder pivots to enable the jaw's motion, too. The tree frog leaps across the page, attempting to snap up a wasp in its jaws, when the reader pulls a tab at the bottom of the page. The movement reveals Meggendorfer's skill. While paper engineers often choreograph several movements all at once on a page, using connected tabs, the different motions are not often linked together plausibly; in *Dean's Moveable Cock Robin,* for instance, the mechanism alone—not the nursery rhyme—dictates that one tab should move fish, beetle, and linnet in a sort of chain reaction. Meggendorfer, by contrast, uses multiple movements to represent cause and effect: the wasp moves out of reach because the frog has leapt toward it.

Like all of Meggendorfer's creations, this tree frog is a rudimentary sort of mechanical toy—a fact recognized by contemporary reviewers, one of whom, for instance, referred to Meggendorfer's mechanical books as "a most ingenious combination of the story-book and the mechanical toy."[8] The tree frog moves back and forth across the page just as a mechanical toy might move back and forth across the nursery floor. The nature of the movement is similar, too: mechanical illustrations move in repetitive circuits governed by a staccato rhythm. There is little smoothness. (The fact that sometimes mechanical books are today reproduced in GIF form, the jerkiest technology for digitally rendering movement, supports the point.)[9]

The mechanical book's relationship to the mechanical toy links it to a rich set of debates about play, machines, and childhood. Today, such discussions may structure thing theory's investigations of subjects and objects, people and things, as when Bill Brown classifies toys as unusual literary objects because they make the subject "a pretext for the object."[10] Mechanical toys blur the boundaries between subject and object, the animate and the inanimate, even more than other toys, especially in the nineteenth century (their peak of popularity), and this means they become key fodder for debates about art and popular culture. It is the mechanical toy in particular that, for instance, Ruskin dismisses as follows: "You destroy the vitality of a toy to [children], by bringing it too near the imitation of life. You never find a child make a pet of a mechanical mouse that runs about the floor—of a poodle that yelps—of a tumbler who jumps upon wires."[11] Ruskin's classic formulation positions the mechanical as a lesser aesthetic category, one not up to the task of representing life. At

FIGURE 5.1. Lothar Meggendorfer's mechanical tree frog from *Curious Creatures* (circa 1890) leaps across the page, but the wasp it chases is always just out of reach. Henrietta Hochschild Collection of Children's Books, Washington University Libraries, Department of Special Collections, St. Louis, Missouri.

the same time, though, he seems fascinated with mechanical toys: the sense of an unnatural "imitation of life" in this passage inheres to vividly recalled objects from contemporary material culture—the tumbler, the mechanical poodle, and so on.

When Ruskin sees the child's relationship to "vitality" as one in which her own animating spirit, rather than a mechanical animation that is ultimately false, must be brought to bear on the object, his ideas foreshadow twentieth-century opinions on the value of the mechanical book: the Opies' critique of novelty books in "Books That Come to Life" heaps especial scorn on those writers who "put life into their books by the crudest of all possible means, by representing life mechanically."[12] There are, though, important limitations to such a viewpoint, which discounts the ways in which children's mechanical books and toys show us what Tamara Ketabgian describes as "forms of feeling and community that combine the vital and the mechanical, the human and the nonhuman"—forms that are particularly associated with the nineteenth century.[13] Such combinations, as Ketabgian and others (notably, in the field of children's literature criticism, Susan Honeyman and Nathalie op de Beeck) have shown, valuably complicate our picture of mechanical culture by showing mechanical feeling and aesthetics as valuable in their own right, rather than as a failed or lesser category of representation.[14]

The second group of implications to consider when parsing the mechanical book and mechanical toy is their relationship to the uncanny. Mechanical toys often feature in early twentieth-century writings on the subject, specifically, Ernst Jentsch's essay "On the Psychology of the Uncanny" (1906) and Freud's more famous engagement, which draws upon Jentsch, in "The Uncanny" (1919). Jentsch writes that "doubt as to whether an apparently living being is animate and, conversely, doubt as to whether a lifeless object may in fact be animate" reliably produces uncanny effects in an observer, and he anatomizes this feeling using E. T. A. Hoffmann's works, the epileptic fit (with its impression of "mechanical processes" at work on or in the body), and children's windup toys.[15] Freud takes up Jentsch's arguments, linking his ideas specifically to Hoffmann's "The Sandman" (1817), with its mechanical doll Olimpia and—more important—its motif of blinding and eyelessness.[16] Both psychologists posit the child as a figure that generates new emotional engagements with lifelike objects. For Jentsch, children's things might be excluded from uncanniness because of their scale and familiarity: "A doll which closes and opens its eyes by itself, or a small mechanical toy, will cause no notable sensation of [the uncanny], while on the other hand, for example, the lifesize automata that perform complicated tasks, blow trumpets, dance, and so forth, very easily give one a feeling of unease." At the same time, though, the child's animism makes her a natural figure to discuss in relation to uncanny feelings: "Small children speak in all seriousness to a chair, to their spoon, to an old rag, and so on, hitting out full of anger at lifeless things in order to punish them."[17] Freud also points out children's animistic tendencies, but he links them to pleasure instead of anger: children differ from other groups in their tendency "not [to] distinguish at all sharply between living and lifeless objects." "Children," writes Freud, "have no fear of their dolls coming to life, they may even desire it."[18] Freud (after Jentsch) hypothesizes a child who might challenge, refuse, or play with the categories of inanimate and animate, drawing pleasure from the recognition of and then possible transgression of the difference. Children's mechanical books and toys work in the same way, muddling the boundaries between subject and object. In the mechanical book, the incorporation of the mechanism into a book—that especially affective childhood object—perhaps inscribed to commemorate a particular moment, as explored in chapter 4, sharpens the effect.

Finally, though, the mechanical toy has a special relationship to time. As Susan Stewart remarks, the mechanical toy offers "a repetition and closure that the everyday world finds impossible. The mechanical toy threatens an infinite pleasure; it does not tire or feel, it simply works or doesn't work."[19] Wound up and set going, a mechanical toy completes one set of actions (if it does not malfunction, that is) before beginning its temporal cycle again. Meggendorfer's mechanical illustrations operate in like fashion: the simple movements of each animated piece give a tiny model of narrative—a beginning and an ending, a telescoped but complete plot. There is, as Jacqueline Reid-Walsh writes, "no possibility of error and variety built into the design. The end results are always the same. Since the actions are 'mechanical' they are also repeatable (until the material of the book breaks down)."[20] The texts that accompany Meggendorfer's illustrations may seek to reconcile these movements, meditating upon what Stewart calls the "repetition and closure" of the mechanized object, with its threat of the infinite and its radical temporal systems.

The mechanical toy's dual preoccupations with aliveness and with time, transmitted also to the mechanical book, are brought together in a final associated object: the automaton. In the eighteenth century, automata shifted, as Jessica Riskin has shown in her work on the inventor Jacques de Vaucanson, from "amusements and feats of technical virtuosity" to "philosophical experiments, attempts to discern which aspects of living creatures could be reproduced in machinery, and to what degree, and what such reproductions might reveal about their natural subjects."[21] Mechanical toys and books are not automata: they overtly require human operation, and hence do not create the same intellectual uncertainty as to whether they are living beings as automata do. Nonetheless, mechanical toys might be marketed as automata by those who seek (in George Speaight's phrase) to make "a mystery of their manipulation," and for Hildegard Krahé, Meggendorfer's creations are paper androids—inheritors to the eighteenth-century automata of Vaucanson and Pierre Jaquet-Droz, no less.[22] The resemblance between the mechanical book and the automaton provides a genealogical precursor for the mechanical book's hyperawareness of time, related in part to the mechanical toy's perpetual lifelikeness.

The title of Meggendorfer's *Aus dem Leben* (From life) already plays on the potentially uncanny relationship between actual life and the lifelike mechanisms between the book's covers; like many of Meggendorfer's books, *Aus dem Leben* is also full of clocks, watches, and other timepieces. One mechanical picture shows a mother, in dirndl and braided coiffure, rocking her baby's cradle (Plate 14). The window behind her opens onto a picturesque alpine scene. When the child reader pulls the tab, the cradle moves from side to side, keeping time with the pendulum of a clock on the wall to the rear of the figure grouping. Meggendorfer's mechanical mother is like an automaton, which is, as Daniel Tiffany writes, "a clock without hands or face," while pulling the tab is like winding a clock, reaffirming what Dolf Sternberger calls the mechanical object's "navel cord"—its connection to the human.[23] But the image comprises multiple other temporal systems and time schemes. There is domestic time, nested within or overlaying the wider historical time in which this moment takes place—the wooden cradle has "1882" carved into its foot—but there is also eternal time, introduced via pictures on the wall of the Holy Family, which draw an implicit parallel between this mother and child and the divine ones. In fact, this picture encompasses three of the crucial temporal modes posed by the narratologist Mieke Bal: a maternal micro time marked by a "routine of small acts of care"; the "long-term sense of time" gleaned from history; and monumental time, which "aspires to eternity."[24] The poem on the page facing the illustration, "An der Wiege" (By the cradle), expands the image's temporal knowledges, as it concerns what we might now call downtime, in that the baby keeps her mother awake, and the mother wonders when she will be able to rest. The written text reveals, though, that the baby has no intention of letting this happen, so that the internal conceit of the poem self-reflexively amplifies the frozenness of the image: mechanical figures wait for something to happen that will not happen. As a corollary, it is the child reader, not the figures within the book, who understands and has power over time.

Other Meggendorfer books engage their own repetitions as a type of futility. Sometimes this occurs by way of mechanical animals. The frog and the wasp, or a weasel and field mice, in *Curious Creatures* short-circuit what might seem certain dynamics between predator and prey, with the text sometimes registering an impasse: "And the frog makes another grasp / But it is no use, whatever he does / He will never catch that wasp." Other animals are trapped in their mechanical positions to more poignant effect, as when a dancing bear in the early editions of *Aus dem Leben* is forced by the ring in his nose to dance forever. In *Comic Actors,* one of the most technically accomplished movable pages shows a hunter who, pursued by a wild boar, has climbed a tree (Figure 5.2). The mechanical action consists of his body movement—hitting the boar with the butt of his rifle—and the boar's own motion upward, which mimics an animal bucking in a remarkably lifelike manner. The English text poses the mechanical movements of these two figures as a sort of existential crisis:

> In vain to beat him or call for aid,
> The boar will not budge from the tree,
> The sportsman a great mistake has made
> And wishes he could be free.

This poem presents actions at once depicted in the image and not depicted in the image. The sense in which the hunter's attempts to save himself are "in vain" derives as much from the mechanical nature of the movements, the inevitability of the characters moving back and forth in a prescribed sweep, as from, say, the fortitude of the boar. While the threat of lifelessness and an inability to progress through time are constant components of the mechanical image, where repetitive movements evoke characters locked within their actions and reactions, the written texts to Meggendorfer's books may, then, narrate these features directly.

At other points in *Comic Actors,* the verbal play with the repetitions and stoppages of mechanical illustrations is related specifically to childhood experiences, as in the page opening showing a mechanical photographer. In the course of its three stanzas, the poem accounts for both the book and its illustration. For example, the mechanical figure has "eyes that are ever awake" in the poem's world but also in the illustration in front of the reader (Figure 5.3). The photographer's mechanical movement to check his pocket watch, which happens when the reader pulls the tab, underscores the ways in which the illustration keeps time. Right arm (riveted at the shoulder and holding the camera cover) moves down, revealing the lens; left arm, holding the watch, moves up and into view; eyes move across (directed at the watch). The verse's plot is once more self-referential: the photographer narrates the poem, with the child reader sitting for her portrait. The long exposure time and static process of posing for even a late nineteenth-century photograph—a textual injunction for the reader (as portrait

FIGURE 5.2. The naturalistic bucking movement of a boar's head in *Lustiges Automaten-Theater/Comic Actors* (circa 1890) shows the complexity of Meggendorfer's paper engineering. Staatsbibliothek zu Berlin.

sitter) to "stand still," just as the photographer himself does—are other modes of timekeeping, further reflecting on the conditions of representation. The direct address to a child reader relates the mechanical book's time schemes to control—instructions to be quiet, to be still, to be patient, and so on—and to social class, given the expense and prestige of having a studio portrait taken. The poem at once naturalistically reproduces boredom and being controlled as reliable childhood feelings and creates a camaraderie between the child reader and the mechanical photographer, whose own movements are so curtailed.

The relationship between childhood, repetition, and time takes on special resonance, though, in the mechanical book's interest in a further, more specific context for marking time in the nineteenth century: what Steven Dillon has called "the oppressive time-consciousness of the workingman's clock."[25] Susan Stewart argues that "the eighteenth and nineteenth centuries mark the heyday of the automaton, just

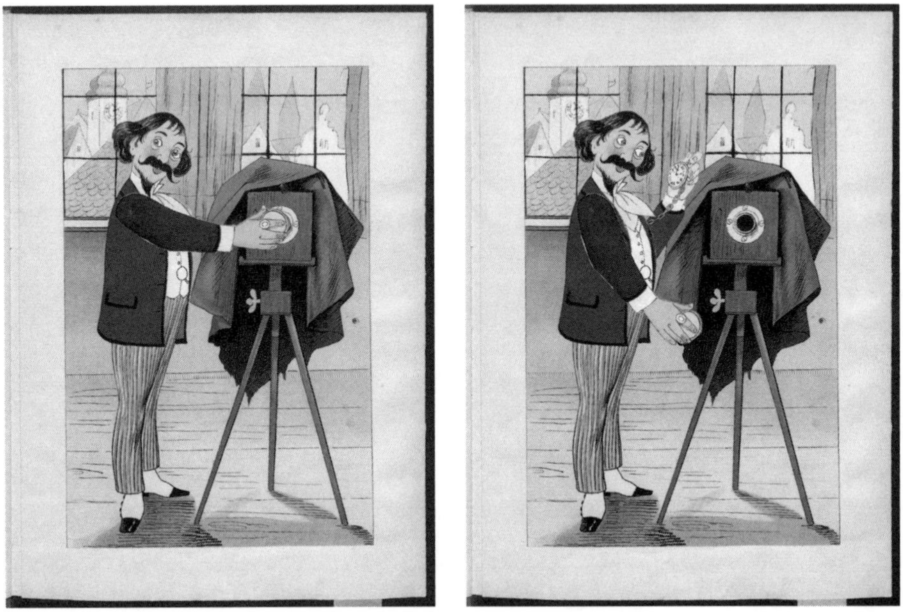

FIGURE 5.3. The photographer in *Lustiges Automaten-Theater/Comic Actors* instructs the child reader, imagined in the text as posing for her portrait as she looks at the book, to keep still. Staatsbibliothek zu Berlin.

as they mark the mechanization of labor: jigging Irishmen, whistling birds, clocks with bleating sheep, and growling dogs guarding baskets of fruit," and mechanical books tend to support her timeline.[26] The full title of one Dean mechanical book, for instance, is *The History of How Ned Nimble Built His Cottage, Showing the Trades of Bricklayer, Sawyer, Carpenter.* The volume socializes boys into manual labor, giving the reader a child avatar in the form of Ned's younger brother, who watches the sawing of logs, the laying of bricks, and so forth. A second example is Darton's *Moveable Trades, Showing the Mechanical Movements in Each Trade to Instruct and Amuse Children.*[27] (In a pleasingly self-conscious gesture, the trades of printer and bookbinder are included.) Other titles, such as Dean's tab-pull version of *This Is the House That Jack Built* from 1860, pick up preexisting tales focused on manual labor. Indeed, in Dean's *House That Jack Built,* the format interprets afresh the rhyme, which comes (like the mechanical book) to seem gripped by action and movement as various figures build, eat, kill, worry, toss, milk, kiss, marry, crow, and finally sow.[28] Even for a book artist working in a format imbricated with work, though, Meggendorfer depicts a breathtaking array of mechanical laborers, from tailors to blacksmiths to domestic workers to cooks (Figure 5.4).[29] Rather than depicting particular sorts of work (factory work, for instance) as mechanized, Meggendorfer's illustrations make all labor seem mechanized by representing it with movable figures.

Supporting this reading, different jobs are often marked, because of the importance of the book's movable parts, by the particular types of actions they entail—"showing the mechanical movements in each trade," as Darton has it. This is particularly evident in *Comic Actors,* where Meggendorfer has (as Higonnet remarks) "captured not only the distinctive garments and products but the *movements* that typify each kind of work."[30] Consider the verse and movable pieces depicting the tailor (see Figure 5.4). Each stanza describes a separate movement on the page: "The iron moves both to and fro / Guided by Mr Snip," "The tailor works with thought and care / And knits his brows as well." Mr. Snip, whose personal name reduces his character to his profession alone, holds the iron in his right hand and moves it across the jacket when the tab is pulled, the left hand smoothing the fabric. (This left arm slides in and out of a slit in the page.) The movements on this page are smaller than those at other points in the book, but in their minuteness of action they evoke the monotonous rhythm of the tailor's labor. This is the world of work as repetition, in which the worker is reduced to one function—one movement—only. In fact, perhaps function and movement collapse into one another.

If the photographer page opening in *Comic Actors* represents its child readers' experiences of time—the bourgeois occasion of having a studio portrait taken, as well as the more generalized childhood experience of being told what to do with one's time—the mechanical book also implies that its child readers have an abundance of leisure. The reader is often a person who does not mark time. This economy is especially notable in Victorian children's literature, where the child bestowed with books to read for pleasure is the child who does not work; the child is excluded from the economies and tasks the books depict, even when a figure such as Ned Nimble provides an induction to them. As op de Beeck has noted of early twentieth-century American picture books, a fascination with mechanical objects and machine labor does not mean that child readers have their attention drawn to the plight of actual laborers, as picture books "seldom, if ever, propose alternatives to class hierarchies,

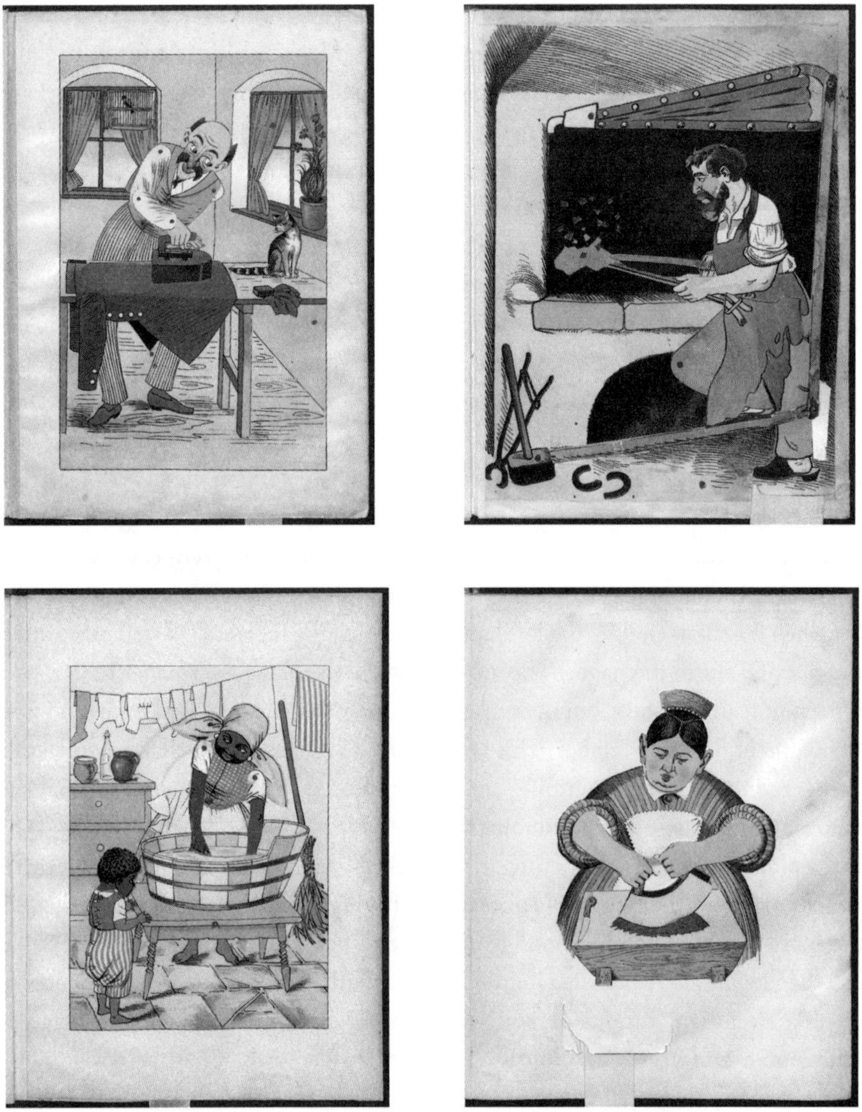

FIGURE 5.4. Meggendorfer's interest in work spans his mechanical books: a tailor irons a coat in *Lustiges Automaten-Theater/Comic Actors*; a blacksmith stokes his fire in the tenth edition of *Aus dem Leben* (From life); a girl does the family washing in *Lustige Ziehbilder* (Merry tab-pull pictures); and a young cook chops spinach in *Lebende Bilder* (Living pictures). Staatsbibliothek zu Berlin.

mind-numbing assembly-line jobs, and industrial production and consumerism."[31] The high prices for mechanical books at many points during the century—as noted in chapter 1, Meggendorfer's mechanical volumes cost seven shillings and sixpence in England—marked them out as status items that would have been inaccessible to any of the workers depicted within their pages. The mechanical book format thus encouraged spectacular pleasure in mechanical movement and repetitive labor without suggesting that the latter was a problem in the world outside the book.

The split between the child reader and Meggendorfer's workers is, then, pronounced. But the format of the mechanical book queers this dynamic. A sort of *contagion* occurs when the reader pulls the tab: the reader performs rudimentary movements, the same actions over and over again, just as the mechanical figures do. Indeed, part of Meggendorfer's vaunted genius as a paper engineer is his ability to convey a sense of the mechanical book's own time scheme—to synchronize book user and illustration. Sendak praises Meggendorfer's control of the temporal schemes of his mechanical pieces: "One *could* speed up the action by pulling the tabs more quickly, but after some experience, one begins to sense the speed at which Meggendorfer must have intended these pictures to move."[32] The rhythm is catching, as the page openings encourage repeated pulling; child readers perform work with the book that matches the smaller repetitive movements—the drudgery—of the mechanical figures' tasks, even as they remain excluded from those tasks in real life.

## Different People: Puppet, Caricature, and Type in the Mechanical Book

Searching for a framing device for the first publication of *Vanity Fair* in volume form in 1848, Thackeray took a friend's suggestion of the puppet show. The resulting preface has the narrator "proud to think that his Puppets have given satisfaction to the very best company in this empire" and reporting the special praise accorded to the "little Becky Puppet [which] has been pronounced to be uncommonly flexible in the joints and lively on the wire."[33] The famous metaphor has a number of effects. First, it is self-deprecating and irreverent, as the narrator-puppeteer is depicted in the novel's frontispiece as little better than a down-on-his-luck showman or fool. This extends from persona to technique, as the attributes of *Vanity Fair*'s puppet-characters, in particular the "flexible" and "lively" Becky, upend criteria for judging the realist novel. Thackeray encourages us not to see Becky as E. M. Forster's prototypical round character, a triumph of literature's ability to represent the world accurately, but rather as artificial—as nonnaturalistic.[34] The analogy reveals the "lively" or lifelike and the natural in literature as nothing more than the puppet's simulation of these things. Second, though, the puppet metaphor stresses the author-artist's control: a version of the ancient metaphors of puppet and puppet master, in which the puppet is "emblem of the human simulacrum as an inferior entity manipulated by a superior entity," couched in terms not of a divine creator but of a literary one.[35] By extension, it places the audience on the same level as the spectator of the puppet show, foregrounding the narrator's mastery over his characters and novelistic world.

Thackeray, however, concludes the novel with different puppeteers. The last sentence of *Vanity Fair* reads: "Come children, let us shut up the box and the puppets, for our play is played out."[36] In Thackeray's original woodcut illustration, the embedded text "FINIS" appears on the inner lid of the toy box, and the puppeteers are two little girls; perhaps they represent Thackeray's two surviving daughters, Annie and Minny, who were around eight and ten years old when the novel was released (Figure 5.5). More broadly, the girls in the picture signal—along with the final line of the novel, with its imperative address to its readers as children—a shift in power dynamics. Thackeray completes *Vanity Fair* not by reiterating the author's mastery over his characters but by providing a symbolic position of power for the reader. The reader becomes a participant in the staging of the puppet show; the puppet metaphor no longer conveys a self-portrait of the author as on the title page but rather a suggestion of the reader's power. Moreover, this occurs by way of the child, who acts as the avatar for all readers.[37]

As with Thackeray's puppets, the analogy between puppets and the figures in the mechanical book raises questions of childhood, control, and being controlled. "A puppet," writes George Speaight, "is an inanimate figure moved by human agency."[38] If the mechanical book is a book of puppets, by extension its child reader is a puppet master—the child's manipulation of the mechanical book provides a metaphor for, and even a form of, control. But what, exactly, does the child control in Meggendorfer's mechanical books? The answer to this question relates in part to the multivalent connections between the puppet and the mechanical book, which range from material form to subject matter to aesthetic allegiances.[39] First of all, mechanical books and puppets share construction materials—nineteenth-century puppeteers often used pasteboard puppets for reasons of economy or portability.

FIGURE 5.5. W. M. Thackeray's final illustration in *Vanity Fair* (1848) shows two little girls putting away their toys, with puppets of Dobbin and Amelia peeking out from the toy chest and the glowering Becky puppet on the floor to the right. Courtesy of Macmillan Brown Library, University of Canterbury, Aotearoa New Zealand.

Indeed, Meggendorfer's figures are *assembled* into books rather than into puppets: before a book is made, the component designs of each of its mechanical figures are laid out like the parts of the flat, jointed *pantin,* or jumping jack.[40] Mechanical books frequently refer to the puppet show, as in *Dean and Son's Moveable Book of the Royal Punch and Judy,* where a showman figure beating a drum appears on each page (Figure 5.6); this includes Meggendorfer's works, which draw on German traditions of the Kasperl puppet show.[41] Moreover, as the examples of Punch, Judy, and Kasperl suggest, both the mechanical book and the puppet show offer *caricatures.*

As with the interest in labor, links between the mechanical book and caricature span from earlier visual and material culture through to Meggendorfer. For example, Dean's *Moveable Shadows for the People: Second Series* (1857) is illustrated by William Newman, a prolific contributor to *Punch*; Newman has rejiggered *Ombres*

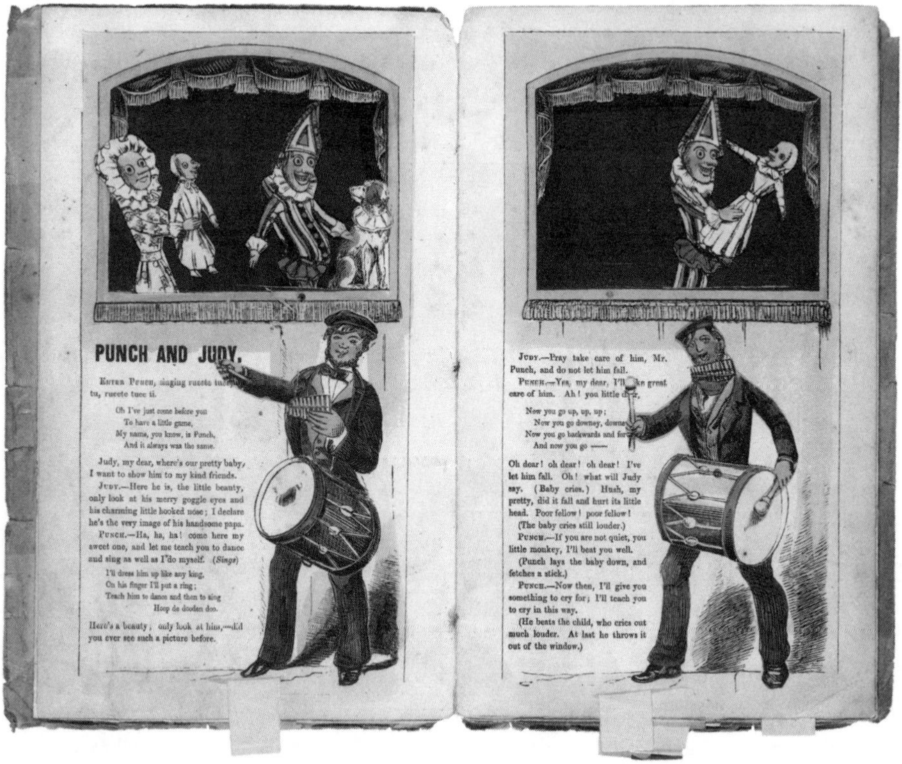


FIGURE 5.6. Titles such as *Dean and Son's Moveable Book of the Royal Punch and Judy* (1861) foreground the connection between mechanical books and puppetry, as each page features a miniature puppet-show tableau. TS 561.1.257 F. Houghton Library, Harvard University.

*portées* (Projected shadows), a series of earlier prints by the French caricaturist J. J. Grandville, for a mechanical format.[42] The shadows of a series of caricatured stock figures, captioned as "Honest John Bull," "The Old Woman," "The Conceited Ass," and so on, reveal their resemblances to different animals when the tabs are pulled. (The fact that Newman illustrated the short-lived satirical magazine *The Puppet Show* completes the syncretic triangulation of mechanical book, puppet, and caricature.) Meggendorfer himself was a caricaturist and cartoonist for two popular German magazines, *Fliegende Blätter* (Flying pages) and its spin-off *Meggendorfer Blätter* (Meggendorfer pages).

Both mechanical book and puppet show frequently adopted exaggerated visual modes that fit Ernst Kris and Ernst Gombrich's foundational definition of a caricatured style based in "conscious distortion."[43] Significantly, mechanical books and puppetry also mined traditions of caricature for a bank of possible subjects for illustration: they adopted the caricature's classificatory, typifying, and physiognomic impulses. The caricature in this mode offers not an individual but rather (to quote Martha Banta) "a type that stands alone," an idea that nineteenth-century mechanical books visualize.[44] Meggendorfer's comical studies, Newman's movable shadows, and the English tourist consulting his guidebook in the French mechanical book *Les Excentriques* (The eccentrics) literally stand or sit alone on the page, their peccadilloes heightened by the fact that each is presented in isolation (Plate 15).[45]

There are many permutations of the type in Meggendorfer's mechanical books. Recall the tree frog: in *Curious Creatures,* the divisions between species are one popular manifestation of the type, and a type constitutively not rounded and individualized, as none of the animals have proper names. The cast of occupations in Meggendorfer's books—tailor, cook, musician, photographer, blacksmith—provides a further example: the type can relate to the workaday function. Leisure activities, rather than professional ones, might serve a similar role, as in the case of a well-to-do gentleman taking his fine horse over a jump in *Aus dem Leben,* who is typified by his glamorous hobby. Meggendorfer's frequent depiction of the dandy is another mode, as demonstrated by the titular figure in *Scenes in the Life of a Masher.* (Abate helpfully glosses *masher* as "a slang term referring to a man of fashion in the late Victorian and Edwardian periods.")[46] Meggendorfer's *Verschiedene Leute* (Different people) smoothly aligns various forms of difference, as occupations such as chambermaid become equivalent to subcultural types, such as the dandy, or ethnicities, such as Japanese (Figure 5.7). The one thing the mechanical figures share across the book is the fact that they are not individualized but rather typified.

As Meggendorfer's illustration of a Japanese woman suggests, one of the most persistent examples of the type in Meggendorfer's works is ethnographic—from "different people" to "other people." In these examples, the conversion from individual to type is a colonizing process. "If the caricature fits," Kris and Gombrich write, "the victim really *is* transformed in our eyes. We learn through the artist to see him as a caricature."[47] While Kris and Gombrich refer to political caricature and celebrity lampoon here, their observations are also germane to racist modes of caricature,

FIGURE 5.7. This mechanical figure of a Japanese woman and child from the second edition of *Verschiedene Leute* (Different people; circa 1902) demonstrates Meggendorfer's interest in human types, whether professional, subcultural, or racialized. Staatsbibliothek zu Berlin.

and to the didactic or otherwise socializing impulses of the children's book. Judith Wechsler remarks that caricature crucially involves "the description of people from without."[48] The mechanical book physicalizes this tendency in its invitation to the reader to *manipulate* figures from without.

Furthermore, the movement that occurs after this manipulation heightens both caricatural mode (distortion) and subject (type). While puppets were called *motions* and puppeteers *motion-men* for centuries, the techniques of the moving parts in the mechanical book—the jerky motion of wiggling eyebrows or a dropping jaw—are grotesque over and above the exaggerated and stylized approach of the illustrations. Moreover, the conjunction of racist caricature, particularly involving black figures, with mechanical movement is highly charged. The nature of the tab-pull book's animatedness corresponds to the discourses of "excessively 'lively' or 'agitated' ethnic subjects" that govern racialized caricatures and animations, as identified by Sianne Ngai. "The affective state of being 'animated,'" says Ngai, "seems to imply the most basic or minimal of all affective conditions: that of being, in one way or another, 'moved.'" Ngai summarizes the transaction by which "the seemingly neutral state of 'being moved' becomes twisted into the image of the overemotional racialized subject, abetting his or her construction as unusually receptive to external control"—that is, as a sort of puppet.[49] The mechanical book formally realizes links between race and animatedness in its black puppet figures, whose exaggerated, racially stereotyped features are animated into outlandish movement. This further means, as Abate and Higonnet have both observed, that the child reader heightens—or becomes directly responsible for—the mockery as she pulls a tab.[50]

Two of Meggendorfer's images of black characters, both featured in *Comic Actors,* provide particularly detailed evidence of the links between racist caricature, puppetry, animation, and the mechanical book for children. Each image—the first showing a black dandy, the second a black nurse with a white child—reprises stereotypes that can be traced through a variety of modes of popular visual culture, including blackface minstrelsy. Contrasting the English, French, and German texts is in the case of these page openings instructive, as these are different versions, not translations stemming from one original text. This is a feature of the international publication of Meggendorfer's books, recently explored by Higonnet, and of the relatively fluid parameters for movable books in general, which divide labor—writer from illustrator; illustrator from paper engineer; writer, illustrator, and paper engineer from printer-publisher-assembler and so on—so as to use movable images as discrete components to be repackaged and reframed as needed.[51] In the case of ethnic caricature, though, the different texts do not always share specifics of plot or tone; as a result, they work unpredictably either to underscore or to undermine the racial politics of the illustrations. In the process, they suggest the tendency Eric Lott finds in the mid-nineteenth-century minstrel show toward "a simultaneous drawing up and crossing of racial boundaries."[52]

The first caricatured mechanical image shows an elaborately dressed black man sitting at a table; he has a long-stemmed pipe in his left hand, and his right hand holds a newspaper that partially obscures his face (Figure 5.8).[53] When the tab is pulled, multiple motions happen at once: the dandy's eyes close and then open in a blinking action, his newspaper moves to reveal the bottom of his face, and his left arm comes up to put the pipe to his now-open mouth. The dandy's clothes are foregrounded: blue-and-black vertical-stripe trousers, red-and-white horizontal-stripe socks, wide-lapelled white jacket and waistcoat, heart-patterned shirt with matching hatband and contrasting cuffs, yellow cravat, large yellow cufflinks, yellow gloves, and two-tone pointy-toed shoes with contrasting laces. The intended effects of this illustration on the child readers of *Comic Actors* seem to be twofold, but linked. First, the illustration aims to initiate (white) child readers into an established visual vocabulary of racist caricatures of black subjects: a child-size incarnation of what Homi Bhabha has identified as the stereotype's vacillation "between what is always 'in place,' already known, and something that must be anxiously repeated"—in this case, visually repeated in front of, or to, children.[54] Second, the illustration promotes an approved response to these conventions, that is, mockery and dismissal of the black dandy.[55] The first aim is achieved by means of caricatural exaggeration—here, the use of a common code drawn from blackface minstrelsy in which, as Michael Harris puts it, "exaggerated red lips, dark skin, and a wide-eyed expression" signify blackness.[56] (Imagery drawn from blackface minstrelsy has underpinned multiple icons of children's culture, from Raggedy Ann to the Cat in the Hat.)[57] The mechanical movement, which consolidates the caricature's othering work, achieves the second aim, as the dandy's moving eyes at times roll back into his head so that he looks eyeless and inhuman, and as it is the mechanical movement that creates his wide-mouthed grin.

At the same time, the stereotypes Meggendorfer inculcates are interwoven: the illustration combines the subcultural stereotype of the dandy with caricatured

FIGURE 5.8. The racist caricature of a dandy from *Lustiges Automaten-Theater/Comic Actors* partially obscures the figure's blackness in the course of the mechanical movement. In this copy, the original newspaper he reads has been replaced with a placeholder piece. Staatsbibliothek zu Berlin.

blackness. This play with linked subcultural and racial types is not new; in fact, one of the two foundational characters in American blackface minstrelsy—the other being the southern slave, Jim Crow—was the northern dandy, Zip Coon, who "exhibited airs beyond his lowly status, dressed as a dandy, and mangled standard English."[58] Dandies were also visually interlaid with black minstrelsy in the illustrations that appeared on the sheet music for popular songs and ballads such as "Dandy Jim, from Caroline" and "The Dandy Broadway Swell."[59] At the same time, though, Meggendorfer's mechanical dandy resembles iconic British images of aesthetic dandies, such as that purveyed in "An Æsthetic Midday Meal," a cartoon by George du Maurier (Figure 5.9).[60] Both illustrations feature an elaborately attired man sitting with legs crossed at a small round pedestal table, a simple vase of flowers adorning the table. More important, where the twinned stereotypes are concerned, Meggendorfer uses the newspaper to pretend at a scene of passing, until the

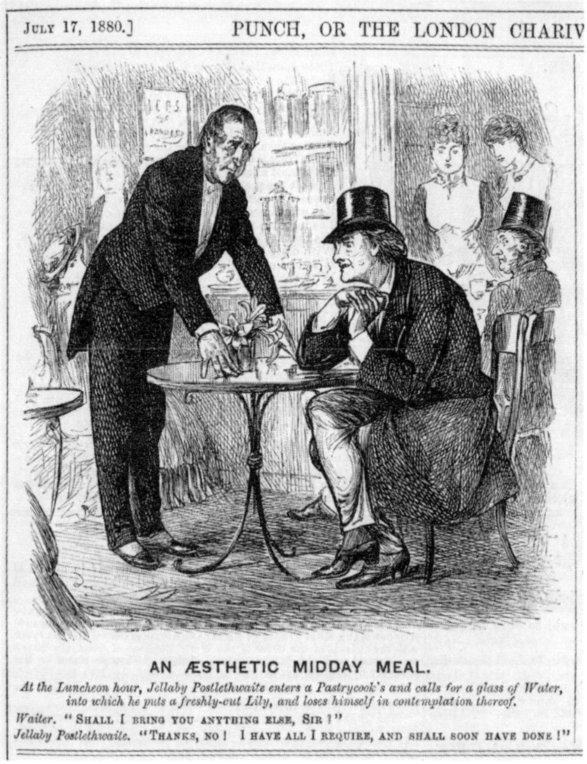


FIGURE 5.9. Meggendorfer's dandy recalls George du Maurier's famous *Punch* cartoon of his recurring aesthetic dandy character, Jellaby Postlethwaite, published on July 17, 1880. Courtesy of Macmillan Brown Library, University of Canterbury, Aotearoa New Zealand.

mechanical movement heightens the racist caricature so that any doubt as to the dandy's race is dispelled.

The different versions of the text approach the Meggendorfer illustration in a variety of ways. In the German poem "Das Negergigerl" (The Negro dandy, *Gigerl* being an obsolete word for dandy or fop) in *Lustiges Automaten-Theater,* the emphasis changes from stanza to stanza. The first stanza stresses the dandy's modishness; the second, his enjoyment of his newspaper; the third, the ingeniousness of the movements engineered by Meggendorfer as the dandy can "even" bring the pipe up to his mouth. While in the German and English versions the text involves a sequence of discrete poems, *Héritiers de Monsieur Babylas,* the French version of the book (written by Ernest d'Hervilly, an acquaintance of Arthur Rimbaud and Paul Verlaine), is a prose narrative notable for linking together the different "comic actors" in one story, and for giving many of them proper names—if typified ones.[61] D'Hervilly has the dandy, named César and given an American backstory as "a charming fop from overseas," protest the superiority of his race, noting that a tobacco pipe is valuable only once it is blackened with smoke. While the specifics of the French and German texts differ—significantly, in the fact that d'Hervilly explicitly links César to the United States—the crux of each poem is comical mockery of the black dandy.

The English text, titled "The Dandy Nigger" in a more pejorative translation of the German "Negergigerl," continues this emphasis, but with a significant adjustment: the verse directly references the way that the mechanics of the illustration can conceal the dandy's race. The image is described thus: "His face is hidden by the book, / We wish it could be seen." Henry Wonham points out that racist caricature typically attempts to present ethnicity as "fixed and discernible."[62] By contrast, this poem hints at a racial *indiscernibility* in the illustration, imagining a hiding of the dandy's blackness. Such play with stereotypes—the threat posed by a mimicry that is also a discrete new form of signification, of cultural know-how—is at the heart of the figure of the black dandy, as Monica Miller has noted.[63] In fact, it could be traced back to the black dandy as a type symbolizing historical challenges to the policing of racial boundaries, by way of the black dandy's earlier association (remarked by Lott) with abolitionism, amalgamation, and miscegenation in the American context.[64]

The black dandy's particular purchase in *Comic Actors* depends on the way the illustration is physically constructed—the mechanics of its composition. The text dramatizes a scene of passing, of troubled distinctions between categories, made possible by the movable parts. As such, the movement comes to challenge the child reader's control of the puppetlike movable figures and the safe associated control of types and stereotypes from which the white child is excluded or immune. The child reader, the English text imagines, has believed she was contemplating one type when she was really contemplating another. At the same time, this playfulness can be countenanced only if any indiscernibility is ultimately dispelled, as when the text describes the changes wrought by a pull of the tab:

> We move the picture up and down
> And then he laughs you see
> Not like a dandy but a clown
> And these do not agree.

Ultimately, the poem splits the black dandy into two types—into dandy and "clown," coded as black—insisting that these are mutually exclusive. The boundaries between races may be troubled, but only if racial hierarchies can be restored at the end of the poem—by the child who pulls a tab to heighten the dandy's stereotyped blackness.

A similar dynamic plays out in the final illustration in *Comic Actors* and its accompanying texts. The mechanical picture shows a black nurse holding a white baby (Plate 16). The scenario is given in the poem's title: "Washing the Black Nurse." A little white girl, the sole mechanical figure in the illustration, hinged at the waist and shoulders, leans toward the nurse and moves a sponge back and forth across her face. ("The Dandy Nigger" and "Washing the Black Nurse" are the only racist caricatures in the book; they are also the only mechanical illustrations in which the movement works to obscure or reveal the figures' faces.) The mise-en-scène implies a colonial context—the figures are pictured in an open-air marbled colonnade, the nurse holds a fan to ward off the hot weather, and the baby is swathed in mosquito netting.[65] A small African gray parrot perches on the chair's rear spindle. The nurse's own accoutrements, including her gold bangle and earrings, Turkish slippers, and beaded necklace with pendant crescent moons, provide further exotic detail.

The English, German, and French texts accompanying this illustration all narrate a scenario of washing the black nurse white. Brian calls the joke about washing the black nurse white an old German one, and Nana Badenberg observes that "the idea of *Mohrenwäsche* (The Whitewashing of the Moor) has been a powerful concept in German-language culture since premodern times, giving rise to stereotypes and idioms that persist to this day."[66] (The title of Meggendorfer's verse is indeed "Die Mohrenwäsche.") In fact, though, the conceit is proverbial in European cultures from the ancient world onward. It echoes Bible verses, such as the book of Jeremiah's "Can the Ethiopian change his skin, or the leopard his spots?" (13:23 KJV), and Aesopic fables, such as number 393 in the Perry Index of Aesopica: "Someone saw a black man from India washing himself in a river and said to him, 'You better keep still and not stir up the mud in the water, or you are never going to turn that body of yours white!' *This fable shows that nothing in this world can change its nature.*"[67] While this is Laura Gibbs's recent translation, titled "The Black Man in the River," nineteenth-century versions derived from the Greek prose of Aesop make the black man or "Æthiop" a servant whose new master, "persuaded that the colour of his skin arose from dirt contracted through the neglect of his former masters," subjects him to a series of "incessant scrubbings" that make the servant sick.[68] The English expression "to wash the blackamoor white" was in popular usage in England from the sixteenth through nineteenth centuries and provoked a number of Victorian variations, as in, for example, "Washing the Maharajah White," a cartoon that appeared in *Punch* on July 17, 1858.[69] The concomitant French phrase appears in Gustave Flaubert's letters. Flaubert writes that he could no more change the name of one of his characters once decided than change the color of the character's skin, and to emphasize (in line with the Aesopic and vernacular English usages) the impossible nature of such an endeavor, he follows up the point thus: "It's like wanting to bleach a Negro."[70]

In its constellation of the black subject, washing, and the child, this illustration also recalls soap advertisements contemporary with *Comic Actors,* as Brian has noted elsewhere.[71] Anne McClintock describes the most famous such image, in an advertising campaign for Pears' soap (Figure 5.10), thus: "A white boy, clothed in a white apron—the familiar fetish of domestic purity—bends benevolently over his 'lesser' brother, bestowing upon him the precious talisman of racial progress." In the fact, however, that the washing is "imperfect"—the black boy's body turns white, but his head remains black—such pictures imagine "a passive racial hybrid, part black, part white, brought to the brink of civilization by the twin commodity fetishes of soap and mirror."[72] According to Tanya Sheehan and Henry Louis Gates Jr., Pears' thus maintained racial boundaries: "Leaving the boy's face black . . . encouraged consumers to laugh at the advertisement and buy Pears' soap rather than perceive it as a threat to the immutability of white dominance."[73] The washing is always doomed to failure, and therein lies the point of both the proverb and the Pears' promotions.

Yet, in a way that parallels the dual-coded black dandy, some of the written texts accompanying Meggendorfer's illustration introduce an ambiguity to the racial hierarchy between white and black. Carol Mavor has argued that the Pears' advertisements envisage an "indeterminable reciprocity between the races" by having a white figure in service to a black one.[74] In the soap advertisements, both the characters are usually children. In *Comic Actors,* the white child washes an adult employee of the family—a servant, in fact. The ambiguity (the "reciprocity," in Mavor's term) of the scene of the child's washing the black nurse is complicated by the possibility that the nurse is a *wet* nurse. While the word *nourrice* in the French text makes this explicit, details of the nurse's pose, including the baby's position near her breast and the deep V of her blouse or shawl, suggest such a reading (as does the colonial context

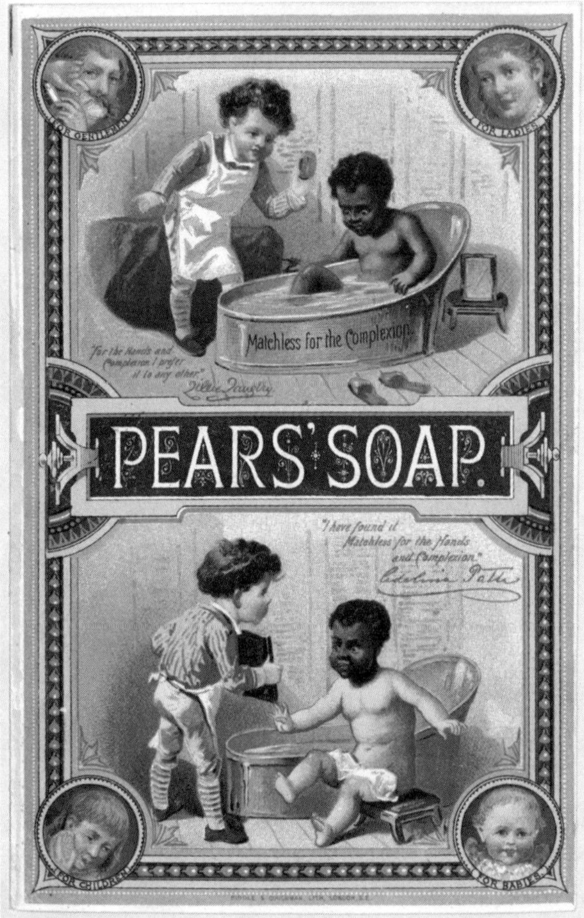


FIGURE 5.10. Meggendorfer's caricature of the black nurse being "washed" echoes a famous fin de siècle advertising campaign for Pears' soap. The Bodleian Libraries, the University of Oxford (2009), John Johnson Collection Soap 8 (11).

for the illustration) even when the text does not state it outright. This is significant because, as Valerie Fildes points out, the black wet nurse is a "strange anomaly" in European colonialism considering the persistent belief "that infants imbibed the wet nurse's physical and mental characteristics together with her milk."[75] The black wet nurse is a servant unlike other servants, a figure that embodies unstable allegiances.

The English and German texts are virtually identical in their approach to the image. The little girl (in English called Elsie; in German, Ilse) tries and fails to wash the black nurse white, with the nurse chiding her that it is impossible to do so. Both texts initially convey the idea that the nurse was "born this way," refusing to make an outright value judgment against blackness, in a moral that echoes the equivocating yet Eurocentric logic of Aesop's fable ("nothing in this world can change its nature"). The conclusion of the poem, however, is in each case straightforwardly derogatory: "And Elsie gave up hope," in English, and in Meggendorfer's German, "The Moor remains a Moor—the blackness remains / Despite all efforts." The references to lost hope and fruitless toil, which recall the boar hunter and the dancing bear from the previous section, racialize the existential crisis of Meggendorfer's mechanical figures while also jettisoning any implication of reciprocity between interlinked white and black characters. Although the mechanical girl's efforts to wash her nurse white fail, *Mohrenwäsche* rests unchallenged as a worthy goal for an imperious, indeed imperial, child.

D'Hervilly's French text begins in like manner to the English and German versions. Although little Alicia diligently washes the nurse, the girl's sponge will wear out before the nurse's face loses "a speck of its color." The narrative takes an unexpected turn, however, when Alicia reveals that she has been whipped for performing a similar ceremonial washing on her mother, after the "sponge had removed the white from her forehead, the pink from her cheeks, the red from her lips, the black from her eyebrows, the blue from the veins at her temples." Alicia's mother, not the black nurse, wants to change her nature, to hide something. The verse ends as the nurse laughs at her young charge's story. D'Hervilly parses the illustration in terms of the intimacy between Alicia and her nurse, who share a secret, as well as the nurse's mockery, implicit in her laughter, of Alicia's mother, as their conversation dramatizes the intimacy between the wet nurse and the child she has fed, proverbial from the Renaissance onward.[76]

But while d'Hervilly uses his text to gesture toward the undermining of not just physical and emotional bonds between white mothers and children but also racial and domestic hierarchies, the mechanical caricature of the black nurse shuts down these ambiguities. This happens in part through links to another black stereotype, that of Aunt Jemima, "the ultimate symbol and personification of the black cook, servant, and mammy." While Meggendorfer's black nurse lacks Jemima's checked head wrap, *mammy* was the term used for wet nurses on slave plantations, and her wide smile evokes that of Jemima.[77] As Harris observes in his detailed account of the stereotype—from minstrel shows at midcentury to redeployment at the end of the nineteenth century in advertisements for pancake flour—fantasies of care are central across the Aunt Jemima figure's American trajectory. By having Alicia better cared for by the black nurse than by her mother, d'Hervilly reproduces these fantasies, whereby "the love of the mammy . . . was a nostalgia for an imagined past, for a carefree period of childhood when this mother/grandmother figure would have cared for him and bestowed an overarching humanity on white children."[78] Here, the nostalgia relates to colonialism rather than to slavery, but the affective links—and the way those links fantasize racial inequality, using it as a balm for the identity of a white child—are similar.

Where both dandy and nurse are concerned, then, ambiguity may be introduced to the mechanical book by way of the differing texts, only to be diminished by the mechanical caricatures themselves. As such, Meggendorfer's mechanical caricatures represent what Robin Bernstein calls "black-and-whiteness": they are image objects "that do not merely mingle blackness and whiteness, but . . . instead keep blackness and whiteness simultaneously in tense distinction and in intimate contact."[79] The republication of the caricatures with texts in different languages demonstrates the persistence and circulation of racist stereotypes across national and linguistic boundaries—a neglected point within the study of visual humor and race, as Sheehan argues.[80] Moreover, what unites readers across these divides is their operation of the mechanical caricatures—a sinister twist to Higonnet's optimistic comparatist assertion that "the manual gestures that 'animate' mechanical books have a universal appeal that crosses the boundaries of language and age."[81] The white child reader's physical participation in animating the book's figures instantiates Bernstein's idea that white children become the "coproducers" of racist culture through their play with, for example, black dolls.[82] Meggendorfer's readers produce the racist implications of his mechanical illustrations as they pull the tabs and change the images.

Being a type means aligning involuntarily with particular behaviors and identifications. It makes individual identity into a mechanical attribute. The mechanical book renders its characters neither more nor less than their particular movements; in turn, these movements link with intractable stereotypes, be they professional or racial, subcultural or zoological. The child reader as puppeteer, however, is the one figure excluded from—indeed, in control of—these economies of character. The mechanical book provides a position of power, one that inculcates a number of adult types while assuring a child reader of her own mastery over the book. At the same time, though, the mechanical movements of the page—as in the obscured face of the black dandy, or the white girl forever moving in service to the black nurse—often express some difficulties in the policing or control of such stereotypes, which materialize in excess of the book's parameters for race.

The mechanical book as toy-book hybrid is one of Bernstein's scriptive things. It presupposes a certain set of actions or behaviors from the user but also allows for the possibility of subversive behavior—here, perhaps, in the way that the mechanism can be slowed down or paused at any point in its arc. Once more, we cannot interpret the caricatures without considering the physical relationship between the child and the book. Although the child is in one sense in control of the mechanical figures, in another she once more becomes like them. "The human agent anthropomorphizes the puppet," argues Ngai, "but the puppet also mechanizes the human, breaking his organic unity into so many functional parts: pressing toe, stretching hand, commanding voice."[83] The reader may become mechanized as she operates the book—may become a type predictable in her actions, operated by the mechanical figures in the book rather than superior to them. In this context, the phrase *to go through the motions,* a nineteenth-century coinage, has multiple applications: the movable book's creators, who draw on established banks of subjects; its child readers, who perform particular automatic operations, sometimes in line with textual instructions; and its characters, mechanical toys whose operation is predefined, invariable.[84]

— Conclusion —

# Novelty Book History

As Seth Lerer notes, "The history of children's literature is a history of image as well as word. It is a history, too, of artifacts: of books as valued things, crafted and held, lived with and loved." It is for this reason, according to Lerer, that children's literature criticism "dovetails beautifully with the discipline of book history."[1] Novelty picture books for children can take this logic one step further: looking more closely at these marginal and marginalized items can help to reveal that book history's most important concepts *inhere* to certain branches of children's literature. To adapt Deborah Thacker's parallel claim regarding children's literature and critical theory: scholars should recognize what children's novelty books can do for book history, rather than what book history can do for children's novelty books.[2]

A general version of the latter formulation—what book history can do for children's literature—has been demonstrated by important work synthesizing the two that I have already engaged. Scholars such as Patricia Crain, M. O. Grenby, and Lissa Paul have adopted the methodologies and habitual concerns of book history and bibliography, altering children's literature criticism in the process. By contrast, novelty books confirm children's literature as an ideal place to do book history, as a place where book history's central tenets are clearly visible between the covers of the books themselves. In line with this idea, I begin this Conclusion by taking up three claims in the history of the book and using the novelty book to explore them, before going on to reprise some of the most significant insights into novelty books gleaned across the chapters.

First claim: *the book is a material object (but not too materialized).* Novelty books for children can aid the book historian by providing an extreme case for the discipline's focus on materiality. Many book historians point out that the book is not just a carrier for ideas—not just a text—but also an object. They may do this in a call to arms, as when Jerome McGann states, "Literary works do not know themselves, and cannot *be* known, apart from their specific material modes of existence/resistance," or they may exercise restraint, as when Roger Chartier asserts that "no text exists outside of the support that enables it to be read."[3] They may generate succinct and carefully worded prescriptions, such as D. F. McKenzie's "forms effect meaning"—that's *effect,* "to bring about . . . to accomplish," not *affect,* "to have an effect on" *(OED).*[4] Materialist literary critics may turn the declaration into a sort of lyric, as when Susan Stewart invokes the duality of "the book as both idea and object, finalizable as meaning and materiality at once."[5] And in work on digital texts, materiality remains a key concern: N. Katherine Hayles identifies "the belief that 'work' and 'text' are immaterial constructions independent of the substrates in which they are instantiated" as a major problem for scholarship on the relationship between print and electronic media.[6]

It is a foundational gesture of book history, then, to remind the reader of the book's physical and material existence. There is often, however, a caveat. Even iconoclastic writers may insist on restoring the book's special dispensations from thingness, as when McKenzie balances statements such as "forms effect meaning" with the emphatic declaration, "For a book is never simply a remarkable object."[7] McKenzie uses "object" in a pejorative sense, while "simply" conveys the idea that books are superior to other things—a reinstatement of the duality between idea and vessel that the initial proposition "book = object" complicates. As when individual novelty books plead with child readers to treat books well, not just in textual imprecations but also in branding apparatuses such as that of the untearable book, this gesture works not so much as a statement of fact as a locus for anxiety: here, worries about what would happen if a book *did* become "simply a remarkable object." It is for this reason that novelties raise a number of pressing questions only partially answered in existing studies of material texts but omnipresent in *Playing with the Book.* Why is it important that the book be revealed as a material object, but not "simply" a material object? What are the ramifications when books become too materialized? What about books whose materiality is achieved at the expense of their texts, both verbal and visual? And, to quote Peter Stallybrass, "What have we done to things to have such contempt for them?"[8] (Nowhere is this question more pertinent than in the world of the book.)

Acknowledging, by way of the novelty book, the qualifications that apply to book history's interest in materiality illuminates current biases in the scholarship surrounding material texts. The adherence to the book's specialness as an object perhaps explains why much of the specialist critical literature on the book as a material object has focused on canonical or elite authors—Shakespeare's plays as pamphlets, say, or postwar fine editions of *Moby-Dick* (1851).[9] To take one example in greater depth: in *Paratexts* (1997), Gérard Genette cements the reader's sense of the importance of paying attention to the material presentation of texts using *Ulysses* as his foundational case. "To indicate what is at stake," he declares, "we can ask one simple question as an example: limited to the text alone and without a guiding set of directions, how would we read Joyce's *Ulysses* if it were not entitled *Ulysses*?"[10] Scholars should pay attention to paratexts—part of the book's material presentation—because they promote better understanding of an individual feted text, which is reinstated as the central topic of investigation.

Perhaps it is because book history's focus is often on canonical texts that book historians still insist on the materiality of the book. This is understandable in many ways: *Ulysses* is the sort of text whose contents are most likely to have slipped free of their associations with particular editions or formats, in part because it has been republished so many times and because its textual value is so well established (and in part perhaps because it has been talked about even by those who have not read it). But regardless, the materiality of print and the book becomes something of a means to an end in these examples—worth discussing only when it has a bearing on a canonical text or hallowed literary movement. That popular or mass-market products, such as the novelty picture book, constitute a signature locale for material understandings of the book remains underexplored, in part because the point seems so obvious: of course children's novelties are material objects. Marginalizing the most decidedly "material" books in this way, however, threatens to uphold the familiar hierarchies of form and content that the discipline of book history hopes, in its characteristic operations, to upset.

Second claim: *the book is a mechanized object (but not too mechanized).* As Jeffrey Masten, Stallybrass, and Nancy Vickers have written, "Even the most interesting theoretical work on reading and writing often assumes a problematic distinction between the manual and the mechanical production of texts."[11] Novelty books shed light on the vexed relationship between the mechanical and the manual within the history of the book, this time through a specific format: the mechanical book. While *mechanical book* refers to the specific format discussed in chapter 5, the phrase has wider significance—any book produced by a machine, which is to say, any printed book, is also in some sense a "mechanical book." Although the rise of mechanized printing in the nineteenth century adds a further layer to this, the compulsion to claim the book for mechanization has a long history. The title page to Stradanus's late sixteenth-century series of engravings *Nova reperta* (New inventions of modern times), memorably discussed by the book historian Elizabeth Eisenstein, includes the printing press alongside the compass and the gunpowder cannon as signal inventions of the early modern period (Figure C.1).[12] But Stradanus's engraving does not show a *whole* book. Instead, we see the book broken down into its fetishized components—printed sheets hung up to dry. The etching visually reminds us of what Stallybrass calls a "counterintuitive" circumstance of book production: "Printers do not print books. It is the process of gathering, folding, stitching, and sometimes binding that transforms printed sheets into a pamphlet or book."[13] It also suggests a paradox: even the book that has arisen *from* the machine is not *of* it.

Much canonical writing on mechanization explores its relation to the book. For example, Walter Benjamin begins "The Work of Art in the Age of Mechanical Reproduction" by opposing visual art in the titular age to print culture: "The enormous changes which printing, the mechanical reproduction of writing, has brought about in literature are a familiar story."[14] The propositions of Benjamin's storied essay apply only to visual art, because the "mechanical reproduction of writing" is already so established as to make the book a characteristic type of mechanical object. Analyzing the effects of the printing press has also formed an important thread in book history. Eisenstein, critiquing media historians such as Marshall McLuhan for assuming an equivalence between print and later technologies, famously contends that the advent of print represents "an event that is *sui generis.*"[15] More recently, Adrian Johns has critiqued Eisenstein for the "self-evidence" of her key idea that "printed texts are identical and reliable." Johns argues that this amounts to a

FIGURE C.1. On the title page to *Nova reperta,* Stradanus charts sixteenth-century progress through mechanical inventions including the printing press, but he does not show a *book.* The Metropolitan Museum of Art, New York, Harris Brisbane Dick Fund, 1934.

"technological order of reality" and questions the "intrinsic cultural consequences of technology" in which Eisenstein believes.[16] Despite their contrasting perspectives, Johns and Eisenstein share a preoccupation with the book's relationship to the technological and the mechanical. (Johns repeatedly uses the phrase "mechanick art.") For both authors, a technologization or otherwise of the book is at stake.

In fetishizing the presence of technology on each page—the tab-pull *is* the novelty—the mechanical book insistently recalls the fact that the book itself is a technology. Indeed, the conditions of the production of the mechanical book—and the experience of reading it—dismantle the seeming schism between the two branches of the word *mechanical,* "I. Senses relating to manual or practical work" and "II.

Senses relating to machines or mechanical processes" *(OED).* In the copy of Lothar Meggendorfer's *Curious Creatures* in the Bodleian, part of the movable image that accompanies the verse "The Weasel" is broken. A cutout of a field mouse, which should move up from a slit in the page when the tab is pulled—the weasel moving up as several mice move down, and vice versa, by means of one of Meggendorfer's signature dual movements—floats free. This is one of the pictures praised in a contemporary review in the *Pall Mall Gazette,* perhaps in part according to the criterion of durability: the reviewer remarks disapprovingly that some of the book's pictures are "not calculated to bear the harsh usage to which they will have to become inured."[17] The usual archival irony aside, the resultant fault exposes the book's mechanics. The cutout mice are mounted on a cardboard disc, which is labeled in exquisite cursive handwriting: "Schneckerl" on one side, the letter *B* on the other. *Schneckerl* (meaning ringlet or curl) is here the word for the piece that holds the mechanical figures to the page, adopted because of the rivet's spiral shape. The word is an instruction—in effect, "fasten here"—while the letter label diagrams the assembly of the movable. The book might have passed through a German library or private collection before coming to the Bodleian, and hence *Schneckerl* could have been written by an owner of the book who intended to fix it. Such a circulation seems unlikely, however, as the Bodleian shelfmark is a standard one for the 1890s, and *Schneckerl* was a term used by Meggendorfer and his publisher.[18]

As the mechanism is exposed, so, too, is the book's status as handmade: the annotations on the moving parts reveal the book's constitution—its prelife, its intimate involvement with *mechanical* in its "senses relating to" both the manual and the machine-made. Complicated movables such as the mechanical book require an unusually "high degree of hand assembly." Indeed, Ann Montanaro uses the suggestive phrase "hand-made mechanicals" to describe movable books.[19] The visible instruction in the Bodleian's copy of *Curious Creatures* reveals not just the mechanics of the tab-pull but also its status as an artifact that challenges a dichotomy between handmade and machine-made products (and between the manual and the mechanical). The most mechanical parts of the book are those that require the most careful, artisanal assembly, transporting the book from its industrial and technological contexts—color printing and German superiority therein, for example—into embodied configurations of book production within these contexts.

Indeed, the reader of mechanical books produced by Meggendorfer finds hands at work everywhere. These include the hands of previous readers, which leave marks on tabs and pages, as well as illustrations of hands, like large-scale versions of the typographical symbol for the index ☞, also known as the printer's fist. Meggendorfer's *Tiny Tim* features a large colored illustration of an upturned hand with cuff at the wrist; Tim, a Tom Thumb character, stands on the palm of the hand, encased by the fingers of his much larger friend. An illustration in *Curious Creatures* is virtually the same, but a cockchafer beetle rests on the large hand instead of a miniature person (Figure C.2). A lack of background, notable given that these books often set figures within detailed environments, heightens the impact of both illustrations. Hands have been important to the readers of these books because of the repeated manipulation; this image layers a printed hand with hands outside the book, so that the mechanical is mediated (always) through the manual.

Third claim: *authors do not write books.* In a parallel assertion to Stallybrass's remark that printers do not print books, Roger Stoddard answers certain misprisions around book production with the following statement: "Whatever they may do, authors do *not* write books. Books are not written at all. They are manufactured by scribes and other artisans, by mechanics and other engineers, and by printing presses and other machines."[20] Nobody who is confronted with Victorian novelty books could forget this fact, and as such, novelty books can contribute to book history's interest in unseating the author as the sole creative agent behind a book—an interest visible, for instance, at the level of the famous communications circuit model proposed by Robert Darnton, which places the author within a network of publisher, printer and supplier, shipper, bookseller, binder, and, of course, reader.[21]

Take, for example, the original movable books for children: harlequinades. When we think about who creates books, harlequinades shift the focus from writers and illustrators to publishers and printers, and from auteur figures (both historical and contemporary) to entrepreneurs. In fact, they suggest considerable slippage between these categories: for instance, the Bodleian catalogs harlequinades using the name of their publisher, Robert Sayer, as "Author/Creator," appending a note to justify this practice: "Robert Sayer is accredited with inventing the first harlequinades."[22] In part, this attribution relates back to the material makeup of the harlequinade: identifying the author of a harlequinade as the person who had written its text would be

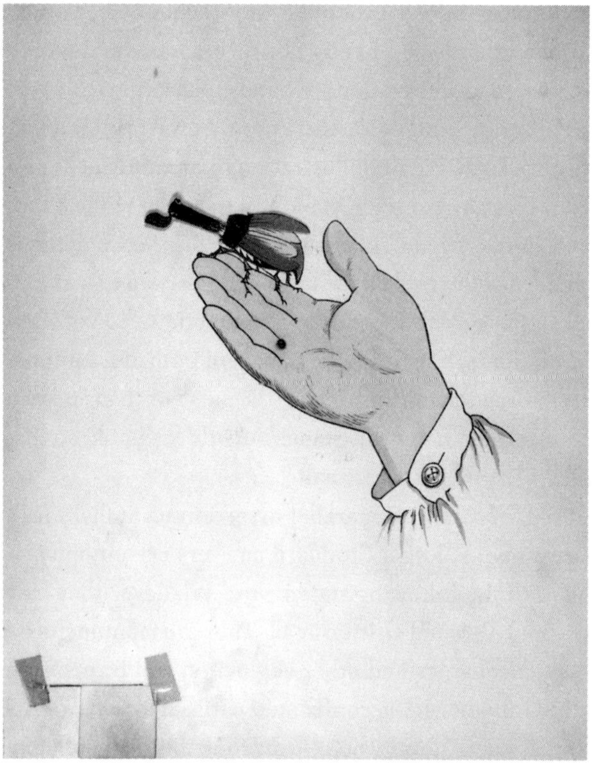

FIGURE C.2. This illustration of a hand in Meggendorfer's *Curious Creatures* evokes both the child reader's hand as she pulls a tab and the painstaking hand assembly of movable books. Henrietta Hochschild Collection of Children's Books, Washington University Libraries, Department of Special Collections, St. Louis, Missouri.

difficult, not just because that person is usually anonymous but also because a written text is not the harlequinade's primary feature—why not list its illustrator, its engraver, or its assembler? The appeal lies in the *format,* not in the text, a reality I encountered again and again while writing this book—asked which children's authors I was working on, I had to reply instead with a list of formats. Children's literature critics may use this state of affairs to dismiss novelty books, as when Alderson describes these items as "attracting their readership through the paper mechanisms rather than any intrinsic merit, . . . a common factor in the exploitation of paper toys that reached high peaks of popularity."[23] In fact, though, the primacy of format over author or even illustrator makes Stoddard's statement about who is responsible for books seem commonplace.

In the trajectory of the Victorian novelty book specifically, the predominance of the publisher—a consistent thread throughout *Playing with the Book*—further decenters the author. The marks of the publisher's centrality range widely. Title pages alone bear witness to it, as when a lift-the-flap book such as *Old Fashioned Mother Goose Melodies* (1879) names no author save Mother Goose herself, although both the publisher (G. W. Carleton) and the designers and printers (Donaldson Brothers) are listed.[24] Think also of the emphasis on series terminology: from Routledge's panoramic Stories Told in Pictures, which perambulate around the English countryside, to the tactile shape books released as Father Tuck's Woolly-Woolly Lifelike Series, to the multifarious series mounted by Dean and Son throughout the century, many of which seem to offer strings of randomly chosen words by way of titles, as in Dean's Word Changing Chromo Picture Toy Books. These series rubrics shape the child reader's knowledge of a text not according to the writer's name but rather according to the publisher's commissioning and marketing of a particular sort of book. Series titles, too, work like Barthesian captions—they dictate to child readers what is important or special about an individual format. There are clear differences, for instance, among pop-ups foregrounded as magic-lantern apparatuses, peepshows, and unspecified scenic views. Meanwhile, the history of copyrighting movable devices places the author of novelty books as a marginal figure in their development. In the Introduction, I mentioned the patents for movable pieces visible on the covers of Nister movables, but other publishers worked in this way, too. The Tuck series of shape books mentioned above was patented, as was the pop-up cage technique used in *The Home Menagerie* (1883).[25] The small Dundee publisher Valentine and Company, early in the twentieth century, trademarked its Book Toys and Wheel Books.[26] In no case do these books indicate that any patent accrued to an author or an illustrator.

Of course, as I have detailed in chapter 4, Ernest Nister provides a particularly strong case study of the publisher's domination in novelty books for children. This is both because of the self-aware insertion of his character into his dissolving-view books and other movables and because of the publishing practices that shaped the presentation of each movable, with images commissioned, chopped, changed, and remixed by the printer-publisher. Nister's case extends the claim that authors do not write books to the illustrators, who do not illustrate them—or, at least, do not know which books they are illustrating as the images are produced. At the same time, the illustrations take precedence over the text in imagined scenarios of book production, such as the introductory poem to *More Pleasant Surprises*: "In such a matter I have no voice, / You pay your money and take your choice." Once consideration is extended to the papermakers who secure movable effects in books and the assemblers who put them together, the network of figures surrounding novelty books becomes hugely complex—and decathected from the author.

Nineteenth-century novelty books for children, then, provide forceful evidence of some of book history's central claims. They also reveal much else besides, as I hope I have shown throughout this volume. Across the preceding chapters, I have used novelty books to demonstrate what is at stake when primary attention is paid to the content of the words and pictures in picture books, with format an afterthought. It is not enough, for instance, to note that Meggendorfer's mechanical figures draw on traditions of ethnic caricature and blackface minstrelsy, transposing these into different cultural contexts by distributing the illustrations alongside texts in different languages. The unusual *format* in which these cartoons are placed must also be taken into account, summoning as it does dynamics of control and movement that are themselves racialized, as certain sorts of animation are, and that involve the white child reader in the production of racist representational discourses. While novelty books are special sorts of books, books that force the critic to confront the way different book formats make meaning, the same is true in other branches of children's literature, and form should not be an afterthought to content, be it verbal or visual.

Novelty books show the multifaceted ways that children's books related to the wider universe of things in Victorian culture, moving beyond the relationship between books and toys (although this remains important). This takes place not just in direct references—as when a mechanical book such as Dean's movable *Royal Punch and Judy* memorializes a production staged before Queen Victoria around 1859—but also by way of formal resemblances. The shapes of children's novelty books resemble the shapes of other objects and media. Following these formal resemblances, as I have in chapter 2 by considering wallpaper alongside the panorama, in chapters 3 and 4 by noting the novelty book's theatricality, and in chapter 5 by counterpointing mechanical books with mechanical toys and puppets, is evocative. These echoes between forms provide a sense of how the materiality of children's books could become densely freighted with associations—intertextual or self-referential, even. Again, this provides a model beyond that usually adopted in (say) bibliography's genetic criticism, as the precursors of the book may not be other book-texts, but other objects.

Nonetheless, considering novelty books primarily *as books* rather than as optical toys can show what is lost in more exclusively visual culture readings of these items. Novelty books provide the child with a rich sensorium as enmeshed with touch as with sight: they make the production of visual illusions a function of the child's body. While they foreground their resemblance to new nineteenth-century visual technologies, they also recur obsessively to the bread-and-butter subjects of Victorian children's literature—the fairy tale, the folktale, the nursery rhyme, the portal fantasy. Within their texts, novelty books also draw parallels between the magical reading experience they offer and earlier modes of reading, such as reading aloud at a *veillée.* As such, novelty books take their meaning in relation to discourses of children as readers as much as in relation to discourses of children as viewers.

This relates, in turn, to the reparative role that the children's picture book, becoming in the Victorian period a treasured marker of a good childhood, might play in mediating the very relationship between children and technology—a role amplified in books that themselves seem technologized, such as novelties. Thus *A Morning Ride* folds out panoramic vistas, deploying two boys' horseback ride to mitigate the impact of the railway on the British landscape. Nister's dissolving-view books make chromolithographic rainbows a gift from the fairies to the child. And mechanical books allow the child reader to enjoy the spectacle of mechanized labor while also controlling workers and time itself. These are just a few of the examples that have recurred across this volume, but they suggest that a reading of novelty books as optical toys *tout court* may marginalize the sorts of fantasies about technology that these books proffer, which tend toward the palliative rather than the triumphal.

Novelty books demonstrate that particular sorts of materialized books promote an embodied reader and link that embodiment to childhood in particular. The split attitude toward this embodiment within individual novelty books, which remind the child reader that paper is not iron while also requiring that paper be manipulated by eager (sometimes overeager) hands, shows the multifaceted attitudes toward children as embodied readers in the nineteenth century. Moreover, novelty books contribute to the increasing sense in book history and literary criticism (derived from the work of Leah Price and others) that the primary purpose of a book may not always be that special activity, reading, or rather that reading might encompass physical activities and motions as well as intellectual processes. The sometimes hostile reception of novelty books by scholars and collectors shows that books as objects, and readers whose enjoyment of books is not based on mental activity and immersion in a textual world, remain threatening.

The corpus of novelty books in the Opie Collection, as the kernel of *Playing with the Book,* also demonstrates the value of unconventional evidence in the history of reading—especially where child readers are concerned. As I have argued in chapter 1, it is important to place nontextual evidence of reading, such as the ripping, tearing, coloring-in, and reconstruction to which novelty books testify, at least on a par with children's marginalia and doodles. Such evidence reflects the embodied reading practices outlined above, and it also challenges the sense of the power dynamics of children's literature. When evidence of children literally ripping up their books—against the wishes of their caregivers as well as those who produced the books—is so prevalent, why do critics persist in examining child readers as lacking in agency? In part, it may be because the literalness of such evidence has until recently been unfashionable, and because of the perils of arguing from it when solid information about the readers involved is lacking. Perhaps it is because, in an antiobject culture, agency itself works best when dematerialized and intellectualized. Nonetheless, children's literature critics must admit that such evidence has powerful potential to reshape the questions we ask about children as readers.

There is perhaps no more dematerialized or disembodied type of book than the academic monograph. But novelty books can have strange effects on even the most august genres. In 1979, the Swedish critic Sten Lindberg published a learned exegesis of historical movable books. The essay focuses not on children's publishing but on scientific works, examining such things as the circular mechanical devices called volvelles in Johannes Schöner's *Opera mathematica* (1551) and seventeenth-century lift-the-flap medical plates. As a sort of centerfold to the article, Lindberg provides a diagram that gives instructions for how to assemble a volvelle.[27] The material awareness of format occasioned by the novelty book is such that even Lindberg's academic article attempts to perform the movable's gesture of being what it describes. As such, I have borrowed the idea: my final illustration is a template for a pop-up rabbit, created by the modern-day pop-up genius Robert Sabuda (Figure C.3). Lindberg advises the reader to make a photocopy of his volvelle diagram before beginning assembly, but that kind of suggestion would not be in the spirit of children's books. So, to end with an instruction: the next page is to be cut or ripped out, and made into a white rabbit, and played with.

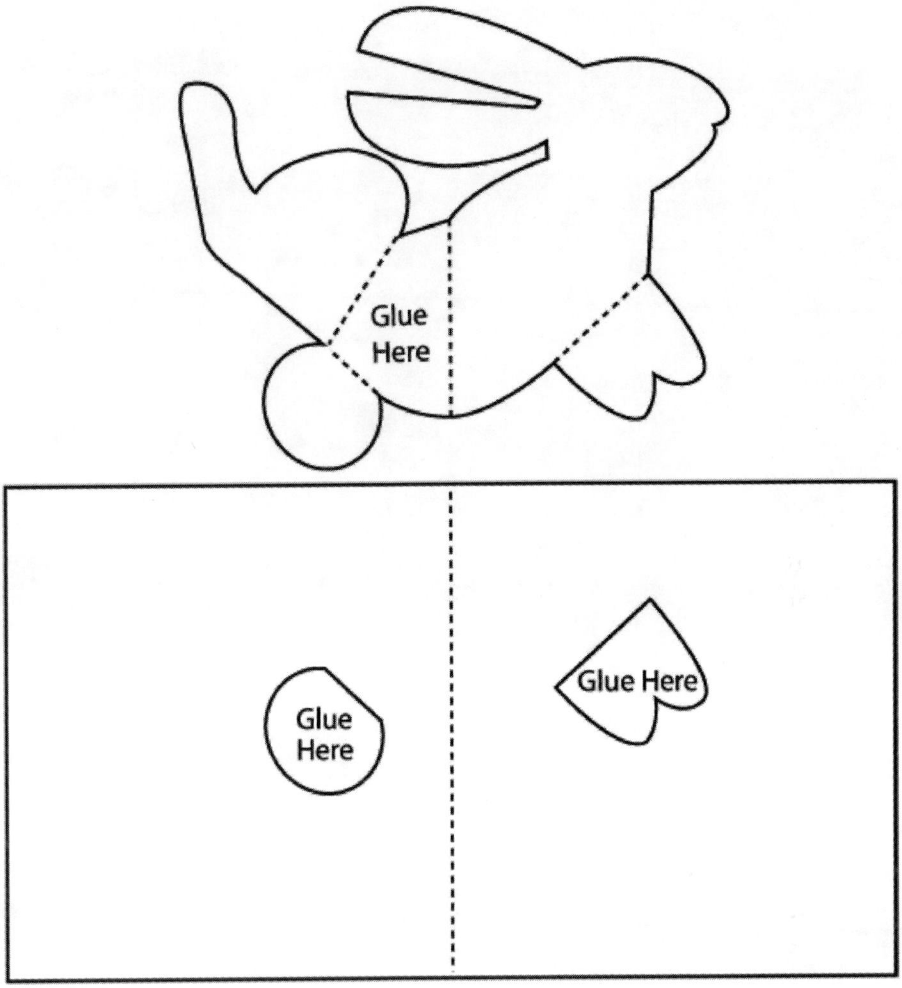


FIGURE C.3. Instructions for assembling this pop-up rabbit by Robert Sabuda can be found, along with the original template, at Sabuda's website. Reproduced by kind permission of Robert Sabuda, http://wp.robertsabuda.com.

# Acknowledgments

This book began while I was a Clarendon Scholar at Somerville College, University of Oxford, so my first thanks go to Somerville, to the Clarendon Fund and the Oxford English Faculty, and to those I worked with while there: my supervisors, Stefano Evangelista and Diane Purkiss; my examiners, Clare Pettitt and Helen Small; and the staff of the Bodleian Libraries (particularly Colin Harris, Clive Hurst, Dunja Sharif, and Sarah Wheale) for granting me access to the Opie Collection of Children's Literature. Numerous other libraries, galleries, and museums also allowed me to reproduce works from their collections; they are acknowledged by name in captions but deserve further gratitude here. The illustration program for the book was supported by a Publications Grant from the Paul Mellon Centre for Studies in British Art and a Research Committee award from the School of English, University of Sussex, for which I am most appreciative.

But *Playing with the Book* is also the product of several other debts, which I gladly acknowledge. At the University of Auckland, Rose Lovell-Smith fostered interests in children's picture books and Victorian literature that have never left me. While I was at Oxford (and since), Ginny Bouillerot, Maria Sachiko Cecire, Broderick Chow, Paul Earlie, Jennifer Juillard Maniece, Racha Kirakosian, Jacques Schuhmacher, and Robert Simpson were all generous in giving their time to read my work or talk over ideas with me. Jacqui Reid-Walsh responded to an over-the-transom inquiry about paper doll books with characteristic warmth, and I am grateful not just for her kindness but also for her excellent scholarship on novelty publishing for children. The opportunity to attend the London Rare Books School at the School of Advanced Study, University of London, was given to me by the Bibliographical Society in 2010, and I benefited greatly from learning about the history of children's books in sessions led by Brian Alderson and Jill Shefrin. At the University of Lincoln, Ruth Charnock, Jim Cheshire, Owen Clayton, Amy Culley, Christine Grandy, Adam Houlbrook, and Rebecca Styler provided sage advice and good friendship; I have been lucky to find the same in my colleagues at Sussex, particularly Natalia Cecire, Andrea Haslanger, Annabel Haynes, Doug Haynes, Rachel O'Connell, Lindsay Smith, Sam Solomon, Bethan Stevens, and Hope Wolf. Generous audiences at Oxford (not just Somerville and the English Faculty but also the Centre for the History of Childhood at Magdalen College); the University of Lincoln; King's College London; the University of Birmingham; Homerton College, University of Cambridge; Roehampton University; the Università degli Studi di Milano; Senate House, University of London; and the Victoria and Albert Museum shaped my readings of the material. Finally, many thanks to Dani Kasprzak, Anne Carter, Judy Selhorst, and the readers at the University of Minnesota Press for making the experience of publishing my first book enjoyable and stimulating.

I also thank those who remind me there is more to life than books (if not much more). My gratitude especially to my parents, Jeff Field and the late Robyn Stewart; my sisters, Bella and Harriet Field; my in-laws Peter, Jennifer, and Meghan Kerr; and my friends Lydia Cowpertwait, Antonia de Vere, Paora Durie, Kylie McKenzie, Celia Phillips, Emma Rosenberg, Josephine Rout, Todd Stratton, Caroline Sturgess, and Jeremy Tapsell. Christabel Field arrived while I was completing final revisions and began chewing her picture books almost right away, which seemed a good omen for the argument of *Playing with the Book,* if not for the actual books in question.

Most important, I cannot express the thanks I owe Matt Kerr—for his enthusiasm and support, not to mention his impeccable knowledge of Victorian literature. This book is for him.

# Notes

## INTRODUCTION

I conducted most of the archival work for this book at the Bodleian Libraries at the University of Oxford, using the Opie Collection of Children's Literature. When discussing copies of novelty picture books with particular evidence of reading (for instance, marginalia or coloring), I provide shelfmarks from this collection in the endnotes. Novelty books published by Ernest Nister are listed by their titles in the notes, because the author bylines often reflect an editorial role.

When the dates of novelty books discussed are uncertain, I report them in the notes and figure captions only. All dates in square brackets are from the Bodleian Libraries unless otherwise stated; where "my date" appears for Dean and Son novelty books, I have used the method for dating the firm's productions proposed by Stephen J. Gertz in "Dean and Son Movable Books and How to Date Them," Booktryst, March 2, 2012, http://www.booktryst.com.

1 *Novelty! Metamorphoses Picture-Book/Neuestes Verwandlungs-Bilder-Buch/Nouveauté! Livre de metamorphoses* (Germany: n.p., [ca. 1895]), publication information from Columbia University Libraries.

2 See Richard F. Abrahamson and Robert Stewart, "Movable Books—A New Golden Age," *Language Arts* 59 (1982): 342.

3 For a collector's summary of the debate over which publisher produced this 1850s book, see Theo Gielen, "*The New Riding-School*: A Movable Picturebook with Rhymes," *Movable Stationery* 16, no. 2 (2008): 1–3, 13–17.

4 Ilgım Veryeri Alaca, "Materiality in Picturebooks," in *The Routledge Companion to Picturebooks,* ed. Bettina Kümmerling-Meibauer (Abingdon: Routledge, 2018), 59–68.

5 See, for instance, Brian Alderson, "The Making of Children's Books," in *The Cambridge Companion to Children's Literature,* ed. M. O. Grenby and Andrea Immel (Cambridge: Cambridge University Press, 2009), 35–54; Andrea Immel, "Frederick Lock's Scrapbook: Patterns in the Pictures and Writing in the Margins," in "Handmade Literacies," ed. Michael Joseph and Lissa Paul, special issue, *The Lion and the Unicorn* 29, no. 1 (2005): 65–85; Katie Trumpener, "City Scenes: Commerce, Utopia, and the Birth of the Picture Book," in *The Victorian Illustrated Book,* ed. Richard Maxwell (Charlottesville: University Press of Virginia, 2002), 332–84.

6 "Learning as Play: An Animated, Interactive Archive of Seventeenth- to Nineteenth-Century Narrative Media for and by Children," ed. Jacqueline Reid-Walsh, Pennsylvania State University, accessed December 10, 2018, http://sites.psu.edu/play. Reid-Walsh's scholarly articles on novelties include "Activity and Agency in Historical 'Playable Media': Early English Movable Books and Their Child Interactors," *Journal of Children and Media* 6 (2012): 164–81; and "Pantomime, Harlequinades and Children in Late Eighteenth-Century Britain: Playing in the Text," in "Cultures of Childhood," ed. M. O. Grenby, special issue, *Journal for Eighteenth-Century Studies* 29, no. 3 (2006): 413–25.

7 See Michelle Ann Abate, "When Clothes Don't Make the Man: Sartorial Style, Conspicuous Consumption, and Class Passing in Lothar Meggendorfer's *Scenes in the Life of a Masher,*" *Children's Literature Association Quarterly* 37 (2012): 43–65; Margaret R. Higonnet, "Orality onto Paper and into Action," in *Intersections, Interferences, Interdisciplines: Literature with Other Arts,* ed. Haun Saussy and Gerald Gillespie (Brussels: Peter Lang, 2014), 125–38.

8 Ann R. Montanaro, *Pop-Up and Movable Books: A Bibliography* (Metuchen, N.J.: Scarecrow Press, 1993); Ann R. Montanaro, *Pop-Up and Movable Books: A Bibliography (Supplement 1, 1991–1997)* (Lanham, Md.: Scarecrow Press, 2000); Peter Haining, *Movable Books: An Illustrated History* (London: New English Library, 1979).

9 Robin Bernstein, *Racial Innocence: Performing American Childhood from Slavery to Civil Rights* (New York: New York University Press, 2011).

10 M. O. Grenby, *The Child Reader, 1700–1840* (Cambridge: Cambridge University Press, 2011); Courtney Weikle-Mills, *Imaginary Citizens: Child Readers and the Limits of American Independence, 1640–1868* (Baltimore: Johns Hopkins University Press, 2012); Patricia

Crain, *Reading Children: Literacy, Property, and the Dilemmas of Childhood in Nineteenth-Century America* (Philadelphia: University of Pennsylvania Press, 2016); Karen Sánchez-Eppler, "Marks of Possession: Methods for an Impossible Subject," *PMLA* 126 (2011): 151–59.

11 Walter Benjamin, "Unpacking My Library: A Talk about Book Collecting," in *Illuminations*, ed. Hannah Arendt, trans. Harry Zorn (London: Pimlico, 1999), 67; Walter Benjamin, "A Glimpse into the World of Children's Books," trans. Rodney Livingstone, in *Selected Writings*, vol. 1, *1913–1926*, ed. Marcus Bullock and Michael W. Jennings (Cambridge, Mass.: Belknap Press, 1996), 435. For an account of Benjamin's collection of children's books, see Kenneth Kidd, "The Child, the Scholar, and the Children's Literature Archive," *The Lion and the Unicorn* 35 (2011): 4–6.

12 F. J. Harvey Darton, *Children's Books in England: Five Centuries of Social Life* (Cambridge: Cambridge University Press, 1932), sec. 5, 151–52. I have written about the Fuller paper doll books elsewhere; see Hannah Field, "'A Story, Exemplified in a Series of Figures': Paper Doll versus Moral Tale in the Nineteenth Century," in "Girls and Dolls," ed. Miriam Forman-Brunell, special issue, *Girlhood Studies* 5, no. 1 (2012): 37–56.

13 F. J. Harvey Darton, *Children's Books in England: Five Centuries of Social Life*, 3rd ed., rev. Brian Alderson (1982; repr., Cambridge: Cambridge University Press, 1999), app. 1, 320.

14 Alderson, "Making of Children's Books," 42; Brian Alderson and Marjorie Moon, *Childhood Re-collected: Early Children's Books from the Library of Marjorie Moon* (n.p.: Provincial Booksellers Fairs Association, 1994), 88.

15 Ann R. Montanaro, "Movable Books and Pop-Up Books," in *The Oxford Encyclopedia of Children's Literature*, ed. Jack Zipes (Oxford: Oxford University Press, 2006), para. 1 of 17, Oxford Reference Online, doi:10.1093/acref/9780195146561.001.0001.

16 Children's Books History Society, "Novelty Books and Movables: Questions of Terminology," *Children's Books History Society Newsletter* 61 (July 1998): 15.

17 Montanaro, *Pop-Up and Movable Books* (1993), xiii.

18 David D. Hall, introduction to *Cultures of Print: Essays in the History of the Book* (Amherst: University of Massachusetts Press, 1996), 1.

19 Percy H. Muir, *English Children's Books, 1600 to 1900* (London: B. T. Batsford, 1954), 204–36.

20 See Seth Lerer, *Children's Literature: A Reader's History, from Aesop to Harry Potter* (Chicago: University of Chicago Press, 2008), chap. 5. For other important reflections on this formula, see Patricia Demers, ed., *From Instruction to Delight: An Anthology of Children's Literature to 1850*, 4th ed. (Don Mills, Ontario: Oxford University Press,

2015); Lissa Paul, *The Children's Book Business: Lessons from the Long Eighteenth Century* (New York: Routledge, 2011), 174.

21 For comprehensive studies of (respectively) Randolph Caldecott and Routledge's Victorian picture books, see Brian Alderson, *Sing a Song for Sixpence: The English Picture-Book Tradition and Randolph Caldecott* (Cambridge: Cambridge University Press, 1986); Tomoko Masaki, *A History of Victorian Popular Picture Books: The Aesthetic, Creative, and Technological Aspects of the Toy Book through the Publications of the Firm of Routledge 1852–1893,* 2 vols. (Tokyo: Kazamashoto, 2006).

22 Beverly Lyon Clark, introduction to *Girls, Boys, Books, Toys: Gender in Children's Literature and Culture,* ed. Beverly Lyon Clark and Margaret R. Higonnet (Baltimore: Johns Hopkins University Press, 1999), 1.

23 Robin Bernstein, "Children's Books, Dolls, and the Performance of Race; or, The Possibility of Children's Literature," *PMLA* 126 (2011): 162.

24 Jacqueline Reid-Walsh, "Books or Toys? A Traveller's Tale: Researching Early Movable Books for and by Children in Material and Virtual Collections," in "Children's Literature Collections and Archives," special issue, *Papers: Explorations into Children's Literature* 22, no. 1 (2012): 156.

25 Gordon N. Ray, *The Illustrator and the Book in England from 1790 to 1914* (New York: Pierpont Morgan Library, 1991), xiii.

26 Maxwell, introduction to Maxwell, *Victorian Illustrated Book,* xxv.

27 Michael R. Booth, *Victorian Spectacular Theatre 1850–1910* (London: Routledge & Kegan Paul, 1981), 8.

28 Martin Meisel, *Realizations: Narrative, Pictorial, and Theatrical Arts in Nineteenth-Century England* (Princeton, N.J.: Princeton University Press, 1983), 3.

29 *Dean's New Book of Dissolving Views* (London: Dean and Son, [1861]), my date. Marsh notes that summer to winter and day to night were well-known Childe dissolves; see Joss Marsh, "Dickensian 'Dissolving Views': The Magic Lantern, Visual Story-Telling, and the Victorian Technological Imagination," *Comparative Critical Studies* 6 (2009): 335.

30 Eric Faden, "Movables, Movies, Mobility: Nineteenth-Century Looking and Reading," *Early Popular Visual Culture* 5 (2007): 71.

31 John Plunkett, "Moving Books/Moving Images: Optical Recreations and Children's Publishing 1800–1900," in "Verbal and Visual Interactions in Nineteenth-Century Print Culture," ed. Luisa Calè and Patrizia Di Bello, special issue, *19: Interdisciplinary Studies in the Long Nineteenth Century* 5 (2007): 1, 21.

32 Helen Groth, *Moving Images: Nineteenth-Century Reading and Screen Practices* (Edinburgh: Edinburgh University Press, 2013), 35.

33 Markman Ellis, "'Spectacles within Doors': Panoramas of London in the 1790s," *Romanticism* 14 (2008): 134.

34 Gerard Curtis, *Visual Words: Art and the Material Book in Victorian England* (Aldershot: Ashgate, 2002), 271.

35 Michael Twyman, *Breaking the Mould: The First Hundred Years of Lithography* (London: British Library, 2001), 129.

36 Lorraine Janzen Kooistra, *Poetry, Pictures, and Popular Publishing: The Illustrated Gift Book and Victorian Visual Culture 1855–1875* (Athens: Ohio University Press, 2011), 4; Kathryn Ledbetter, "'BeGemmed and BeAmuletted': Tennyson and Those 'Vapid' Gift Books," *Victorian Poetry* 34 (1996): 235.

37 See Nathalie op de Beeck, *Suspended Animation: Children's Picture Books and the Fairy Tale of Modernity* (Minneapolis: University of Minnesota Press, 2010), chap. 1.

38 *Report from the Select Committee on Fourdrinier's Patent*. . . , 1837, HC Parliamentary Papers 351, p. iv.

39 Alderson, "Making of Children's Books," 42.

40 Lothar Meggendorfer, *Always Jolly! A Movable Toybook* (London: H. Grevel, [ca. 1891]), date from Lilly Library, Indiana University.

41 Iona Opie and Peter Opie, "Books That Come to Life," *Saturday Book* 34 (1975): 64. For a recent collector's essay on Dean and Son, see Jo Tisinger, "Dean and Son Publishers—A Short History," *Movable Stationery* 21, no. 2 (2013): 3–7.

42 The dates for Dean's premises at Ludgate Hill are from Geoffrey Wakeman and Gavin D. R. Bridson, *A Guide to Nineteenth Century Colour Printers* (Loughborough: Plough Press, 1975), 34.

43 Gertz, "Dean and Son Movable Books." With characteristic acerbity, Alderson remarks the "undistinguished and debased" productions of Dean in his history of English picture books, *Sing a Song for Sixpence*, 57.

44 "Books for Children," *Myra's Journal*, January 1, 1895, 28. The title reviewed is Dean's *Surprise Animal Picture Book*.

45 Opie and Opie, "Books That Come to Life," 74.

46 Julia Hunt and Frederick Hunt, *Peeps into Nisterland: A Guide to the Children's Books of Ernest Nister* (Chester: Casmelda, 2006), 10–11.

47 Appendix to "Report on the Recent Progress of Technical Education in Germany," in *Forty-Fourth Report of the Department of Science and Art of the Committee of Council on Education, with Appendices*, 1897, HC Parliamentary Papers C.8581, p. 73.

48 Wilhelm Ruland, *Beilage zur Allgemeinen Zeitung* [Supplement to the general newspaper], 1902, cited in Maurice Sendak, "Lothar Meggendorfer," in *Caldecott and Co.: Notes on Books and Pictures* (London: Reinhardt Books, 1989), 56.

49 Michael Dawson, "S. Louis Giraud and His Development of Pop-Ups," *Antiquarian Book Monthly Review* 18, no. 205 (1991): 218. Geoff Fox gives an account of the celebrated creator of movables, Jan Pieńkowski, visiting a factory where his books were made and remarking, "All the girls seem to have very delicate hands and fingers which is why I think they're so good at doing these books." Geoff Fox, "Movable Books," in *Children's Book Publishing in Britain since 1945,* ed. Kimberley Reynolds and Nicholas Tucker (Aldershot: Scolar Press, 1998), 100.

50 E. Nister, "New Patent Process for Mechanically Producing Chromographs in Three or More Printings," *Process Year Book* 3 (1897): 105.

51 Wakeman and Bridson, *Guide to Nineteenth Century Colour Printers,* 86. On book history and technicist skepticism, see John O. Jordan and Robert L. Patten, "Introduction: Publishing History as Hypertext," in *Literature in the Marketplace: Nineteenth-Century British Publishing and Reading Practices,* ed. John O. Jordan and Robert L. Patten (Cambridge: Cambridge University Press, 1995), 13.

52 Walter Crane, *Of the Decorative Illustration of Books Old and New* (1905; facsimile repr., Detroit: Gale Research Group, 1968), 155–56. This book was originally published in 1896.

53 *Minutes of Evidence Taken before the Select Committee on the Copyright Acts . . . ,* 1818, HC Parliamentary Papers 280, p. 280; E. Fenwick, *Visits to the Juvenile Library; or, Knowledge Proved to Be the Source of Happiness* (London: Barnard and Sultzer for Tabart, 1805), 66. Paul discusses Fenwick's *Visits* throughout *Children's Book Business.*

54 Darton, *Children's Books in England* (1999), 202; Andrew W. Tuer, *Pages and Pictures from Forgotten Children's Books* (London: Leadenhall Press, 1898–99), 6.

55 Tuer begins his book, "The love of things rendered quaint by lapse of time and change of surroundings seems to grow on one imperceptibly." Tuer, *Pages and Pictures,* 5.

56 *Playtime Surprises,* by Clifton Bingham (London: Ernest Nister; New York: E. P. Dutton, [ca. 1900]), date from Hunt and Hunt, *Peeps into Nisterland,* 297. The book's title is given as *Playtime Surprises for the Children* on the cover.

57 Ernest Robert Nister, "Improvements in So-Called Revolving Changing Pictures," UK Patent 189910870. Faden notes that early cinema pioneer Theodore Brown patented both cinematic technologies and movable parts for books. Faden, "Movables, Movies, Mobility," 71.

58 Clare Pettitt, *Patent Inventions: Intellectual Property and the Victorian Novel* (Oxford: Oxford University Press, 2004), 33; Mark Rose, *Authors and Owners: The Invention of Copyright* (Cambridge, Mass.: Harvard University Press, 1993), 131–32. The phrase "style and sentiment" comes from the eighteenth-century legal commentator William Blackstone.

59 Simon Eliot, *Some Patterns and Trends in British Publishing 1800–1919* (London: Bibliographical Society, 1994), 3.

60 Kathy Piehl, "Books in Toyland," *Children's Literature Association Quarterly* 12 (1987): 79.

61 On private collections as a frequent provenance for children's literature archives, see Kidd, "The Child, the Scholar," 4–10.

62 Gillian Avery, "The Opie Collection Appeal," *Signal* 53 (1987): 145.

63 See Francisca Goldsmith, "Opie, Iona and Peter," in *The Continuum Encyclopedia of Children's Literature,* ed. Bernice E. Cullinan and Diane G. Person (New York: Continuum, 2005), 603.

64 See Iona Opie, Peter Opie, and Brian Alderson, *The Treasures of Childhood: Books, Toys, and Games from the Opie Collection* (London: Pavilion, 1989), 18.

65 Brian Alderson, "Collecting Children's Books: Self-Indulgence and Scholarship," in *Children and Their Books: A Celebration of the Work of Iona and Peter Opie,* ed. Gillian Avery and Julia Briggs (Oxford: Clarendon Press, 1989), 15.

66 Alderson, 9.

67 Opie and Opie, "Books That Come to Life," 61.

68 Sianne Ngai, "Theory of the Gimmick," in "Comedy: An Issue," ed. Lauren Berlant and Sianne Ngai, special issue, *Critical Inquiry* 43, no. 2 (2017): 481.

69 As Higonnet observes, "The moveable book has been viewed by major students of children's literature as a trivial, ephemeral, and even tasteless 'gimmick' or toy." Higonnet, "Orality onto Paper," 132.

70 Martha L. Carothers, "Novelty Books: Accent of Images and Words," in *A Book of the Book: Some Works and Projections about the Book and Writing,* ed. Jerome Rothenberg and Steven Clay (New York: Granary Books, 2000), 319.

71 The Kate Greenaway Medal is awarded by the United Kingdom's Chartered Institute of Library and Information Professionals. Robert Sabuda's essay is "Making the Paper Listen and Obey," in Joseph and Paul, "Handmade Literacies," 9–11.

72 Leah Price, *How to Do Things with Books in Victorian Britain* (Princeton, N.J.: Princeton University Press, 2012), 8.

73 Perry Nodelman, *Words about Pictures: The Narrative Art of Children's Picture Books* (Athens: University of Georgia Press, 1988), 2.

74 Lawrence Sipe and Caroline McGuire, "Picturebook Endpapers: Resources for Literary and Aesthetic Interpretation," in *Talking beyond the Page: Reading and Responding to Picturebooks,* ed. Janet Evans (London: Routledge, 2009), 77; Barbara Kiefer, "What Is a Picturebook, Anyway? The Evolution of Form and Substance through the Postmodern Era and Beyond," in *Postmodern Picturebooks: Play, Parody, and Self-Referentiality,* ed. Lawrence R. Sipe and Sylvia Pantaleo (New York: Routledge, 2008), 18.

75 W. J. T. Mitchell, "Beyond Comparison: Picture, Text, and Method," in *Picture Theory: Essays on Verbal and Visual Representation* (Chicago: University of Chicago Press, 1994), 89–90.

76 Julia Thomas, *Pictorial Victorians: The Inscription of Values in Word and Image* (Athens: Ohio University Press, 2004), 8.

77 Maria Nikolajeva, "Play and Playfulness in Postmodern Picturebooks," in Sipe and Pantaleo, *Postmodern Picturebooks,* 67.

78 Jordan and Patten, "Introduction," 3.

79 Brian Alderson, "Bibliography and Children's Books: The Present Position," *The Library,* 5th ser., 32, no. 3 (1977): 206.

80 For scholarly discussions of the harlequinade, see Reid-Walsh, "Activity and Agency"; Reid-Walsh, "Pantomime, Harlequinades"; Brian Alderson and Felix de Marez Oyens, *Be Merry and Wise: Origins of Children's Book Publishing in England, 1650–1850* (New York: Pierpont Morgan Library, 2006), 118–20; George Speaight with Brian Alderson, "From Chapbooks to Pantomime," in *Popular Children's Literature in Britain,* ed. Julia Briggs, Dennis Butts, and M. O. Grenby (Aldershot: Ashgate, 2008), 87–91; George Speaight, "Harlequinade Turn-Ups," *Theatre Notebook* 45 (1991): 70–84.

81 Reid-Walsh gives a clear technical account of how harlequinades were made in "Pantomime, Harlequinades," 414.

82 See Alderson, *Sing a Song for Sixpence,* 31.

83 See Cathy Lynn Preston and Michael J. Preston, eds., *The Other Print Tradition: Essays on Chapbooks, Broadsides, and Related Ephemera* (New York: Garland, 1995).

84 Maurice Rickards and Michael Twyman, *The Encyclopedia of Ephemera: A Guide to the Fragmentary Documents of Everyday Life for the Collector, Curator, and Historian* (London: British Library, 2000), 218–19, 221.

85 Timothy G. Young, "Evidence: Toward a Library Definition of Ephemera," *RBM: A Journal of Rare Books, Manuscripts, and Cultural Heritage* 4 (2003): 16.

86 Cathy Lynn Preston, introduction to Preston and Preston, *Other Print Tradition,* ix.

87 Ifan Kyrle Fletcher, "Harlequinades," *Theatre Notebook* 1, no. 4 (1946): 46.

88 Susan Stewart, *On Longing: Narratives of the Miniature, the Gigantic, the Souvenir, the Collection* (Durham, N.C.: Duke University Press, 1993), 137–38; Nelson Lee, *The Royal Acting Punch and Judy: As Played before the Queen* (London: Dean and Son, [not before 1873]).

89 On the possibility that harlequinades commemorated children's theater trips in the early nineteenth century, see Reid-Walsh, "Pantomime, Harlequinades," 413–14.

90 Notable exceptions to this rule, in addition to the works cited above in note 5, include

the essays in Bettina Kümmerling-Meibauer, ed., *Picturebooks: Representation and Narration* (New York: Routledge, 2014).

91 *Harlequin's Metamorphoses* (London: E. Tringham, 1780); *Harlequin Skeleton* (London: Robert Sayer, 1772).

92 Maria Nikolajeva and Carole Scott, *How Picturebooks Work* (New York: Garland, 2001), 152.

93 Walter Benjamin, "A Child's View of Color," trans. Rodney Livingstone, in *Selected Writings*, 50.

94 Leah Price, "From *The History of a Book* to a 'History of the Book,'" *Representations* 108 (2009): 120.

### 1. THE THREE RS

1 Although some copies of *The Nursery "Alice"* were published in 1889 and dated thus, these early copies were held back. See Morton N. Cohen, "Another Wonderland: Lewis Carroll's *The Nursery 'Alice,'*" *The Lion and the Unicorn* 7/8 (1983–84): 121.

2 Grenby, *Child Reader*, 9, 255, 281.

3 Sánchez-Eppler, "Marks of Possession," 151.

4 David Lewis, *Reading Contemporary Picturebooks: Picturing Text* (London: Routledge, 2001), 98.

5 *The Children's Wonderland*, by Helen Marion Burnside, illus. Florence Hardy (London: Ernest Nister; New York: E. P. Dutton, [ca. 1900]), date from Hunt and Hunt, *Peeps into Nisterland*, 297.

6 However, Hunt and Hunt trace attributions for many of these pictures in *Peeps into Nisterland*.

7 Georges Perec, "Reading: A Socio-physiological Outline," in *Species of Spaces and Other Pieces*, rev. ed., ed. and trans. John Sturrock (London: Penguin Books, 1999), 175.

8 Michel de Certeau, *The Practice of Everyday Life*, trans. Steven Rendall (Berkeley: University of California Press, 1984), 175.

9 Garrett Stewart, *The Look of Reading: Book, Painting, Text* (Chicago: University of Chicago Press, 2006), 3.

10 Price, *How to Do Things with Books*, 14.

11 Price, 5, 75, 90.

12 Nodelman, *Words about Pictures*, 22.

13 Catherine E. Snow and Anat Ninio, "The Contracts of Literacy: What Children Learn from Learning to Read Books," in *Emergent Literacy: Writing and Reading*, ed. William H.

Teale and Elizabeth Sulzby (Norwood, N.J.: Ablex, 1986), 122. See also Lewis, *Reading Contemporary Picturebooks,* 78.

14 Lian Beveridge, "Chewing on Baby Books as a Form of Infant Literacy: Books Are for Biting," in *More Words about Pictures: Current Research on Picture Books and Visual/Verbal Texts for Young People,* ed. Naomi Hamer, Perry Nodelman, and Mavis Reimer (New York: Routledge, 2017), 19, 28.

15 Armando Petrucci, "Reading to Read: A Future for Reading," in *A History of Reading in the West,* ed. Guglielmo Cavallo and Roger Chartier, trans. Lydia G. Cochrane (Cambridge: Polity Press, 1999), 364. Petrucci includes both children and adolescents in this category of reader, specifying that he speaks about "young people under twenty."

16 See Crain, *Reading Children,* 1.

17 Reid-Walsh, "Activity and Agency," 166; Janet H. Murray, *Hamlet on the Holodeck: The Future of Narrative in Cyberspace* (New York: Free Press, 1997).

18 Marah Gubar, *Artful Dodgers: Reconceiving the Golden Age of Children's Literature* (New York: Oxford University Press, 2009), 4–5. For two recent retrospective surveys of debates concerning agency in children's literature, see "Divergent Perspectives on Children's Agency," special forum, *Jeunesse: Young People, Texts, Cultures* 8, no. 1 (2016): 248–310; David Rudd and Anthony Pavlik, eds., "The (Im)Possibility of Children's Fiction: Rose Twenty-Five Years On," special issue, *Children's Literature Association Quarterly* 35, no. 3 (2010).

19 Margaret Higonnet, "Narrative Fractures and Fragments," *Children's Literature* 15 (1987): 40; Reid-Walsh, "Activity and Agency," 177.

20 Bernstein, *Racial Innocence,* 71, 74.

21 Bernstein, 75, 71, 79; for the larger discussion of *A Coon Alphabet,* see 74–81.

22 Walter Benjamin, "'Old Forgotten Children's Books,'" trans. Rodney Livingstone, in *Selected Writings,* 411.

23 Joyce Irene Whalley and Tessa Chester, *A History of Children's Book Illustration* (London: John Murray, 1988), 150.

24 Benjamin, "'Old Forgotten Children's Books,'" 407. Benjamin's discussion indicates his relative disdain for Victorian children's literature, as opposed to earlier productions including J. F. Bertuch's juvenile encyclopedia (discussed in chapter 2) and the illustrated books of Johann Peter Lyser; nonetheless, his interest in novelties—mentioned in the Introduction—evokes quintessentially *Victorian* children's books. See, for example, Benjamin, "'Old Forgotten Children's Books,'" 407, 408; "Glimpse into the World," 244; and "Notes for a Study of the Beauty of Colored Illustrations in Children's Books: Reflections on Lyser," trans. Rodney Livingstone, in *Selected Writings,* 264–66.

25 Anne Higonnet, *Pictures of Innocence: The History and Crisis of Ideal Childhood* (London: Thames and Hudson, 1998), 8.

26 Patricia Crain, "Postures and Places: The Child Reader in Nineteenth-Century U.S. Popular Print," *ELH* 80 (2013): 343–72. Crain also discusses the trope of the child reading in a window seat at the beginning and end of *Reading Children*, 2–4, 173–74.

27 Lewis Carroll, *"Alice's Adventures in Wonderland" and "Through the Looking-Glass,"* ed. Peter Hunt (Oxford: Oxford University Press, 2009), 25.

28 Grenby, *Child Reader*, 203; Crain, "Postures and Places," 356–58.

29 Stewart, *Look of Reading*, 268.

30 See Crain, *Reading Children*, coda.

31 Carroll, *Alice's Adventures in Wonderland*, 162.

32 Carroll, *Nursery "Alice,"* 1, 56.

33 Lerer, *Children's Literature*, 328.

34 Garrett Stewart, *Dear Reader: The Conscripted Audience in Nineteenth-Century British Fiction* (Baltimore: Johns Hopkins University Press, 1996), 276; Grenby, *Child Reader*, 257.

35 *Comical Kittens and Their Frolics*, by Clifton Bingham (London: Raphael Tuck and Sons, [ca. 1896]), date from University of Connecticut Library.

36 The inscription is "Mast. Jno / Adams 5th Class, / No. 15 Third Desk." Grenby, *Child Reader*, 205.

37 *The Magic Toy Book* (London: E. Nister; New York: E. P. Dutton, [ca. 1890]), date and publication information from Hunt and Hunt, *Peeps into Nisterland*, 292.

38 *Our Peepshow*, by F. E. Weatherly (London: Ernest Nister; New York: E. P. Dutton, [ca. 1897]), date from Hunt and Hunt, *Peeps into Nisterland*, 295. The title on the cover is *Our Peepshow: A Novel Panorama Book.*

39 Verity Hunt, "Technologies of Wonder: Optical Devices, Perception and the Book, 1851–1895" (PhD thesis, University of Reading, 2009), 209.

40 Kate Flint, "Afterword: Women Readers Revisited," in *Reading Women: Literary Figures and Cultural Icons from the Victorian Age to the Present*, ed. Janet Badia and Jennifer Phegley (Toronto: University of Toronto Press, 2005), 284.

41 *The Robins at Home*, by F. E. Weatherly (London: E. Nister; New York: E. P. Dutton, [189-?]), date from Columbia University Libraries.

42 Crain discusses siblings reading together in "Postures and Places," 353–54.

43 Stewart, *Look of Reading*, 14.

44 *Peeps into Fairyland*, by F. E. Weatherly (London: E. Nister; New York: E. P. Dutton, [ca. 1896]), n.p., date from Hunt and Hunt, *Peeps into Nisterland*, 294.

45 Roger Chartier, "Texts, Printings, Readings," in *The New Cultural History,* ed. Lynn Hunt (Berkeley: University of California Press, 1989), 160.

46 Chartier, 158–59.

47 Leah Price, "Reading: The State of the Discipline," *Book History* 7 (2004): 310.

48 Kate Flint, *The Woman Reader, 1837–1914* (Oxford: Clarendon Press, 1995), 194.

49 *Fireside Pictures* (London: Raphael Tuck and Sons, [ca. 1900]).

50 See Stewart, *Look of Reading,* 13.

51 Stewart dubs the process by which the viewer's eyes are drawn to the cover of a book in pictures of reading "the decipherable urge" (8).

52 Maria Tatar, *Enchanted Hunters: The Power of Stories in Childhood* (New York: W. W. Norton, 2009), 51.

53 *The Fairies' Playtime,* by Clifton Bingham (New York: E. P. Dutton; London: E. Nister, [ca. 1896]), date from Hunt and Hunt, *Peeps into Nisterland,* 294.

54 Mary Carbery, *Happy World: The Story of a Victorian Childhood* (London: Longmans, Green, 1941), quoted in Flint, *Woman Reader,* 200.

55 The four books in the original Surprise Model series are *Surprise Model Picture Book*; *Tale of an Old Sugar Tub: With Surprise Model Pictures*; *Seaside Fun: With Surprise Model Pictures*; and *A Visit to the Country: With Surprise Model Pictures.* All of the books were published in London by Dean and Son in 1891 (my date). *The Surprise Animal Picture Book,* which was of similar design, was released around 1895.

56 F. C. Westley, *The Paignion* ([London]: F. C. Westley, [ca. 1830]).

57 *The Sleeping Beauty and Little Snowdrop,* Father Tuck's "Panorama" Series (London: Raphael Tuck and Sons, [19—]).

58 *The Motograph Moving Picture Book,* illus. F. J. Vernay, Yorick, et al. (London: Bliss, Sands, 1898). Contemporary reviews show that the book, despite its sophisticated cover, was understood as children's literature, as when the *Spectator*'s reviewer commends the *Motograph* album thus: "Parents and guardians who have to amuse little boys with a turn for nursery-science will do well to buy this book." "Current Literature," *Spectator,* January 1, 1898, 32.

59 *Cinderella and the Glass Slipper and the Pantomime* (London: R. March, [19-?]).

60 Mrs. M. J. Wells, *Living Nursery Rhymes: Newly Treated with Moving Pictures,* Dean's New Surprise Picture Books (London: Dean and Son, [not before 1873]).

61 Bernstein, *Racial Innocence,* 71.

62 These lines come from the verse drama *Richelieu,* first published in 1839; see Andrew Brown, "Lytton, Edward George Earle Lytton Bulwer, First Baron Lytton (1803–1873)," *Oxford Dictionary of National Biography Online,* accessed March 20, 2017, doi:10.1093/

ref:odnb/17314. For "RECOLLECT THAT PAPER IS NOT IRON," see also Faden, "Movables, Movies, Mobility," 74; Haining, *Movable Books,* 32.

63 See Immel, "Frederick Lock's Scrapbook," 67.

64 See Grenby, *Child Reader,* 177, 27.

65 The Author of "The Heir of Redclyffe," "Heartsease," etc. [Charlotte M. Yonge], *The Young Step-mother; or, A Chronicle of Mistakes* (London: Parker, Son, and Bourn, 1861), 309.

66 Unsigned review of *The Young Stepmother: A Chronicle of Mistakes,* by the Author of "The Heir of Redclyffe" &c., *The Athenæum,* December 21, 1861, 838.

67 Yonge, *Young Step-mother,* 309, 311, 314.

68 Charlotte M. Yonge, *What Books to Lend and What to Give* (London: National Society's Depository, [1887]), 12, date from Charlotte Mary Yonge Fellowship, Durham University.

69 For example, an advertisement for the indestructible primers appeared on the back cover of Darton's *Jack the Giant-Killer* (ca. 1860). See Linda David, *Children's Books Published by William Darton and His Sons: A Catalogue of an Exhibition at the Lilly Library, Indiana University, April–June, 1992* (Bloomington: Lilly Library, Indiana University, 1992), 14, entry 16, http://www.indiana.edu/~liblilly.

70 These advertisements appeared, respectively, on the back covers of Sarah Catherine Martin, *A New Story about Mother Hubbard and Her Dog,* movable ed. (London: Ward and Lock, [between 1854 and 1861]), and Dean's *Old Sugar Tub.*

71 Darton, *Children's Books in England* (1999), 208. For an image of the logo, see "Dean's Rag Book Company Trade Advert (Games and Toys 1956)," Brighton Toy and Model Index, Brighton Toy and Model Museum, June 15, 2014, http://www.brightontoy museum.co.uk/index.

72 *Dean's New Moveable Book of the Popular Performance of Galanti Show* (London: Dean and Son, [ca. 1861]), endpapers, date from the *Penny Illustrated Paper,* December 21, 1861, 176.

73 *Dean and Son's Moveable Book of the Royal Punch and Judy, as Played before the Queen at Windsor Castle and the Crystal Palace* (London: Dean and Son, [1861]), endpapers, date from Houghton Library, Harvard University.

74 Lothar Meggendorfer, *Comic Actors: A New Movable Toy Book* (London: H. Grevel, [1890]).

75 Lothar Meggendorfer, *Aus dem Leben: Lustiges Ziehbilderbuch* [From life: A merry tab-pull picture book], 2nd ed. (Munich: Braun and Schneider, [ca. 1890]), date from Bayerische Staatsbibliothek. I discuss a subsequent edition of this book, with different images, in chapter 5.

76 See Weikle-Mills, *Imaginary Citizens,* chap. 2.

77 Sánchez-Eppler, "Marks of Possession," 155.

78 H. J. Jackson, *Marginalia: Readers Writing in Books* (New Haven, Conn.: Yale University Press, 2001), 14, 21.

79 Jackson, 19.

80 Seth Lerer, "Devotion and Defacement: Reading Children's Marginalia," *Representations* 118 (2012): 127, 128.

81 Gillian Adams, "In the Hands of Children," in Joseph and Paul, "Handmade Literacies," 38.

82 Grenby, *Child Reader,* 28; Crain, *Reading Children,* 123.

83 On the example of *Wuthering Heights,* see Jackson, *Marginalia,* 120–21; Lerer, "Devotion and Defacement," 142.

84 Lerer, "Devotion and Defacement," 128.

85 Crain, *Reading Children,* 9.

86 H. J. Jackson, *Romantic Readers: The Evidence of Marginalia* (New Haven, Conn.: Yale University Press, 2005), 60.

87 Grenby, *Child Reader,* 227–31.

88 Jacqueline Reid-Walsh, "Artifactual Memory: Fragmentary 'Memoirs' of Three Eighteenth- and Nineteenth-Century Moveable Books about Their Child Owners," in *Productive Remembering and Social Agency,* ed. Teresa Strong-Wilson, Claudia Mitchell, Susann Allnutt, and Kathleen Pithouse-Morgan (Rotterdam: Sense, 2013), 198. Some of the modifications that Reid-Walsh charts involved producing new illustrations as well as new written texts.

89 Price, *How to Do Things with Books,* 19.

90 Collins links the grubbiness of this book to juvenile reading—"a beautiful girl" sullies a copy of *The Catcher in the Rye* with "'egg salad stains.'" Billy Collins, "Marginalia," in *Picnic, Lightning* (Pittsburgh: University of Pittsburgh Press, 1998), 16.

91 Price, *How to Do Things with Books,* 20.

92 *This Is the House That Jack Built* (London: Dean and Son, [1860]), shelfmark Opie EE 117, date from *The Literary and Educational Year Book.*

93 Lothar Meggendorfer, *Curious Creatures: A New Movable Toybook of All Kinds of Animals* (London: H. Grevel, [1890]), shelfmark Rec. d.516.

94 *Visit to the Country,* shelfmark Opie EE 300.

95 Lothar Meggendorfer, *Tiny Tim, Prince of Liliput* (London: H. Grevel, [1898]), shelfmark 252 c.146.

96 *Playtime Surprises,* shelfmark Opie EE 29; *Pleasant Surprises* (London: E. Nister; New York: E. P. Dutton, [ca. 1891]), shelfmark Opie EE 30; *Something New for Little Folk,*

by Clifton Bingham (London: Ernest Nister; New York: E. P. Dutton, [ca. 1899]), shelfmark Opie EE 31, dates for *Pleasant Surprises* and *Something New* from Hunt and Hunt, *Peeps into Nisterland,* 292, 297. The title of *Pleasant Surprises* is given as *Pleasant Surprises for Folks of All Sizes* on the book's cover.

97 *Sleeping Beauty,* shelfmark Opie EE 256.

98 Grenby, *Child Reader,* 205.

99 Benjamin, "'Old Forgotten Children's Books,'" 411.

100 Sánchez-Eppler also notes the ambiguity of coloring-in as part of her discussion of the Dickinson children. Sánchez-Eppler, "Marks of Possession," 153.

101 Benjamin, "'Old Forgotten Children's Books,'" 406.

102 See Curtis, *Visual Words,* 274.

103 Randolph Caldecott to Frederick Locker, unpublished letter, November 17, 1883, quoted in Trumpener, "City Scenes," 362–63.

104 Mary Denson Pretlow, "The Opening Day—and after—in a Children's Library," *Library Journal* 33 (1908): 179, quoted in Kathleen McDowell, "Toward a History of Children as Readers, 1890–1930," *Book History* 12 (2009): 258.

105 For the price of Meggendorfer's books, see, for example, two advertisements placed by his British publisher, H. Grevel and Company, in 1889, in *Publishers' Circular and General Record of British and Foreign Literature,* August 15, 1889, 994, and December 6, 1889, 404. Simon Eliot has proposed eleven price bands for nineteenth-century books, with seven shillings and sixpence at the top of the seventh band. Eliot, *Some Patterns,* 60.

106 [W. Roberts], "Life on a Guinea a Week," *The Nineteenth Century,* March 1888, 465, author attribution from the Wellesley Index to Victorian Periodicals.

107 Viviana A. Zelizer, *Pricing the Priceless Child: The Changing Social Value of Children* (New York: Basic Books, 1985), 6.

108 Marta Gutman and Ning de Coninck-Smith, "Introduction: Good to Think with—History, Space, and Modern Childhood," in *Designing Modern Childhoods: History, Space, and the Material Culture of Children,* ed. Marta Gutman and Ning de Coninck-Smith (New Brunswick, N.J.: Rutgers University Press, 2008), 13.

109 See Field, "'A Story, Exemplified,'" 54.

110 *Transformation Pictures and Comical Fixtures* (London: Ernest Nister; New York: E. P. Dutton, [ca. 1891]), shelfmark Opie EE 32, date from Hunt and Hunt, *Peeps into Nisterland,* 292.

111 *Old Sugar Tub,* shelfmark General Reference 12806b.l.74, British Library.

112 Sánchez-Eppler points out that provenances in private collections make the children's archive a home for "the scrap and the scribble as well as the tome," even in the

most august libraries. Karen Sánchez-Eppler, "In the Archives of Childhood," in *The Children's Table: Childhood Studies and the Humanities,* ed. Anna Mae Duane (Athens: University of Georgia Press, 2013), 215.

113 *Dean's Moveable Cock Robin* (London: Dean and Son, [1857]), shelfmark Opie EE 57, my date.

114 *The History of How Ned Nimble Built His Cottage . . .* (London: Dean and Son, [1860]), shelfmark Opie EE 113, date from *The Literary and Educational Year Book.*

115 *A Morning Ride mid Country Scenes,* Stories Told in Pictures—First Story (London: G. Routledge, 1852), shelfmark Opie EE 190.

116 Martin, *New Story,* shelfmark Opie EE 198.

117 The term *scissorizing* comes from Ellen Gruber Garvey, *Writing with Scissors: American Scrapbooks from the Civil War to the Harlem Renaissance* (New York: Oxford University Press, 2013).

118 Lerer, *Children's Literature,* 90.

119 Sánchez-Eppler, "In the Archives of Childhood," 223.

## 2. AGAINST THE WALL

1 For instructions on making the cockhat fold (including a diagram), see Lina Orman Cooper, "Paper Folding," *Girl's Own Paper,* 1900, 797. For an early nineteenth-century puzzle-purse Valentine, see Cynthia V. A. Schaffner and Susan Klein, *Folk Hearts: A Celebration of the Heart Motif in American Folk Art* (New York: Alfred A. Knopf, 1984), 98–99.

2 For an example of *cadavre exquis,* see Yves Tanguy, Joan Miró, Max Morise, and Man Ray, *Nude,* 1926–27, composite drawing, 35.9 × 22.9 cm, Museum of Modern Art, New York, object number 260.1935.

3 Keith A. Smith, *Structure of the Visual Book,* 3rd ed. (Rochester: Keith Smith Books, 1994), 23. Smith prefers the term *oriental fold book* to *panorama*; however, the formats are identical. For a recent discussion of contemporary artists' book panoramas and their intersection with children's picture books, see Carole Scott, "Artists' Books, Altered Books, and Picturebooks," in Kümmerling-Meibauer, *Picturebooks,* 42–48.

4 Jeffrey Masten, Peter Stallybrass, and Nancy J. Vickers, "Introduction: Language Machines," in *Language Machines: Technologies of Literary and Cultural Production,* ed. Jeffrey Masten, Peter Stallybrass, and Nancy J. Vickers (New York: Routledge, 1997), 2.

5 See, for instance, Nodelman's statement that "stories, which are about movements and changes, necessarily take place in time, whereas most pictures depict only how

things look at one moment separated from the flow of time." Nodelman, *Words about Pictures,* 158.

6 Here I build on Mieke Bal's refutation of the illusion that taking in a picture "can be done in a blink"; in fact, says Bal, "still artifacts also 'take time.'" Mieke Bal, *Narratology: Introduction to the Theory of Narrative,* 3rd ed., trans. Carol Van Boheemen (Toronto: University of Toronto Press, 2009), 77.

7 "Specification of the Patent Granted to Mr. Robert Barker . . . ," in *The Repertory of Arts and Manufactures,* vol. 4 (London, 1796), 165.

8 For a detailed analysis of Barker's panoramas of London and the Grand Fleet, neither of which survives, see Ellis, "'Spectacles within Doors,'" 137–44. For the Colosseum panoramas, see Richard D. Altick, *The Shows of London* (Cambridge, Mass.: Belknap Press, 1978), 141–62.

9 Charles Dickens, "The American Panorama," in *Dickens' Journalism,* vol. 2, *"The Amusements of the People" and Other Papers: Reports, Essays and Reviews, 1834–1851,* ed. Michael Slater (London: Dent, 1997), 135.

10 Rickards and Twyman, *Encyclopedia of Ephemera,* s.v. "Panorama, newspaper give-aways," 219.

11 Maria Edgeworth to Mrs. Ruxton, June 1813, in *The Life and Letters of Maria Edgeworth,* ed. Augustus J. C. Hare (Boston: Houghton, Mifflin, 1895), 1:227; Maria Edgeworth to Mrs. Edgeworth, May 28, 1822, in *Life and Letters,* 2:427.

12 Bernard Comment, *The Panorama,* trans. Anne-Marie Glasheen (London: Reaktion Books, 1999), 8. Walter Benjamin's famous statement "The interest of the panorama is in seeing the true city—the city indoors," which Ellis uses as an epigraph to his article, also points to the metropolitan character of the panorama. Walter Benjamin, "Q: [Panorama]," in *The Arcades Project,* ed. Rolf Tiedemann, trans. Howard Eiland and Kevin McLaughlin (Cambridge, Mass.: Belknap Press, 1999), 532; Ellis, "'Spectacles within Doors,'" 133.

13 Maria Edgeworth to Mrs. Edgeworth, October 1812, in *Life and Letters,* 1:194.

14 Unsigned review of *What Will He Do with It?,* by Edward Bulwer Lytton, *Sharpe's London Magazine of Entertainment and Instruction,* July 1859, 106.

15 Benjamin, "Q: [Panorama]," 531.

16 Meisel, *Realizations,* 374.

17 Hayden White, "The Value of Narrativity in the Representation of Reality," in "On Narrative," ed. W. J. T. Mitchell, special issue, *Critical Inquiry* 7, no. 1 (1980): 11.

18 "Banvard's Panorama of the Mississippi and Missouri Rivers," *Illustrated London News,* December 9, 1848, 364.

19 Altick, *Shows of London,* 205.

20 "Banvard's Panorama," 364. *Jonathanism* comes from the word *Jonathan* as a "generic name for the people of the United States" *(OED)*: a verbal genre to match the American sights that Banvard brought before his British viewers.

21 Scott D. Wilcox, "Unlimiting the Bounds of Painting," in Ralph Hyde, *Panoramania! The Art and Entertainment of the "All-Embracing" View* (London: Trefoil/Barbican Art Gallery, 1988), 36.

22 Ellis, "'Spectacles within Doors,'" 138.

23 For a valuable collection of panoramic texts, see Laurie Garrison, ed., *Panoramas, 1787–1900: Texts and Contexts,* 5 vols. (London: Pickering and Chatto, 2012).

24 Katie Trumpener, "Picture-Book Worlds and Ways of Seeing," in Grenby and Immel, *Cambridge Companion to Children's Literature,* 64.

25 Emma Bosch, "Texts and Peritexts in Wordless and Almost Wordless Picturebooks," in Kümmerling-Meibauer, *Picturebooks,* 71–90.

26 Tom Gunning, "The Cinema of Attraction: Early Film, Its Spectator and the Avant-Garde," *Wide Angle* 8 (1986): 64.

27 Gilles Deleuze, *Cinema 1: The Movement-Image,* trans. Hugh Tomlinson and Barbara Habberjam (Minneapolis: University of Minnesota Press, 1986), 1.

28 Ellis, "'Spectacles within Doors,'" 134.

29 Rickards and Twyman, *Encyclopedia of Ephemera,* s.v. "ABC primer," 2; Alderson, *Sing a Song for Sixpence,* 17.

30 Patricia Crain, *The Story of A: The Alphabetization of America from "The New England Primer" to "The Scarlet Letter"* (Stanford, Calif.: Stanford University Press, 2001), 18.

31 George Cruikshank, *A Comic Alphabet* (London: published by author, 1836). For details of Honoré Daumier's panoramic alphabet, also produced in 1836, see the Daumier Register, ed. Dieter Noack and Lilian Noack, no. 323, last updated November 15, 2016, http://www.daumier-register.org/werkview.php?key=323. Daumier's alphabet was part of the series Petites Macédoines d'Aubert (Aubert's little medleys).

32 A. Robin Hoffman has argued that the *Comic Alphabet* "manipulate[s] publishing practices and formal conventions in order to *evoke* a child audience while primarily addressing an *adult* audience." A. Robin Hoffman, "George Cruikshank's *Comic Alphabet* (1836) and the Audience 'à la Mode,'" *Nineteenth-Century Contexts* 36 (2014): 138. The *Comic Alphabet*'s physical format (panoramic frieze), genre (ABC), and content (including the focus on animals), however, are all germane to juvenile publishing—hence my discussion of it alongside other children's panoramas here.

33 See, in order, Alderson, *Sing a Song for Sixpence,* 56; Alexander M. Cohn, *George Cruikshank: A Catalogue Raisonné of the Work Executed during the Years 1806–1877 . . .*

(London: Office of the Bookman's Journal, 1924), 62; W. C. B., "Toothache," *Notes and Queries,* 10th ser., 10, no. 242 (1908): 122.

34 Hoffman also makes this point in "George Cruikshank's *Comic Alphabet,*" 143.

35 The pairing of *I* with *J* and *U* with *V* reflects earlier typographical conventions that treated the letters in these pairs as interchangeable.

36 One rare vertical panorama plots a trip to the moon; see Aliquis, *The Flight of the Old Woman Who Was Tossed Up in a Basket* (London: D. Bogue, [1844]).

37 Crain analyzes a similar alphabet as "a republic of ABCs whose citizen-letters are identified and categorized according to trade . . . , state . . . , or station." Crain, *Story of A,* 68.

38 Hoffman reads the image as a gentleman and a "squat, soot-covered laborer," but I believe there is also a racial dimension to the satire. Hoffman, "George Cruikshank's *Comic Alphabet,*" 159.

39 Laura Brown, *Homeless Dogs and Melancholy Apes: Humans and Other Animals in the Modern Literary Imagination* (Ithaca, N.Y.: Cornell University Press, 2010), chap. 4.

40 *Alfred Crowquill's Comic History of the Kings and Queens of England from William the Conqueror to the Present Time: Containing 36 Illustrations* (London: Read, [1856 or 1857]), date from Lilly Library, Indiana University. Alfred Crowquill was the pseudonym of the illustrator and writer Alfred Forrester; before 1850, Forrester and his brother Charles used the moniker for collaborative publications.

41 Altick, *Shows of London,* 232.

42 Plunkett, "Moving Books," 13.

43 *Panorama of the Kings and Queens of England: From William the Conqueror to Queen Victoria* (Leeds: Webb and Millington, [between 1840 and 1860]).

44 See, for example, treatments of Cromwell and the Commonwealth in roughly contemporaneous children's histories as follows: the Author of "General Reading for Schools," &c. [Emily Taylor], *England and Its People; or, A Familiar History of the Country . . .* (London: Houlston, 1839), pt. 5, 1–20; Anne Lydia Bond, *The History of England: For the Use of Young Persons* (London: David Bogue, 1848), 191–96; Miss Edmonds, *Tegg's First Book of English History . . .* (London: William Tegg, 1862), 56–59; H. W. Dulcken, *A Handy History of England for the Young* (London: George Routledge and Sons, [1874]), 392–408.

45 Paul Ricoeur, "Narrative Time," in Mitchell, "On Narrative," 169–70.

46 *Playtime Panorama* (London: Dean and Son, [ca. 1880–1900]).

47 Lerer, *Children's Literature,* 107.

48 Nikolajeva, "Play and Playfulness," 63.

49 De Certeau, *Practice of Everyday Life,* 115, 120.

50 Andrea Henderson, "Mastery and Melancholy in Suburbia," in "Technologies of Emotion," ed. Laura Mandell, special issue, *The Eighteenth Century* 50, nos. 2–3 (2009): 225.

51 *A Morning Ride,* 8. Further page references to *A Morning Ride* will appear parenthetically in the body of the chapter.

52 See Éric de Kuyper and Émile Poppe, "Voir et regarder" [To see and to look], *Communications* 34 (1981): 85–96.

53 Alf Seegert, "'Steam of Consciousness': Technology and Sensation in Dickens' Railway Sketches," *Philament,* August 2009, 102, http://www.philamentjournal.com.

54 Wolfgang Schivelbusch, *The Railway Journey: Trains and Travel in the 19th Century,* trans. Anselm Hollo (Oxford: Basil Blackwell, 1980), 63–65.

55 Nicholas Daly, *Literature, Technology, and Modernity, 1860–2000* (Cambridge: Cambridge University Press, 2004), 2.

56 Daly, 3.

57 Ray argues that the picturesque trains in John Cooke Bourne's illustrated *History and Description of the Great Western Railway* (1846) were a departure from Bourne's preceding volume, *Drawings of the London and Birmingham Railway* (1839). See Ray, *Illustrator and the Book,* 55.

58 Altick, *Shows of London,* 231.

59 Trumpener, "City Scenes," 363.

60 The Bodleian's copy is shelfmark Opie EE 190. For biographical information about Eleanor Portal, see Charles Mosley, ed., *Burke's Peerage, Baronetage, and Knightage . . . ,* 107th ed. (Wilmington: Burke's Peerage and Gentry, 2003), 3:3178–79.

61 William Goodall, *The Adventures of Capt. Greenland . . .* (London: R. Baldwin, 1752), 1:32.

62 Schivelbusch, *Railway Journey,* 58.

63 *A New Illustrated Edition of J. S. Rarey's Art of Taming Horses . . .* (London: Routledge, Warnes, and Routledge, 1859), 206–7.

64 Nikolajeva and Scott, *How Picturebooks Work,* 153.

65 [William Cowper], "The Entertaining and Facetious History of John Gilpin . . . ," *Public Advertiser,* November 14, 1782; William Cowper, "The Diverting History of John Gilpin, Shewing How He Went Farther Than He Intended and Came Home Safe Again," in *The Task: A Poem, in Six Books* (London: printed for J. Johnson, 1785), 342–59. Further page references to "John Gilpin" as revised in *The Task* will appear parenthetically in the body of the chapter.

66 Charles Ryskamp, "The First Illustrations to *John Gilpin,*" *Notes and Queries* 53 (2006): 210–11.

67 Geoffrey Hartman, "The Psycho-aesthetics of Romantic Moonshine: Wordsworth's Profane Illumination," *Wordsworth Circle* 37 (2006): 9.

68 Tony Voss, "Mazeppa-Maseppa: Migration of a Romantic Motif," *Tydskrif vir Letterkunde* 49 (2012): 111.

69 See Samuel Collings, "Gilpin Going Farther Than He Intended," 1784, print on laid paper, 17 × 20 cm, call number 784.08.01.01, Lewis Walpole Library, Yale University.

70 Immel, "Frederick Lock's Scrapbook," 67.

71 "[Sheet with 30 small images, mostly of horses]," [1800–1810?], single-sheet woodcut, 22.0 × 27.6 cm, shelfmark Trade in Prints and Scraps 20 (31), John Johnson Collection of Printed Ephemera, Bodleian Library, University of Oxford.

72 "John Gilpin," [1880–90?], shelfmark Scraps 8 (24), John Johnson Collection of Printed Ephemera, Bodleian Library, University of Oxford.

73 A. D. R. Tompkins, "A Nursery Version of 'John Gilpin,'" *Notes and Queries* 9 (1962): 460.

74 Richard D. Altick, *Paintings from Books: Art and Literature in Britain, 1760–1900* (Columbus: Ohio State University Press, 1985), 116. The phrase *amiable humorist* comes from Stuart Tave's book *The Amiable Humorist: A Study in the Comic Theory and Criticism of the Eighteenth and Early Nineteenth Centuries* (Chicago: University of Chicago Press, 1960).

75 Randolph Caldecott, illus., *The Diverting History of John Gilpin,* by William Cowper ([London]: G. Routledge and Sons, [1878]); Brian Alderson, "Picture Book Anatomy," review of *Words about Pictures: The Narrative Art of Children's Picture Books,* by Perry Nodelman, *The Lion and the Unicorn* 14 (1990): 113.

76 Peter Brooks, *Reading for the Plot: Design and Intention in Narrative* (Cambridge, Mass.: Harvard University Press, 1992), 104.

77 [Leigh Hunt], "Sketches of the Living Poets, No. 1: The Rev. William Lisle Bowles," *Examiner,* July 15, 1821, 445.

78 Cowper, "Entertaining and Facetious History," n.p., emphasis added.

79 Percy Cruikshank, illus., *Cowper's Diverting History of John Gilpin* (London: Read, [1850?]). The Bodleian possesses two different copies of the panorama version of Percy Cruikshank's *John Gilpin*: one has text blocks above and below the images, and one (shown in Figures 2.6 and 2.7) has text below the images only. The illustrations were reused in a conventional picture-book version also held in the Opie Collection, shelfmark Opie P 12.

80 Jeffrey T. Schnapp, "The Mass Panorama," *Modernism/modernity* 9 (2002): 243.

81 Alderson and de Marez Oyens, *Be Merry and Wise,* 285.

82 F. Scott and Son, "Wallpaper," ca. 1862, color machine print, 96.5 × 55.6 cm, museum number 21249, Victoria and Albert Museum, London; E. A. Entwisle, *Wallpapers of the Victorian Era* (Leigh-on-Sea: F. Lewis, 1964), plate 43.

83 Advertisement for *Findens' Royal Gallery of British Art, Literary Gazette,* May 25, 1839, 335.

84 Examples of all these designs are held at the Victoria and Albert Museum, London: David Walker, "The Months; Wallpaper," 1893, color print from engraved rollers, 76.2 × 54.9 cm, museum number E.1823-1934; Walter Crane and Jeffrey, "The Sleeping Beauty," 1879, color machine-print wallpaper, 310 × 56.8 cm, museum number E.60-1968; Walter Crane and Lightbown, Aspinall, and Company, "Mistress Mary," 1903, wallpaper frieze machine printed from engraved rollers, 53.3 × 64.7 cm, museum number E.5161-1919. For an illuminating discussion of the difference between Greenaway's licensing of her images to Walker and Crane's artisanal design of patterns for Jeffrey, see Sarah Hyde, *Exhibiting Gender* (Manchester: Manchester University Press, 1997), 89–91.

85 Walter Crane and Jeffrey, "Briar Rose," 1880, color woodblock print wallpaper, 50.3 × 50.8 cm, museum number E.5090-1919, Victoria and Albert Museum, London.

86 For larger discussions of the Greenaway phenomenon, see Michael Patrick Hearn, "Mr. Ruskin and Miss Greenaway," *Children's Literature* 8 (1980): 22–34; Anne Lundin, "Sensational Designs: The Cultural Work of Kate Greenaway," in *Literature and the Child: Romantic Continuations, Postmodern Contestations,* ed. James Holt McGavran (Iowa City: University of Iowa Press, 1999), 155–87.

87 See Charlotte Perkins Gilman, "The Yellow Wallpaper," *New England Magazine*, n.s., January 1892, 647–48; Honoré de Balzac, *Le Père Goriot* [Old Goriot], in *Scènes de la vie privée* [Scenes from private life], vol. 1, *La Comédie humaine* [The human comedy] (Paris: Éditions Garnier, 2008), 70. *Papiers panoramiques* offered "a continuous landscape without any repetition of scenes or of motifs"; some time after they were adopted in England, they were criticized as "widely removed from true principles of taste." See Lesley Hoskins, ed., *The Papered Wall: History, Pattern, Technique* (London: Thames and Hudson, 1994), 94; Charles Eastlake, *Hints on Household Taste in Furniture, Upholstery and Other Details,* 4th ed. (1878; repr., New York: Dover, 1969), 115. The *papiers panoramiques* in *Père Goriot* are emblazoned with scenes from François Fénelon's *Les Aventures de Télémaque* [The adventures of Telemachus] (1699).

88 Charles Dickens, *Hard Times,* ed. Fred Kaplan and Sylvère Monod (New York: W. W. Norton, 2001), 8.

89 Hoskins, *Papered Wall,* 144.

90 Colette, *L'Enfant et les sortilèges: Fantaisie lyrique, en deux parties* [The child and the spells: A lyric fantasy, in two parts], music by Maurice Ravel (Paris: A. Durand et Fils, n.d.), 33, my translation.

91 William Makepeace Thackeray, *Vanity Fair: A Novel without a Hero,* ed. Peter L. Shillingsburg (New York: Garland, 1989), 338.

92 David McKitterick, introduction to *The Cambridge History of the Book in Britain,* vol. 6, *1830–1914,* ed. David McKitterick (Cambridge: Cambridge University Press, 2009), 51.

93 F. J. Bertuch, preface to *Bilderbuch für Kinder: Enthaltend eine angenehme Sammlung von Thieren, Pflanzen, Früchten, Mineralien . . .* [Picture book for children: Containing a pleasant collection of animals, plants, fruits, minerals . . .], 2nd ed. (Weimar: Industrie-Comptoirs, 1801), 1:n.p. Benjamin discusses Bertuch's instructions in "'Old Forgotten Children's Books,'" 408.

94 *Cassell's Household Guide: Being a Complete Encyclopaedia of Domestic and Social Economy, and Forming a Guide to Every Department of Practical Life* (London: Cassell, Peter, and Galpin, [1869]), 1:110.

95 Robert W. Edis, *Decoration and Furniture of Town Houses* (1881; facsimile, Wakefield: EP Publishing, 1972), 228, 229.

96 Garvey, *Writing with Scissors,* 11.

97 Sánchez-Eppler, "Marks of Possession," 156.

98 *Panoramic Alphabet: Second Series* (Leeds: Webb and Millington, [between ca. 1842 and 1899]); *The Sea* (Leeds: Webb, Millington, [between 1840 and 1860?]); *Panoramic Keepsake* (Leeds: Webb and Millington, [ca. 1855]); *Panoramic Museum* (Leeds: Webb and Millington, [between 1840 and 1860?]); *Panorama of Horses* (London: Webb, Millington, [between ca. 1853 and 1857]); *Beasts,* Indestructible Panoramas (London: Webb, Millington, [ca. 1850–60]), date from David Miles Books, Canterbury. An advertisement on the back of *Beasts* lists titles in the Indestructible Panoramas series, including two alphabet panoramas, *Birds, Beasts,* the *Keepsake,* the *Museum, The Sea,* and *Horses.*

99 The Baldwin Library's copy of the *Keepsake,* which is pictured in Plate 9, differs from that in the Bodleian—Webb and Millington's panoramas reuse illustrations in different combinations, including, it seems, in different editions under the same title. The panels in the Bodleian foldout show the following animals: horse, snake, parrot, squirrel, frog, jay, goat, magpie, cat, turkey, sheep, goose, cow, owl, duck, zebra, bullfinch, pony.

100 As a rough comparative guide, all nineteenth-century books costing less than three shillings are classified as low price by Eliot in *Some Patterns,* 60.

101 An advertisement showing this price for the Crane paper is held at the Victoria and Albert Museum. Walter Crane and James Akerman, "The Peacock Garden," ca. 1889, process halftone engraving on paper, museum number E.4054-1915, Victoria and Albert Museum, London.

102 See the advertisements on the back cover of the *Playtime Panorama.*

103 *Art and Architecture Thesaurus Online,* s.v. "ephemera (general)," Getty Research Institute, accessed April 20, 2017, http://www.getty.edu.

104 Young, "Evidence," 16.

105 Sánchez-Eppler, "Marks of Possession," 156.

106 Michel Foucault, "Different Spaces," trans. Robert Hurley, in *Essential Works of Foucault, 1954–1984,* vol. 2, *Aesthetics, Method, and Epistemology,* ed. James D. Faubion (New York: New Press, 1998), 182.

107 "Miss Miles' House," 1890, wooden dollhouse, museum number W.146-1921, Victoria and Albert Museum, London.

## 3. THE MOVABLE BOOK IN 3-D

1 Roger E. Stoddard, "Morphology and the Book from an American Perspective," *Printing History* 17 (1987): 8.

2 David Bland, *A History of Book Illustration: The Illuminated Manuscript and the Printed Book* (London: Faber and Faber, 1958), 65.

3 "Glossary," ArchBook: Architectures of the Book, University of Saskatchewan Humanities and Fine Arts Digital Research Centre, accessed April 24, 2017, http://drc.usask.ca/projects/archbook.

4 Dawson, "S. Louis Giraud," 219.

5 Altick, *Shows of London,* 56. For a richly illustrated account of early peepshows, see Richard Balzer, *Peepshows: A Visual History* (New York: Harry N. Abrams, 1998).

6 Kimberley Reynolds and Nicholas Tucker, introductory note to Fox, "Movable Books," 86.

7 See Haining, *Movable Books,* 30.

8 Unsigned review of *The Land of Long Ago,* by L. L. Weedon, *Spectator,* December 10, 1898, 877; "Dutton's Books and Calendars," *New York Observer and Chronicle,* December 1, 1890, 710.

9 For summaries of different pop-up techniques, see Children's Books History Society, "Novelty Books," 18–19; Booktrust, *Pop-Ups! A Guide to Novelty Books* (London: Booktrust, 2002), 20–21.

10 Rickards and Twyman, *Encyclopedia of Ephemera,* s.v. "Christmas card," 91; Mrs. Edith E. Cuthell, "Where the Christmas Cards Are Made," *Hearth and Home,* December 30, 1897, 334.

11 *Fun at the Circus,* Combined Expanding Toy and Painting Book Series (London: Raphael Tuck and Sons, [1892]), date from University of Florida Libraries; Raphael Tuck and Sons, "[Only to Say How Do You Do / And Introduce Myself to You]," [1880–1900?], embossed chromolithographed scraps, 11.5 × 22.5 cm, shelfmark Scraps 10 (33b)—Circuses, Fairs etc., John Johnson Collection, Bodleian Library, University of Oxford.

12 Lothar Meggendorfer, *Internationaler Circus* [International circus] (Munich: J. F. Schreiber, [1887]), date from facsimile edition of 1979; Margaret Higonnet, "Movable Books: Transnational Publication and Cultural Translations," in *Kinder- und Jugendliteraturforschung international: Ansichten und Ausstichten . . .* [International children's and young adult literature: Views and prospects . . .], ed. Ute Dettmar, Gabriele von Glasenapp, and Bernd Dolle-Weinkauff (Frankfurt: Peter Lang, 2014), 417.

13 Sendak, "Lothar Meggendorfer," 59.

14 Lindsay Smith, *Victorian Photography, Painting and Poetry* (Cambridge: Cambridge University Press, 1996), 44. Smith's point is part of a discussion of Ruskin's critique of illusionism in *Modern Painters.*

15 *Country Life* (London: R. Tuck and Sons, [ca. 1896]); *Seaside Pleasures* (London: R. Tuck and Sons, [ca. 1896]); *Summer Surprises* (London: R. Tuck and Sons, [ca. 1896]). Information about these works, including the estimated date of publication and the bookseller's description, comes from Ann Montanaro, "Raphael Tuck and Sons," supplement, *Movable Stationery* (May 2005): S4, S1.

16 For a description of the floating-layer technique, see Children's Books History Society, "Novelty Books," 19–20.

17 Jesse Edward, *Scenes and Occupations of Country Life, with Recollections of Natural History* (London: John Murray, 1844); Miles Henry Downes, *English Country Life* (London: n.p., [1870]); Sabine Baring Gould, *Old Country Life,* 2nd ed. (London: n.p., 1890).

18 John Ruskin, *The Elements of Drawing: In Three Letters to Beginners,* in *The Works of John Ruskin,* vol. 15, *"The Elements of Drawing," "The Elements of Perspective," and "The Law of Fésole"* (London: George Allen, 1904), 207, sec. 244.

19 William Wordsworth, *A Guide through the District of the Lakes in the North of England . . .,* 5th ed. (Kendal: Hudson and Nicholson, 1835), 16–17; Christopher Wood, *Paradise Lost: Paintings of English Country Life and Landscape 1850–1914* (London: Barrie and Jenkins, 1988), 92.

20 Andrew Hemingway, *Landscape Imagery and Urban Culture in Nineteenth-Century Britain* (Cambridge: Cambridge University Press, 1992), 92.

21 Alison Byerly, *Realism, Representation, and the Arts in Nineteenth-Century Literature* (Cambridge: Cambridge University Press, 1997), 21.

22 Victoria Ford Smith, *Between Generations: Collaborative Authorship in the Golden Age of Children's Literature* (Jackson: University Press of Mississippi, 2017), 217.

23 Booktrust, *Pop-Ups!,* 7.

24 Charles Harrison, "On the Surface of Painting," *Critical Inquiry* 15 (1989): 296.

25 Information on Raphael Tuck in this paragraph comes from Adrian Room, "Tuck, Raphael (1821–1900)," *Oxford Dictionary of National Biography Online,* accessed

March 22, 2013, doi:10.1093/ref:odnb/39039; Wakeman and Bridson, *Guide to Nineteenth Century Colour Printers,* 101.

26 See "Evans, Edmund," in *The Oxford Companion to Children's Literature,* 2nd ed., ed. Daniel Hahn (Oxford: Oxford University Press, 2015), 189–90.

27 Wakeman and Bridson, *Guide to Nineteenth Century Colour Printers,* v.

28 Alderson, *Sing a Song for Sixpence,* 98; Edward Ardizzone, "Creation of a Picture Book," in *Only Connect: Readings on Children's Literature,* 2nd ed., ed. Sheila Egoff, G. T. Stubbs, and L. F. Ashley (Toronto: Oxford University Press, 1980), 291.

29 Benjamin, "'Old Forgotten Children's Books,'" 410.

30 Michael Taussig, *My Cocaine Museum* (Chicago: University of Chicago Press, 2004), 28.

31 John Murray, *Practical Remarks on Modern Paper* (Edinburgh: William Blackwood, 1829), 67; William Morris, *The Ideal Book: A Paper* (London: Central School of Arts and Crafts, 1908), 11.

32 Christopher Daven Chamberlain, "Paper," in *The Oxford Companion to the Book,* ed. Michael F. Suarez and H. R. Woudhuysen (Oxford: Oxford University Press, 2010), 1:84.

33 Nodelman, *Words about Pictures,* 47.

34 Kate Flint, *The Victorians and the Visual Imagination* (Cambridge: Cambridge University Press, 2000), 165.

35 Maurice Merleau-Ponty, *The Phenomenology of Perception,* trans. Colin Smith (London: Routledge, 2002), 297.

36 Figures 3.4 and 3.6 are taken from a German facsimile that reproduces the same pop-up illustration because no copy of *Seaside Pleasures* in a public collection is intact. *Am Meeresstrand: Nach einem 100 Jahre alten Stehaufbilderbuch* [At the seashore: After a hundred-year-old pop-up book] ([ca. 1896]; facsimile, Esslingen: J. F. Schreiber, [ca. 1987]).

37 Merleau-Ponty provides careful, complicated explanations of these properties, noting, for example, that apparent size and convergence "do not act miraculously as 'causes' in producing the appearance of organization in depth." Merleau-Ponty, *Phenomenology of Perception,* 302.

38 Hemingway, *Landscape Imagery,* 164; William Powell Frith, *Ramsgate Sands (Life at the Seaside),* 1851–54, oil on canvas, 77.0 × 155.1 cm, RCIN 405068, Royal Collection.

39 John Ruskin, "Notes on Some of the Principal Pictures Exhibited in the Rooms of the Royal Academy . . . ," no. 4, 1858, in *The Works of John Ruskin,* vol. 14, *"Academy Notes," Notes on Prout and Hunt, and Other Art Criticisms, 1855–1888* (London: George Allen, 1904), 162.

40 Merleau-Ponty, *Phenomenology of Perception,* 298.

41 This may have been part of a larger trend in the Victorian illustrated book, whereby illustrators imitated theatrical set design and theatrical set designs reciprocated; see Maxwell, introduction, xxii.

42 For the authoritative account of the juvenile drama, see George Speaight, *The History of the English Toy Theatre,* rev. ed. (London: Studio Vista, 1969); for a more recent critical perspective, see Liz Farr, "Paper Dreams and Romantic Projections: The Nineteenth-Century Toy Theater, Boyhood and Aesthetic Play," in *The Nineteenth-Century Child and Consumer Culture,* ed. Dennis Denisoff (Aldershot: Ashgate, 2008), 43–61. Rickards and Twyman also review the toy theater in *Encyclopedia of Ephemera,* s.v. "Toy theatre," 332–33.

43 *Little Red Riding Hood,* Dean's New Scenic Books 1 (London: Dean and Son, [ca. 1856]), date from Lilly Library, Indiana University.

44 Nodelman, *Words about Pictures,* 160.

45 See Richard W. Schoch, *Shakespeare's Victorian Stage: Performing History in the Theatre of Charles Kean* (Cambridge: Cambridge University Press, 1998), 30; Oscar G. Brockett and Franklin J. Hildy, *History of the Theatre,* 10th ed. (Boston: Pearson Education, 2008), 344.

46 The first production of a play based on the story of Robinson Crusoe was staged at Drury Lane in 1781. On the importance of theatrical Robinsonnades to childhood cultures, see Andrew O'Malley, *Children's Literature, Popular Culture, and "Robinson Crusoe"* (Basingstoke: Palgrave Macmillan, 2012), chap. 4.

47 Nicola Bown, *Fairies in Nineteenth-Century Art and Literature* (Cambridge: Cambridge University Press, 2001), 1.

48 Diane Purkiss, *Troublesome Things: A History of Fairies and Fairy Stories* (London: Allen Lane, 2000), 225.

49 Tracy C. Davis, "What Are Fairies For?," in *The Performing Century: Nineteenth-Century Theatre's History,* ed. Tracy C. Davis and Peter Holland (Basingstoke: Palgrave Macmillan, 2007), 32.

50 Stephen Orgel, "The Poetics of Spectacle," in "Performances in Drama, the Arts, and Society," ed. Ralph Cohen, special issue, *New Literary History* 2, no. 3 (1971): 381.

51 The Victoria and Albert Museum holds images of the sets for this production under the museum number S.869-2010.

52 Children's Books History Society, "Novelty Books," 19.

53 See Brockett and Hildy, *History of the Theatre,* 216.

54 Booth, *Victorian Spectacular Theatre,* 80.

55 Meisel, *Realizations,* 184.

56 Meisel, 38.

57 Meisel, 64.

58 Hildegard E. Krahé, "The Importance of Being Ernest Nister," trans. Sibylle Fraser, *Phaedrus* (1988): 76.

59 Booth, *Victorian Spectacular Theatre*, 77.

60 Higonnet, "Narrative Fractures," 40; Reid-Walsh, "Activity and Agency," 172; Carothers, "Novelty Books," 319.

61 *Theatrical Picture-Book* ([Fürth: Gustav Loewensohn, 1883]), publication information from Theo Gielen, "Questions and Answers," *Movable Stationery* 15, no. 3 (2007): 14. Gielen explains multiple different configurations of this work. For a description of the copy held at the Metropolitan Museum of Art, see Andrea Rawle, "Once upon a Time," *Metropolitan Museum of Art Bulletin*, n.s., 29 (1971): 373–79.

62 Shauna Vey, *Childhood and Nineteenth-Century American Theatre: The Work of the Marsh Troupe of Juvenile Actors* (Carbondale: Southern Illinois University Press, 2015), 16.

63 Marah Gubar, "Entertaining Children of All Ages: Nineteenth-Century Popular Theater as Children's Theater," *American Quarterly* 66 (2014): 6, 4.

64 *Peter Pan's Postbag: Letters to Pauline Chase* (London: Heinemann, 1909), 3, quoted in Marah Gubar, "*Peter Pan* as Children's Theatre: The Issue of Audience," in *The Oxford Handbook of Children's Literature*, ed. Lynne Vallone and Julia Mickenberg (Oxford: Oxford University Press, 2011), 485.

65 Orgel, "Poetics of Spectacle," 378.

66 Peter Hulme, *Colonial Encounters: Europe and the Native Caribbean, 1492–1797* (London: Methuen, 1986), 198.

67 Crary notes (as does Meisel) that such a mode of arranging depth is theatrical. Jonathan Crary, *Techniques of the Observer: On Vision and Modernity in the Nineteenth Century* (Cambridge: MIT Press, 1990), 125; Meisel, *Realizations*, 45.

68 Ruskin, *Elements of Drawing*, 215n1, sec. 247.

69 Ruskin, 68, sec. 75.

70 David Trotter, "Stereoscopy: Modernism and the 'Haptic,'" in "Low Modernism," ed. Rachel Potter and David Trotter, special section, *Critical Quarterly* 46, no. 4 (2004): 39.

71 Charles Wheatstone, "Contributions to the Physiology of Vision—Part the First: On Some Remarkable, and Hitherto Unobserved, Phenomena of Binocular Vision," *Philosophical Transactions of the Royal Society of London* 128 (1838): 372.

72 Sir David Brewster, *The Stereoscope: Its History, Theory, and Construction . . .* (1856; facsimile, Hastings-on-Hudson: Morgan and Morgan, 1971), 1, 31, 166.

73 Rudolf Kingslake, introduction to Brewster, *Stereoscope*, n.p.; Trotter, "Stereoscopy," 48–51; Lynda Nead, *The Haunted Gallery: Painting, Photography, Film, c. 1900* (New Haven, Conn.: Yale University Press, 2007), 181ff.

74 John Waldsmith, *Stereo Views: An Illustrated History and Price Guide,* 2nd ed. (Iola, Wis.: Krause, 2002), 140–41, 79–83.

75 Trotter, "Stereoscopy," 39.

76 Sheenagh Pietrobruno, "The Stereoscope and the Miniature," *Early Popular Visual Culture* 9 (2011): 173. For reproductions of multiple horror stereographs, see Brian May, Denis Pellerin, and Paula Fleming, *Diableries: Stereoscopic Adventures in Hell* (London: Stereoscopic Company, 2013).

77 James Elliott, *One O'clock: Children at Table,* [ca. 1860s], stereoscopic photograph, museum number 654-1943, Victoria and Albert Museum, London.

78 "Catalogue of Binocular Pictures of the London Stereoscopic Company . . . ," in Brewster, *Stereoscope,* n.p.

79 Rayna Green, "The Tribe Called Wannabee: Playing Indian in America and Europe," *Folklore* 99 (1988): 39.

80 Smith, *Victorian Photography,* 8.

81 Crary, *Techniques of the Observer,* 19.

82 Laura Burd Schiavo, "From Phantom Image to Perfect Vision: Physiological Optics, Commercial Photography, and the Popularization of the Stereoscope," in *New Media, 1740–1915,* ed. Lisa Gitelman and Geoffrey B. Pingree (Cambridge, Mass.: MIT Press, 2003), 116.

83 Trotter, "Stereoscopy," 39.

84 Schiavo, "From Phantom Image," 127.

## 4. ERNEST NISTER CHRISTOPHER COLUMBUS

1 Hunt and Hunt, *Peeps into Nisterland,* 5.

2 Wakeman and Bridson, *Guide to Nineteenth Century Colour Printers,* 86.

3 "Report on the Recent Progress," 73, 97, 98.

4 "Calendars and Cards," *New York Observer and Chronicle,* December 30, 1909, 882.

5 Sigmund Freud, "Family Romances," trans. James Strachey, in *Jensen's "Gradiva" and Other Works,* vol. 9 of *The Standard Edition of the Complete Psychological Works of Sigmund Freud,* ed. James Strachey and Anna Freud (London: Hogarth Press/Institute of Psychoanalysis, 1959), 237.

6 Brian Alderson and Andrea Immel, "Mass Markets: Children's Books," in McKitterick, *Cambridge History of the Book,* 6:401.

7 Krahé, "Importance of Being Ernest Nister," 76.

8 Michael Twyman, *A History of Chromolithography: Printed Colour for All* (London: British Library, 2013), 343.

9 *More Pleasant Surprises for Chicks of All Sizes,* by Fred E. Weatherly (London: Ernest Nister; New York: E. P. Dutton, [ca. 1893]), date from Hunt and Hunt, *Peeps into Nisterland,* 292.

10 Hunt, "Technologies of Wonder," 211.

11 Price, *How to Do Things with Books,* 90.

12 *Here and There: A Book of Transformation Pictures,* by F. E. Weatherly (London: Ernest Nister; New York: E. P. Dutton, [ca. 1893]), date from Hunt and Hunt, *Peeps into Nisterland,* 292.

13 "Some Old Friends in New Dresses," *Literary World,* November 28, 1896, 418.

14 The poem "Fairies," better known by its first line (and later title) "There Are Fairies at the Bottom of Our Garden!," is a famous late example of the association between the fairy and doggerel. [Rose Fylcman], "Fairies," *Punch,* May 23, 1917, 341.

15 Twyman, *History of Chromolithography,* 569–71.

16 See "Bingham, Clifton (1859–1913)," in "Modern British Literary Authors," British Library, accessed April 25, 2017, http://www.bl.uk. Clifton Bingham's "Love's Old Sweet Song" is mentioned by name in the "Calypso," "Sirens," "Circe," and "Ithaca" episodes of *Ulysses.*

17 See John D. Pickles, "Weatherly, Frederic Edward (1848–1929)," *Oxford Dictionary of National Biography Online,* accessed July 28, 2013, doi:10.1093/ref:odnb/46652; Fred E. Weatherly, *Piano and Gown* (London: G. P. Putnam's Sons, [1926]).

18 On H. M. Burnside, see "Woman's Who's Who," in *Every Woman's Encyclopædia* (London: n.p., [1910–12]), 3:2819; Charlotte Mitchell, "Carey, Rosa Nouchette (1840–1909)," *Oxford Dictionary of National Biography Online,* accessed August 28, 2013, doi:10.1093/ref:odnb/32288. (Carey, a novelist, lived with Burnside; both had worked for the *Girl's Own Paper.*) My account of Nesbit's productivity comes from Julia Briggs, "Nesbit, Edith (1858–1924)," *Oxford Dictionary of National Biography Online,* accessed September 29, 2016, doi:10.1093/ref:odnb/31919.

19 For detailed discussions of the transformation scene, see Booth, *Victorian Spectacular Theatre,* 80; Purkiss, *Troublesome Things,* 225.

20 Jeffrey Richards, "E. L. Blanchard and 'The Golden Age of Pantomime,'" in *Victorian Pantomime: A Collection of Critical Essays,* ed. Jim Davis (Basingstoke: Palgrave Macmillan, 2010), 28.

21 For this illustration of a star trap, see "Victorian Pantomime," Victoria and Albert Museum, accessed February 24, 2018, https://www.vam.ac.uk.

22 Purkiss, *Troublesome Things,* 225–26, 227.

23 John Ruskin, "Fairy Land: Mrs. Allingham and Kate Greenaway," in *The Works of John Ruskin,* vol. 33, *"The Bible of Amiens," "Valle Crucis," "The Art of England," "The Pleasures of England"* (London: George Allen, 1908), 327, sec. 89.

24 Trumpener, "City Scenes," 365.

25 Bown, *Fairies in Nineteenth-Century Art,* 82.

26 *Princess Mary's Gift Book* (London: Hodder & Stoughton, [1914]).

27 Purkiss, *Troublesome Things,* 288.

28 Carol Mavor, *Reading Boyishly: Roland Barthes, J. M. Barrie, Jacques Henri Lartigue, Marcel Proust, and D. W. Winnicott* (Durham, N.C.: Duke University Press, 2007), 231–33.

29 This phrase draws from Leah Price's call for "accounts of print culture . . . narrated from the point of view not of human readers and users, but of the book." Price, "From *The History of a Book,*" 120.

30 Kimberley Reynolds, "Rewarding Reads? Giving, Receiving and Resisting Evangelical Reward and Prize Books," in Briggs, Butts, and Grenby, *Popular Children's Literature,* 189.

31 Yonge, *What Books to Lend,* 10–11.

32 Maxwell, introduction, xxii.

33 See Kooistra, *Poetry, Pictures,* 111–23.

34 *Pleasant Surprises: A Novel Picture Book,* by Sheila E. Braine (London: Ernest Nister; New York: E. P. Dutton, [ca. 1914]), date from Hunt and Hunt, *Peeps into Nisterland,* 301. I refer to this volume as *Pleasant Surprises* (ca. 1914) to distinguish it from the earlier volume published around 1891.

35 Mark Connelly, *Christmas: A Social History* (London: I. B. Tauris, 1999), 162, 199.

36 "Ernest Nister's Publications," *Morning Post,* November 17, 1899, 7.

37 J. L. Williams, "The Christmas Tree at Windsor Castle," *Supplement to the Illustrated London News,* Christmas 1848, 409–10.

38 Gary Cross, *Kids' Stuff: Toys and the Changing World of American Childhood* (Cambridge, Mass.: Harvard University Press, 1997), 46.

39 Cindy Dickinson, "Creating a World of Books, Friends, and Flowers: Gift Books and Inscriptions, 1825–60," *Winterthur Portfolio* 31 (1996): 53.

40 Grenby, *Child Reader,* 30–31.

41 *Les Aventures de Robinson Crusoë* [The adventures of Robinson Crusoe] (Paris: Librairie Franco Hollandaise, [ca. 1880]), shelfmark Opie EE 245.

42 Frederick Perigal, *Some Account of the Perigal Family* (London: Harrison and Sons, 1887), 29, app. H. On Henry Perigal's dissection, see M. E. Mortimer and R. W. Ball, "Pythagoras and the Dissection of Polygons," *Mathematics in Schools* 13 (1984): 2–3.

43 *Transformation Pictures,* shelfmark Opie EE 32; *Children's Wonderland,* shelfmark Opie EE 42; *Here and There,* shelfmark Opie EE 310.

44 *Something New,* shelfmark Opie EE 31.

45 Pettitt, *Patent Inventions,* 21.

46 Op de Beeck, *Suspended Animation,* 43.

47 *All the Way Round Pictures,* by Maud Carlton (London: Ernest Nister; New York: E. P. Dutton, [ca. 1899]), date from Hunt and Hunt, *Peeps into Nisterland,* 297.

48 Stewart, *On Longing,* 10.

49 Roland Barthes, *S/Z,* trans. Richard Howard (Oxford: Blackwell, 1990), 15–16; Deborah Thacker, "Disdain or Ignorance? Literary Theory and the Absence of Children's Literature," *The Lion and the Unicorn* 24 (2000): 4.

50 Roland Barthes, "Rhetoric of the Image," in *Image, Music, Text,* trans. Stephen Heath (London: Fontana Paperbacks, 1977), 39.

51 There is also at least one Nister title that uses *dissolving view* to describe the format; see Hunt and Hunt, *Peeps into Nisterland,* 295.

52 Marsh, "Dickensian 'Dissolving Views,'" 334.

53 See W. J. Harrison, "Childe, Henry Langdon (1781–1874)," rev. Robert Murphy, *Oxford Dictionary of National Biography Online,* accessed July 28, 2013, doi:10.1093/ref:odnb/5293.

54 Deac Rossell, *Living Pictures: The Origins of the Movies* (Albany: State University of New York Press, 1998), 13.

55 See "Ernest Nister's Publications," 7.

56 *Wonderland Pictures,* by Helen Marion Burnside, illus. "Gar" [Raymond H. Garman] (London: Ernest Nister; New York: E. P. Dutton, [ca. 1899]), date from Hunt and Hunt, *Peeps into Nisterland,* 297.

57 Christian Metz, *The Imaginary Signifier: Psychoanalysis and the Cinema,* trans. Celia Britton (Bloomington: Indiana University Press, 1986), 277.

58 Torben Grodal, *Moving Pictures: A New Theory of Film Genres, Feelings, and Cognition* (Oxford: Clarendon Press, 1997), 271. Marsh applies a similar line of argument to literature by way of the dissolving view, finding a "lantern-like effect of sudden movement through time and space" in Dickens's works; her formulation seems indebted to Sergei Eisenstein's analysis of Dickens's technique of "deliberate 'montage' displacement of . . . time-continuity," although she does not cite him. See Marsh, "Dickensian 'Dissolving Views,'" 338; Sergei Eisenstein, "Dickens, Griffiths, and the Film Today," in *Film Form: Essays in Film Theory,* ed. and trans. Jay Leyda (San Diego: Harcourt, 1977), 211.

59 Roman Jakobson, "Two Aspects of Language and Two Types of Aphasic Disturbances," in *On Language,* ed. Linda R. Waugh and Monique Monville-Burston (Cambridge, Mass.: Harvard University Press, 1990), 119.

60 Metz, *Imaginary Signifier,* 194.

61 This rhyme is number 16150 in the Roud Folk Song Index. The first printed version of the rhyme appeared around 1843, but it is probably older. See Iona Opie and Peter

Opie, *The Oxford Dictionary of Nursery Rhymes,* new ed. (Oxford: Oxford University Press, 1997), 257.

62 See also dissolving pictures in *The Children's Wonderland, More Pleasant Surprises, Here and There,* and *Little Folk's Peep Show* (London: Ernest Nister; New York: E. P. Dutton, [ca. 1898]), date from Hunt and Hunt, *Peeps into Nisterland,* 297.

63 Nikolajeva and Scott, *How Picturebooks Work,* 139.

64 Marsh, "Dickensian 'Dissolving Views,'" 335.

65 Bal, *Narratology,* 218.

66 Higonnet, "Movable Books," 422.

67 Hunt and Hunt, *Peeps into Nisterland,* 292, 297.

68 Altick, *Paintings from Books,* 184.

69 For a discussion of Martin and the rhyme, see Opie and Opie, *Oxford Dictionary of Nursery Rhymes,* 317–22.

70 *Grimm's Household Tales,* trans. and ed. Margaret Hunt, 2 vols. (London: George Bell and Sons, 1884); *Perrault's Popular Tales,* ed. Andrew Lang (Oxford: Clarendon Press, 1888).

71 Andrew Lang, ed., *The Blue Fairy Book* (London: Longmans, Green, 1889).

72 Andrew Lang, ed., *The Yellow Fairy Book* (1894; repr., London: Longmans, Green, 1906), n.p.

73 Molly Clark Hillard, "Trysting Genres: Andrew Lang's Fairy Tale Methodologies," in "The Andrew Lang Effect: Essays in Form, Method, and Discipline," ed. Nathan Hensley and Molly Clark Hillard, special issue, *Romanticism and Victorianism on the Net* 64 (October 2013): para. 30, http://www.erudit.org.

74 Andrew Lang, ed., *The Pink Fairy Book* (1897; repr., New York: Longmans, Green, 1904), vii; Andrew Lang, ed., *The Brown Fairy Book* (1904; repr., New York: Longmans, Green, 1914), viii.

75 Clark, "Trysting Genres," para. 24.

76 Andrew Lang, ed., *The Grey Fairy Book* (1900; repr., New York: Longmans, Green, 1905), n.p.

77 Barthes, *S/Z,* 4.

## 5. GOING THROUGH THE MOTIONS

1 Sendak, "Lothar Meggendorfer," 51–60.

2 Ellen G. K. Rubin, "The Meggendorfer Prize," The Pop-Up Lady: Specializing in Movable Paper, accessed April 25, 2017, http://www.popuplady.com/mbs11-meggprizes.shtml.

3 For example, one volume cherry-picks movable figures from a number of different titles and packages them with an appreciation by Maurice Sendak: *The Genius of Lothar Meggendorfer* (New York: Random House, 1985).

4 Abate, "When Clothes Don't Make the Man," 43–65; Amanda M. Brian, "Beasts within and Beasts Without: Colonial Themes in Lothar Meggendorfer's Children's Books," *German Studies Review* 37 (2014): 253–74; Amanda M. Brian, "Imagining the World in Bavarian Children's Books: Place and Other as Engineered by Lothar Meggendorfer," in *Imagining Sameness and Difference in Children's Literature: From the Enlightenment to the Present Day,* ed. Emer O'Sullivan and Andrea Immel (London: Palgrave Macmillan, 2017), 89–110.

5 On Meggendorfer as caricaturist of race and nationality, see Brian, "Imagining the World." On the culture of caricature around Meggendorfer, see Higonnet, "Movable Books," 417–18.

6 Lothar Meggendorfer, *Verschiedene Leute: Ein Ziehbilderbuch* [Different people: A tab-pull picture book], 2nd ed. (Esslingen: J. F. Schreiber, [1902]), date from Staatsbibliothek zu Berlin. All translations from the German- and French-language versions of movable books by Meggendorfer are my own, unless otherwise stated.

7 Lothar Meggendorfer, *Lustiges Automaten-Theater: Ein Ziehbilderbuch* [Merry machine theater: A tab-pull picture book] (Esslingen: J. F. Schreiber, [1890]), date from facsimile edition of 1993; Lothar Meggendorfer, illus., *Les Héritiers de Monsieur Babylas des Entrechats ancien professeur de danse*... [The heirs to Monsieur Babylas des Entrechats, former dance teacher...], by Ernest d'Hervilly (Paris: Capendu, [ca. 1890]).

8 "Christmas Books," *Glasgow Herald,* November 9, 1898, 4.

9 For a sequence of GIFs of mechanical and other movable books, see Peggy Nelson, "Pop-Up Apotheosis," HiLobrow, February 7, 2011, http://hilobrow.com.

10 Bill Brown, "How to Do Things with Things (A Toy Story)," *Critical Inquiry* 24 (1998): 940.

11 Ruskin, "Fairy Land," 329.

12 Opie and Opie, "Books That Come to Life," 61.

13 Tamara Ketabgian, *The Lives of Machines: The Industrial Imaginary in Victorian Literature and Culture* (Ann Arbor: University of Michigan Press, 2011), 1.

14 Susan Honeyman, "Manufactured Agency and the Playthings Who Dream It for Us," in "Questions of Agency," ed. Richard Flynn, special issue, *Children's Literature Association Quarterly* 31, no. 2 (2006): 109–31; op de Beeck, *Suspended Animation,* chap. 3.

15 Ernst Jentsch, "On the Psychology of the Uncanny," trans. Roy Sellars, *Angelaki* 2 (1997): 11, 14.

16 Sigmund Freud, "The Uncanny," trans. Alix Strachey, in *"An Infantile Neurosis" and Other Works* (1955), vol. 17 of Strachey and Freud, *Standard Edition of Freud,* 226–32.

17 Jentsch, "On the Psychology," 12, 13.

18 Freud, "Uncanny," 225, 232.

19 Stewart, *On Longing,* 57.

20 Reid-Walsh, "Activity and Agency," 173.

21 Jessica Riskin, "The Defecating Duck, or, the Ambiguous Origins of Artificial Life," *Critical Inquiry* 29 (2003): 601. Riskin expands on the automaton's relationship to time and life in *The Restless Clock: A History of the Centuries-Long Argument over What Makes Living Things Tick* (Chicago: University of Chicago Press, 2015).

22 George Speaight, *History of the English Puppet Theatre* (New York: John de Graff, 1950), 261; Hildegard Krahé, "Erscheinungsformen der Spielbilderbücher durch die Jahrhunderte" [Manifestations of the novelty picture book through the centuries], in Peter Laub, *Spielbilderbücher: Aus der Spielzeugsammlung des SMCA* [Novelty picture books: From the toy collection at the Salzburg Museum] (Salzburg: Salzburg Museums Carolino Augusteum, 2002), 21. Speaight is discussing puppets, but the same assertion holds true for mechanical toys.

23 Daniel Tiffany, *Toy Medium: Materialism and Modern Lyric* (Berkeley: University of California Press, 2000), 42; Dolf Sternberger, *Panorama of the Nineteenth Century,* trans. Joachim Neugroschel (Oxford: Basil Blackwell, 1977), 37.

24 Bal, *Narratology,* 77–78.

25 Steven Dillon, "Illustrations of Time: Watches, Dials, and Clocks in Victorian Pictures," in Maxwell, *Victorian Illustrated Book,* 85.

26 Stewart, *On Longing,* 57.

27 *Moveable Trades, Showing the Mechanical Movements in Each Trade to Instruct and Amuse Children* (London: Darton, [ca. 1859]), date from Princeton University Library. See Alderson and Oyens, *Be Merry and Wise,* 242.

28 I have taken these verbs from the version of the rhyme in James Orchard Halliwell, ed., *The Nursery Rhymes of England, Collected Principally from Oral Tradition* (London: Percy Society, 1842), 161–63.

29 References for those works not yet mentioned: for the blacksmith, *Aus dem Leben: Lustiges Ziehbilderbuch* [From life: A merry tab-pull picture book], 10th ed. (Munich: Braun and Schneider, [ca. 1890]); for the black girl and her brother, Lothar Meggendorfer, *Lustige Ziehbilder* [Merry tab-pull pictures], 3rd ed. (Munich: Braun and Schneider, [1906]); for the cook chopping, Lothar Meggendorfer, *Lebende Bilder* [Living pictures], 12th ed. (Munich: Braun and Schneider, [1887]). All dates from Staatsbibliothek zu Berlin.

30 Higonnet, "Orality onto Paper," 133.

31 Op de Beeck, *Suspended Animation,* 122.

32 Sendak, "Lothar Meggendorfer," 57.

33 Thackeray, *Vanity Fair,* xiv.

34 See E. M. Forster, *Aspects of the Novel,* ed. Oliver Stallybrass (London: Penguin, 1974), 74.

35 Victoria Nelson, *The Secret Life of Puppets* (Cambridge, Mass.: Harvard University Press, 2001), 42.

36 Thackeray, *Vanity Fair,* 624.

37 Compare Andrew H. Miller's more pessimistic reading, in which he writes that *Vanity Fair*'s "readers are *reduced* to children" by this ending. Andrew H. Miller, *Novels behind Glass: Commodity Culture and Victorian Narrative* (Cambridge: Cambridge University Press, 1995), 49, emphasis added.

38 Speaight, *History of the English Puppet Theatre,* 22.

39 Higonnet provides an alternative angle on puppets and the mechanical book in "Orality onto Paper," 130–31, 135–37.

40 For images of the flat figures in their individual parts, see *The Publishing Archive of Lothar Meggendorfer: Original Drawings, Hand-Colored Lithographs and Production Files . . .* (New York: J. G. Schiller, 1975).

41 See Brian, "Beasts within," 258, 267–70.

42 W. Newman, *Moveable Shadows for the People: Second Series* (London: Dean and Son, [1857]).

43 Ernst Kris and Ernst Gombrich, "The Principles of Caricature," *British Journal of Medical Psychology* 17 (1938): 319.

44 Martha Banta, *Barbaric Intercourse: Caricature and the Culture of Conduct, 1841–1936* (Chicago: University of Chicago Press, 2003), 4.

45 Pierre Delcourt, *Les Excentriques* [The eccentrics] (Paris: A. Capendu, [1900?]), date from University Library, University of Illinois at Urbana–Champaign.

46 Abate, "When Clothes Don't Make the Man," 45.

47 Kris and Gombrich, "Principles of Caricature," 339.

48 Judith Wechsler, *A Human Comedy: Physiognomy and Caricature in Nineteenth Century Paris* (London: Thames and Hudson, 1982), 13.

49 Sianne Ngai, *Ugly Feelings* (Cambridge, Mass.: Harvard University Press, 2005), 93, 91.

50 Abate, "When Clothes Don't Make the Man," 53–54, 56; Higonnet, "Orality onto Paper," 130–31.

51 See Higonnet, "Movable Books," 415–27.

52 Eric Lott, *Love and Theft: Blackface Minstrelsy and the American Working Class,* 20th anniversary ed. (New York: Oxford University Press, 2013), 7.

53 For discussions of this illustration by other scholars, see Brian, "Imagining the World," 103; Higonnet, "Orality onto Paper," 135. Brian valuably counterpoints the figure with another black dandy illustration by Meggendorfer.

54 Homi K. Bhabha, *The Location of Culture* (London: Routledge Classics, 2004), 95.

55 Compare the process at work in *Scenes in the Life of a Masher,* where the titular persona "is showcased for the purposes of derision: each scene shows the title character as inept, awkward, and even foolish." Abate, "When Clothes Don't Make the Man," 47.

56 Michael D. Harris, *Colored Pictures: Race and Visual Representation* (Chapel Hill: University of North Carolina Press, 2003), 41.

57 On Raggedy Ann, see Bernstein, *Racial Innocence,* chap. 4; on the Cat in the Hat, see Philip Nel, *Was the Cat in the Hat Black? The Hidden Racism of Children's Literature and the Need for Diverse Books* (New York: Oxford University Press, 2017), 40–45.

58 Tanya Sheehan and Henry Louis Gates Jr., "Marketing Racism: Popular Imagery in the United States and Europe," in *The Image of the Black in Western Art,* ed. David Bindman and Gates, vol. 5, pt. 1, *The Twentieth Century: The Impact of Africa* (Cambridge, Mass.: Belknap Press, 2014), 30.

59 "Dandy Jim, from Caroline" and "The Dandy Broadway Swell" are numbers 13924 and V1718, respectively, in the Roud Folk Song Index. For an illustrated copy of "Dandy Jim," see "Dandy Jim, from Caroline: A Celebrated Ethiopian Song," Lester S. Levy Sheet Music Collection, Sheridan Libraries Special Collections, Johns Hopkins University, accessed April 14, 2017, http://levysheetmusic.mse.jhu.edu.

60 My thanks to Michèle Mendelssohn for suggesting the comparison to "An Æsthetic Midday Meal."

61 Henri Fantin-Latour's painting *Un Coin de table* (By the table; 1872) shows d'Hervilly with Arthur Rimbaud, Paul Verlaine, and others.

62 Henry B. Wonham, *Playing the Races: Ethnic Caricature and American Literary Realism* (New York: Oxford University Press, 2004), 26.

63 Monica L. Miller, *Slaves to Fashion: Black Dandyism and the Styling of Black Diasporic Identity* (Durham, N.C.: Duke University Press, 2009), 15.

64 Lott, *Love and Theft,* 137–38.

65 In her article "Beasts within," Brian focuses on direct colonial themes in German-language Meggendorfer titles, in particular, the associations among animals, racial difference, and didacticism.

66 Brian, 265; Nana Badenberg, "Mohrenwäschen, Völkerschauen: Der Konsum des Schwarzen um 1900" [Whitewashing the Moor and human ethnological displays: The

consumption of blackness in 1900], in *Colors 1800/1900/2000: Signs of Ethnic Difference,* ed. Birgit Tautz (Amsterdam: Rodopi, 2004), 163.

67 "The Black Man in the River," in *Aesop's Fables,* trans. Laura Gibbs (Oxford: Oxford University Press, 2002), 171.

68 "The Æthiop," in *Three Hundred Æsop's Fables, Literally Translated from the Greek,* trans. George Fyler Townsend (London: George Routledge and Sons, 1871), 64. Information about the fable in this paragraph comes from "Aesopica: Aesop's Fables in English, Latin and Greek," MythFolklore.net, ed. Laura Gibbs, accessed February 13, 2017, http://mythfolklore.net/aesopica.

69 George Latimer Apperson, "To Wash (or Make) the Blackamoor White," in *Dictionary of Proverbs,* new ed., rev. Martin Manser and Stephen Curtis (Ware: Wordsworth Editions, 2006), 59. William A. Cohen discusses the *Punch* cartoon of the maharaja in *Embodied: Victorian Literature and the Senses* (Minneapolis: University of Minnesota Press, 2009), 83–84.

70 Gustave Flaubert to Louis Bonenfant, [1868?], in *The Letters of Gustave Flaubert, 1857–1880,* ed. and trans. Francis Steegmuller (Cambridge, Mass.: Belknap Press, 1982), 121. The original French is "C'est vouloir blanchir un nègre."

71 Brian, "Beasts within," 265.

72 Anne McClintock, "Soft-Soaping Empire: Commodity Racism and Imperial Advertising," in *Imperial Leather: Race, Gender and Sexuality in the Colonial Contest* (Abingdon: Routledge, 1995), 214.

73 Sheehan and Gates, "Marketing Racism," 29. Sheehan and Gates also link the image to the Aesopic fable.

74 Carol Mavor, *Pleasures Taken: Performances of Sexuality and Loss in Victorian Photographs* (London: I. B. Tauris, 1996), 95.

75 Valerie Fildes, *Wet Nursing: A History from Antiquity to the Present* (Oxford: Basil Blackwell, 1988), 141.

76 See Fildes, 62, 186.

77 Harris, *Colored Pictures,* 84, 93.

78 Harris, 84, 103, 92.

79 Bernstein, *Racial Innocence,* 181.

80 Tanya Sheehan, *Study in Black and White: Photography, Race, Humor* (University Park: Pennsylvania State University Press, 2018).

81 Higonnet, "Movable Books," 415.

82 Bernstein, "Children's Books, Dolls," 167.

83 Ngai, *Ugly Feelings,* 113.

84 According to the *OED,* the first usage of *going through the motions* is found in Walter Scott's *Old Mortality* (1816).

## CONCLUSION

1 Lerer discusses movable books in relation to this assertion in *Children's Literature,* 322, 327–29.

2 Thacker's statement is as follows: "While critics of children's literature *use* theory to argue the case for children's literature, theoreticians in general seem slow to *use* children's literature, despite its relevance." Thacker, "Disdain or Ignorance?," 1.

3 Jerome J. McGann, *The Textual Condition* (Princeton, N.J.: Princeton University Press, 1991), 11; Chartier, "Texts, Printings, Readings," 161.

4 D. F. McKenzie, *Bibliography and the Sociology of Texts* (Cambridge: Cambridge University Press, 1999), 13. I have made this point elsewhere; see Field, "'A Story, Exemplified,'" 49.

5 Stewart, *On Longing,* 31.

6 N. Katherine Hayles, *My Mother Was a Computer: Digital Subjects and Literary Texts* (Chicago: University of Chicago Press, 2005), 97.

7 McKenzie, *Bibliography and the Sociology of Texts,* 4.

8 Peter Stallybrass, "Marx's Coat," in *Border Fetishisms: Material Objects in Unstable Spaces,* ed. Patricia Spyer (New York: Routledge, 1998), 203.

9 See Peter Stallybrass and Roger Chartier, "What Is a Book?," in *The Cambridge Companion to Textual Scholarship,* ed. Neil Freistat and Julia Flanders (Cambridge: Cambridge University Press, 2013), 195–98; Megan L. Benton, *Beauty and the Book: Fine Editions and Cultural Distinction in America* (New Haven, Conn.: Yale University Press, 2000).

10 Gérard Genette, *Paratexts: Thresholds of Interpretation,* trans. Jane E. Lewin (Cambridge: Cambridge University Press, 1997), 2.

11 Masten, Stallybrass, and Vickers, "Introduction," 4.

12 A. Jan Collaert after Jan van der Straet, called Stradanus, title page to *Nova reperta* (New inventions of modern times), ca. 1600, 27 x 20 cm, accession number 34.30(1), Metropolitan Museum of Art, New York; Elizabeth L. Eisenstein, *The Printing Press as an Agent of Change: Communications and Cultural Transformations in Early-Modern Europe* (Cambridge: Cambridge University Press, 1979), 20–21.

13 Peter Stallybrass, "'Little Jobs': Broadsides and the Printing Revolution," in *Agent of Change: Print Culture Studies after Elizabeth L. Eisenstein,* ed. Sabrina Alcorn Baron, Eric

N. Lindquist, and Eleanor F. Shevlin (Amherst: University of Massachusetts Press, 2007), 315.

14 Walter Benjamin, "The Work of Art in the Age of Mechanical Reproduction," in *Illuminations,* 213.

15 Eisenstein, *Printing Press,* 31.

16 Adrian Johns, *The Nature of the Book: Print and Knowledge in the Making* (Chicago: University of Chicago Press, 1998), 2, 4. For further debate between Eisenstein and Johns, see "How Revolutionary Was the Print Revolution?," special forum, *American Historical Review* 107, no. 1 (2002): 84–128.

17 "Christmas Books," *Pall Mall Gazette,* December 14, 1889, 7.

18 The shelfmark (subsequently changed to "Recentiores," the classification for post-1850 books that would be unsuitably dispersed throughout the current collection) came from the Nicholson system adopted in 1883 and explained in Michael Heaney, "The Bodleian Classification of Books," *Journal of Librarianship and Information Science* 10 (1978): 274–82. On Meggendorfer's use of *Schneckerl,* see Hildegard Krahé, afterword to *Lebendes Affentheater: Ein Ziehbilderbuch* [Living animal show: A pull-tab picture book] (1892; facsimile, Vienna: Österreichischer Bundesverlag, 1992), n.p.

19 Dawson, "S. Louis Giraud," 218; Ann R. Montanaro, "A Concise History of Pop-Up and Movable Books," The Pop-Up World of Ann Montanaro, online exhibition, Rutgers University Libraries, accessed February 1, 2018, https://www.libraries.rutgers.edu/rul/libs/scua/montanar/p-intro.htm.

20 Stoddard, "Morphology and the Book," 4.

21 Robert Darnton, "What Is the History of Books?," in "Representations and Realities," ed. Stephen Greenblatt, themed issue, *Daedalus* 111, no. 3 (1982): 68.

22 See Search Oxford Libraries Online, University of Oxford, accessed April 29, 2017, http://solo.bodleian.ox.ac.uk.

23 Alderson, "Making of Children's Books," 42–43.

24 *The Old Fashioned Mother Goose Melodies: Complete with Magic Colored Pictures* (n.p.: G. W. Carleton, 1879).

25 For notices of these patents, see *Farmside Ways: A Book of Stories in Prose and Verse Illustrated throughout in Colour* (London: R. Tuck and Sons, [19—]); *The Home Menagerie* (Boston: Forbes, 1883).

26 See *The Railway Engine* (Dundee: Valentine, [not before 1913]).

27 Sten G. Lindberg, "Mobiles in Books: Volvelles, Inserts, Pyramids, Divinations, and Children's Games," trans. William S. Mitchell, *Private Library,* 3rd ser., 2, no. 2 (1979): 64–66.

# Index

Page numbers in italics refer to figures.

HANNAH FIELD is lecturer in Victorian literature at the University of Sussex. She is coeditor of *Space and Place in Children's Literature, 1789 to the Present.*